D0998536

THE RESPONSORIAL PSALM TONES FOR THE MOZARABIC OFFICE

NUMBER THREE IN THE PRINCETON STUDIES IN MUSIC

Responsorial Psalm Tones for the Mozarabic Office

BY DON MICHAEL RANDEL

PRINCETON UNIVERSITY PRESS
PRINCETON, NEW JERSEY
1969

L.C. Card 68-27410

Publication of this book has been aided by
the Whitney Darrow Publication Reserve Fund of
Princeton University Press and
the Elsie and Walter W. Naumburg Fund in the
Department of Music, Princeton University.

Printed in the United States of America
by Princeton University Press

For Mary

Preface

The research for this study was carried out in Spain during the academic years 1964-65 and 1965-66, thanks to a Fulbright grant. I am, therefore, very much indebted to Mr. Ramón Bela and his staff at the Fulbright Commission in Madrid for their considerable assistance in making my two years in Spain both fruitful and pleasant. Miss Matilde Medina was especially helpful in arranging access to various libraries and introductions to numerous people. Also very helpful in this respect was Professor Luis Vázquez de Parga. The Benedictine community at Santo Domingo de Silos could not have been more generous. The warmth of their hospitality made working with their manuscript treasures an extremely pleasant experience. Dom Ismael Fernández de la Cuesta saw to my every need in the library there and very freely gave me the benefit of his own studies on Mozarabic Chant. Dom Germán Prado, who now resides in Madrid, was also very generous with his time and his counsel. In León, I was very graciously assisted by D. Luis López Santos and in Santo Domingo de la Calzada by D. Mariano Santamaría Alonso. I must also thank D. José López Toro in Madrid and D. Juan Francisco Rivera Recio in Toledo for facilitating the use of the collections which they oversee.

Special thanks are due to Professors Kenneth Levy and Lewis Lockwood for having read an earlier draft of this material and having offered some helpful suggestions. Professor Oliver Strunk inspired this project and oversaw its earliest stages, and to him go my profoundest thanks and admiration.

Mr. John Fonda, of the Department of Geography at Syracuse University, very kindly prepared the map which appears in this book, and I should like to record here my sincere thanks. At the Princeton University Press I owe thanks to Mrs. E. C. Taylor for overseeing all of the matters which editors must oversee.

I wish to thank, finally, my wife Mary for the culinary delights which sustained the latter stages of this project and for her help with preparing the appendix.

CONTENTS

FIGURES

THE RESPONSORIAL PSALM TONES FOR THE MOZARABIC OFFICE

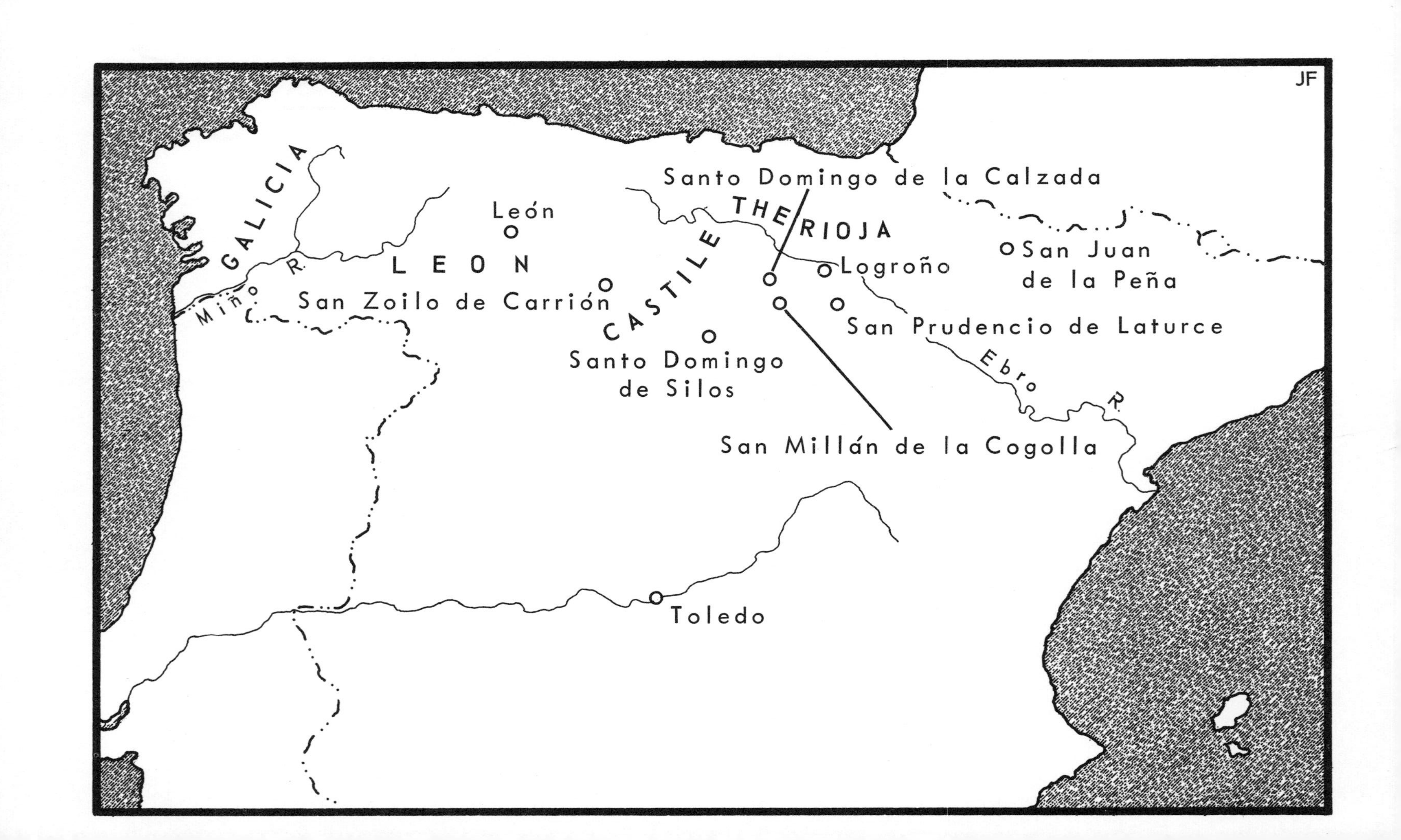
JF
GALICIA
Miño R.
León
LEON
San Zoilo de Carrión
CASTILE
Santo Domingo de Silos
Santo Domingo de la Calzada
THE RIOJA
Logroño
San Juan de la Peña
San Prudencio de Laturce
Ebro R.
San Millán de la Cogolla
Toledo

CHAPTER I

INTRODUCTION

In 1930, Peter Wagner published what has remained the only study to appear in print of the responsorial psalm tones of the Mozarabic office.[1] This study was based primarily on that portion of the Santiago manuscript (the Book of Hours of Ferdinand I) which contains the night office, although comparison was made with manuscript 2.668 of the University of Salamanca Library (formerly Royal Palace manuscript 2 j 5), a source of a similar nature. In addition to making a classification of the tones employed, Wagner arrived at two principal conclusions. First, he concluded that because the notation of his two sources was "identical" there must have been a well-founded tradition in the Spanish Church from which individual singers did not vary. Second, he concluded that within these psalmodic forms there was much freedom in the adaptation of the melodies to the texts--a freedom never found within the forms of Gregorian music and thus suggesting a greater antiquity for the Mozarabic repertory. This freedom was such that a single intonation might appear with any one of several different mediants and final cadences.

Dom Casiano Rojo and Dom Germán Prado had reached a similar conclusion with regard to the freedom of application of psalm tones to texts in their brief remarks on the subject in *El Canto Mozárabe*, published only a year earlier. They asserted, furthermore, that in the León antiphoner a single tone accounted for 372 of a total 476 responds.[2]

Further study of the matter, taking into account more sources, indicates that these conclusions are in need of fundamental revision. It is evident, first of all, that the so-called northern sources transmit two clearly distinguishable traditions for these melodies. Despite incomplete information about the provenance of these sources, it appears that the two

---

[1] "Untersuchungen zu den Gesangstexten und zur responsorialen Psalmodie der altspanischen Liturgie," *Spanische Forschungen der Görresgesellschaft*, Erste Reihe, II (1930), 67-113.

[2] *El Canto Mozárabe* (Barcelona, 1929), p. 91.

traditions correspond to two regions in northern Spain: one the kingdom of León, the other the Ebro river basin above and below Logroño, known as the Rioja, plus neighboring Castile. Wagner's sources belong to the León tradition and are, of all the sources in either tradition, the two in closest agreement. The León tradition is the more developed of the two in that, although the melodies clearly correspond to those in the Rioja manuscripts, the formulas are somewhat more elaborate and more consistently applied. Certain of the Rioja sources show a tendency to elaborate the formulas after the fashion of the León manuscripts, and sources from both traditions contain an occasional piece notated in every detail after the opposed tradition. But there are features of the two traditions which serve unambiguously to identify them.

The application of the more common melodies to their texts, especially in the León sources, follows clearly defined principles. These principles are similar to those embodied in the Gregorian *responsoria prolixa* in that the melodies are generally bipartite, certain formulas remaining fixed while others are adjusted to the structure of the text involved. Adjustments are made much as adjustments of the Gregorian formulas are made: by the addition of puncta and by the suppression, contraction, and division of other elements. Even the adjustable formulas, however, are modified within rather narrowly drawn boundaries in most cases. Within these boundaries, the accentuation of the text is clearly the guiding principle. The text also exercises a strong influence over the melody in its grammatical construction, for clauses and phrases in the text are punctuated through the introduction of secondary mediants and intonations in the melody. Each psalm tone has its own formulas for this purpose, and these are applied according to the accentuation and the lengths of the phrases. What Wagner considered freely interchangeable variants of a single tone are clearly separate tones, each with its own intonations, cadences, and principles for adjustment.

The sources generally identified with Toledo do not present a unified practice with respect to these melodies either. Those with northern notation follow the Rioja tradition. But those with Toledan notation transmit two traditions distinct from both traditions of the north. The two Toledo traditions differ markedly not only from those of the north, but from each other. In general, the psalmody of the Toledo sources is much less elaborate and systematic than that of León.

Finally, in order to arrive at any conclusions about the number of psalm tones in general use for the responds in any of the traditions, both monastic and secular sources must be taken into account. Except in Lent and a few other periods during the year, when certain of the lesser hours are included, the secular office consists of Matins and Vespers, the monks being obliged to observe both of these in addition to their own round of services. Thus, neither type of source contains the entire repertory of responds for the office. In the north, certain melodies occur only once or not at all in the purely monastic repertory, but numerous times in the secular services. One melody, on the other hand, occurs only once in the antiphoner of León, but is common in the monastic sources.

In developing the preceding notions in detail, the present study will deal with the following sources, each preceded here by the abbreviation with which it will be referred to henceforth:[3]

---

[3] The dating of the sources here is generally that of Agustín Millares Carlo and Dom Jorge M. Pinell, who are in accord with the majority opinion among paleographers. Nevertheless, Dom Anscari M. Mundó has recently suggested the following (in his words, "somewhat daring") dates for certain of the Toledo manuscripts of interest for this study: *BN10001*, mid-11th cent.; *BN10110*, 13th-14th cent.; *Cinc*, *ca.* 1200; *MSC*, 13th cent.; *T33.3*, end of 12th cent.; *T35.4*, *ca.* 1192-1208; *T35.5*, 13th cent.; *T35.7*, 11th-12th cent. See Anscari M. Mundó, O.S.B., "La datación de los códices litúrgicos visigóticos toledanos," *Hispania Sacra*, XVIII (1965), 1-25.

Northern Sources

AL León Cathedral Archive, MS 8 (León Antiphoner), 10th cent.

A30 Royal Academy of History, Madrid, *Aemil.* 30 (San Millán Antiphoner), 10th cent.

A56 Royal Academy of History, Madrid, *Aemil.* 56 (San Millán *Liber ordinum*), 10th cent.

A60 Royal Academy of History, Madrid, *Aemil.* 60, 10th cent.

BM45 British Museum Add. MS 30845, 10th cent.

BM51 " Add. MS 30851, 11th cent.

BN11556 Biblioteca Nacional, Madrid, MS 11.556 (binding), 11th cent.

Calz Cathedral of Santo Domingo de la Calzada (fragment), 10th-11th cent.

LF-5 León Cathedral Archive, Fragment F-5, 10th-11th cent.[4]

Sal University of Salamanca Library, MS 2.668 (olim Madrid Real Palacio 2 j 5, *Liber canticorum et psalmi*), 1059

Sant University of Santiago de Compostela Library, reservado 5 (*Psalterium et liber canticorum,* Book of Hours of Ferdinand I), 1058

Silos 3 Santo Domingo de Silos, Bibl. del Monasterio MS 3 (olim B, *Ritus et Missae*), 1039

Silos 4 " MS 4 (olim A, *Liber ordinum*), 1052

Silos 5 " MS 5 (olim D, *Lectiones et officia*), 1009

Silos 6 " MS 6 (olim E, *Breviarium mozarabicum*), 11th cent.

Silos 7 " MS 7 (olim C, *Rituale antiquissimum*), 11th cent.

SJP University of Zaragoza, Library of the Faculty of Law, *Libro de San Voto* (eight folios of an antiphoner from San Juan de la Peña), 10th cent.

---

[4] For notice of the existence of this fragment I am indebted to the work of Clyde Waring Brockett, Jr., "Antiphons, Responsories, and Other Chants of the Mozarabic Rite," unpubl. diss. (Columbia, 1965).

Toledo Sources

BN10001 Biblioteca Nacional, Madrid, MS 10.001 (olim Biblioteca Capitular, Toledo, cajón 35, number 1, binding), 9th-10th cent.

BN10110 Biblioteca Nacional, Madrid, MS 10.110 (olim Biblioteca Capitular, Toledo, cajón 35, number 2, *Officia feriarum Quadragesimae*), 10th-11th cent.

BN13060 Biblioteca Nacional, Madrid, MS 13.060, an 18th century copy of a manuscript belonging to the Cathedral of Toledo, but now lost. The pieces with notation were executed by Don Francisco Javier Santiago de Palomares.

Cinc Library of Hebrew Union College, Cincinnati, Ohio (fragment), 9th-10th cent.

MSC Museo de Santa Cruz, Toledo, Inventario General 1325 (olim Museo de San Vicente, fragment 2), 9th cent.

T33.3 Biblioteca Capitular, Toledo, cajón 33, number 3 *(Liber horarum)*, 9th cent.

T35.4 Biblioteca Capitular, Toledo, cajón 35, number 4 *(Officia et Missae)*, 9th-10th cent.

T35.5 Biblioteca Capitular, Toledo, cajón 35, number 5 *(Officia et Missae)*, 9th-10th cent.

T35.7 Biblioteca Capitular, Toledo, cajón 35, number 7 *(Officia et Missae)*, 9th-10th cent.

Lest there be any confusion about the matter, a few words are in order about the abbreviations for the responds of the office employed in the sources. I am of the opinion that these abbreviations are always to be read as *RS* despite their rather varied forms even within single sources. Such confusion as has existed in the past has developed largely from the abbreviation which appears in manuscripts *BM51, Sal*, and *Silos 4*.[5] Gilson and Wagner read this as *PS*, the former

---

[5] The last of these may be seen in plate 6 of Rojo's and Prado's *El Canto Mozárabe*.

for *Psalmus*, the latter for *Psallendum* or *Psallendo*; and Ferotin read it in *Sal* as *LS* for *Laudes*.[6] As all three of these writers noticed, this abbreviation is at one time or another associated with a rubric specifying *Responsum* or *Responsuria*. Furthermore, the *Laudes* and the *Psallendo* are pieces with different structures and with their own distinct rubrics. The *Laudes* of the office is indeed a responsorial piece, but its form is quite different from that of the responds properly so called. The abbreviation employed for it is *LDS*.[7] The term *Psallendum* is best avoided altogether as a confusion of the *Psalmo* of the Mass and the *Psallendo* of Matins and Vespers. The former is the Mozarabic analogue of the Roman Gradual and is abbreviated in the sources as *PSLM* or *PSLMO*, the latter being employed consistently in *A30* and occasionally in *AL*. The *Psallendo* does not usually have a responsorial form and is generally abbreviated *PSLD* or *PSLDO*, the latter appearing consistently in *A30* as well as occasionally in *AL* and *Silos 6*. The abbreviation *PSLDM* occurs very rarely (never in *AL*) and only at Vespers. The abbreviation *RS* is reserved exclusively for the responds of the office and for the *Ad confractionem panis* of the Mass, e.g., on *AL* fol. 111. The latter, however, is of a different form from the pieces under consideration here, for it lacks a verse. In the office responds, this verse is set off by the abbreviation *VR*.

In order to facilitate discussion, the following list presents the neumes appearing most frequently in the psalm tones in question, their Latin names being provided after the tables of Rojo and Prado. The Mozarabic notation includes a

---

[6] *Liber Mozarabicum Sacramentorum, Monumenta Ecclesiae Liturgica*, Vol. VI (Paris, 1912), p. xxxvii.

[7] The form is identical in manuscripts *Sal* and *Sant*, the latter of which may be seen in plate IX of Dom Louis Brou's "Notes de paléographie musicale mozarabe," *Anuario Musical*, VII (1952), 51-76.

wide variety of neumes, many of which are apparently interchangeable. Nevertheless, it is essential that all of these forms be distinguished.[8]

	Northern	Toledan
Punctum		
Virga		
Podatus		
Clivis		
Torculus		
Scandicus (3 notes)		
Scandicus (4 notes)		
Climacus		

[8] Wagner transcribes the figures as , e.g., in his types III and VIb.

CHAPTER II

THE LEÓN TRADITION AND ITS SOURCES

Owing to the completeness of *AL*, the repertory of responds in the León tradition is rather more extensive than that of the Rioja tradition or either of the Toledo traditions. This manuscript alone includes almost 500 responds with musical notation for their verses. To these must be added about thirty pieces which are peculiar to the night office found in *Sant* and *Sal*.[9] This total repertory is also more homogeneous than that of the Rioja sources, for the León sources are more consistent and more closely related to each other. Even in questions of notational detail, the León sources present a much more unified practice, the sources *Sant* and *Sal* being virtually identical. Nevertheless, *AL* differs from the other two sources in one detail. The vast majority of its respond verses end with the figure , a figure which is never part of the psalm tones as they are presented in the other two sources. The appearance of this figure in *AL* has doubtless contributed to the impression that there is really only one psalm tone being employed. Certain details, however, suggest that this figure was not found in the model from which *AL* was copied and should not be regarded as an essential part of the León tradition.

Throughout *AL*, a second hand has made occasional additions in the margins or between lines. Five times this second hand has supplied a respond verse with notation--once (fol. 251^v *RS Vir dilectus)* by erasing the original notation and four times (fol. 38 *RS Montes filie Syon,* fol. 93 *Propter honorem,* fol. 214 *Me oportet,* fol. 254 *Egredere inter lilia*) by making

---

[9] Mons. Dr. Theophilo Ayuso Marazuela has thus far been the only person to suggest that *Sal* actually proceeds from León: *Psalterium Uisigothicum-Mozarabicum, Biblia Polyglotta Matritensia*, Series VII, *Uetus Latina* L. 21 (Madrid, 1957), p. 13, Codex 38. Whatever its provenance, it belongs, for the present purposes, in a group with *AL* and *Sant*, both of which are generally regarded as products of León.

additions in the margin. Where the original notation has remained, the figure is a part of it, but this figure is always omitted by the second hand. In two of the pieces (fol. 38 *RS Montes filie Syon* and fol. 214 *RS Me oportet*), the second hand indicates a repetition of the same portion of the refrain as that indicated by the first hand. Thus, the figure is apparently not even designed to smooth the transition from the end of the verse to the repetition of the final portion of the refrain, so far as the second scribe was concerned.

There are also extensive erasures throughout *AL*. Generally they affect only the music, the correcting hand being indistinguishable from the original hand appearing elsewhere. At times, however, the erasures involve both text and music, the new text being supplied by the same hand which made the marginal additions. It seems likely, therefore, that the erasures and the marginal additions are the work of the same scribe. In any case, the respond verses with erasures show characteristics in common with those added in the margins. For example, fol. 228 *VR De fructu,* fol. 272v *VR Domine probasti,* and fol. 229 *VR Quum intenderes* all end with simple puncta, the original having been erased, but remaining dimly visible.[10] Only on fol. 82v *VR Converte nos* does it appear that the second hand wrote the , but here the punctum is present too.

Even the pieces notated entirely by the first hand show inconsistencies in the use of this final figure. The first hand has omitted it altogether in at least fifteen pieces, e.g., fol. 36 *VR Ponam iudicium,* fol. 46v *VR Precipitabit Dominus,* fol. 142 *VR Scio quod redemptor,* and fol. 162 *VR Filius quidem.* All of the tones represented here appear

---

[10] Unfortunately, it is impossible to discern the erasures, much less what has been erased, from the facsimile edition. Even first hand examination of the manuscript does not always reveal the original notation.

elsewhere in the manuscript with the final figure. In addition, a number of pieces provide the final syllable of text with both a punctum and the figure in question, thus, . The following are examples: fol. 127 *VR Domine miserere*, fol. 279v *VR Ne irascaris*, fol. 97v *VR Infixus sum*, and fol. 121v *VR Non secundum*. Since we possess sources lacking the altogether, namely *Sant* and *Sal*, and since the second hand in *AL* seems not to have employed it, with the one exception mentioned above, these peculiarities in the original hand suggest that *AL* was copied from a model which also lacked it. The copyist generally supplied it, but occasionally forgot to do so and occasionally remembered to do so only after copying the final punctum of his model. But why should he have bothered to supply it at all? The Rioja sources invariably make this the final figure in tones which, in *Sant* and *Sal*, end with a punctum. Furthermore, *AL*, unlike *Sant* and *Sal*, includes an occasional piece notated after the Rioja tradition. Thus, the original scribe in *AL*, while following the León tradition in all of its essential details, apparently had some knowledge of the Rioja tradition and sought to adopt this one feature from it, adding it wherever he found a psalm tone ending with a punctum.

What applies to also applies to , a figure which appears occasionally in both *AL* and the Rioja sources. In all probability, the difference between the two is related to the problem of making a smooth connection between the end of the verse and the portion of the refrain which is to be repeated. The notation of the refrains, however, does not make this obvious, and the sources do not always agree in their use of the one and the other. Thus, in discussing the individual tones as they appear in the León tradition, I shall not consider the presence or absence of either figure as significant.

In the León tradition, there are seven tones which appear more than once for the respond verses. The frequency with which they appear, however, varies greatly. The least common appears in *AL* only five times, the most common more than 200. The structural plan also varies from tone to tone. For example, some tones have a six element final cadence, but another tone has a two element final cadence. In this sense the Mozarabic repertory does present a much greater freedom of forms than the Gregorian, suggesting that the Mozarabic tones developed separately without any full-blown modal system in view. But in the more common tones of the Mozarabic repertory, whatever the structure of a particular tone, that structure is respected scrupulously.

Tone A[11]

AL includes 150 verses notated with this melody. Its first intonation consists of a maximum of ten elements, these being adjusted to the text accent. The following examples illustrate the placing of the first accent.

	1	2	3	4	5	6	7	8	9	10
fol.127^{v}			Vi-	de	hu-	mi-	li-	tá-	tem	me-(am)
fol.100^{v}	Be-		á-	ti	qui	per-	se-	quu-	ti-	ó-(nem)
fol.157^{v}	Con-	lo-	cá-	bit	me	in	ob-	scú-	ris	sic-(ut)
fol.54^{v}	E-		gre-		di-	é-	tur	vir-	ga	de
fol.39	Quis	re-	mi-		nis-	cí-	mi-	ni		Dó-(minum)

[11] In order to avoid implications of modality and confusion with Wagner's classification of the tones in *Sant* and *Sal*, the seven tones will be identified with the letters A through G. Tones A, B, and C correspond roughly to Wagner's tones VIa, VIb, and VIc, except that the second halves are not interchangeable as in his scheme. His first example under tone IV (piece 13) belongs to my tone D, although it is an exceptional case as we shall see. His second example under tone IV (piece 33) belongs to my tone E. His tone V corresponds to my tone F. Tone G occurs in *Sant*, but not

If the first accent falls on one of the first three syllables, it is placed in column 3. If it falls on the fourth or fifth syllable, it is placed in column 6. Elements 1 and 2 serve to make the adjustment, all other elements up through 8 (except 4) being invariably present. Thus, there are clear limits to the adjustability of the melody. Column 3 is never preceded by more than two syllables, the podatus always being added before the punctum is added. In this respect, the Gregorian formulas are somewhat more flexible, for in the eighth tone, there may be as many as four introductory puncta.[12]

The most basic rule governing this intonation is that a clivis may never bear an accent. If podatus 1 and punctum 2 serve to make the necessary adjustments with respect to the first accent, punctum 4 makes them with respect to the second in those cases where the first accent is placed in column 3. The following examples illustrate the placing of the second accent in such cases.

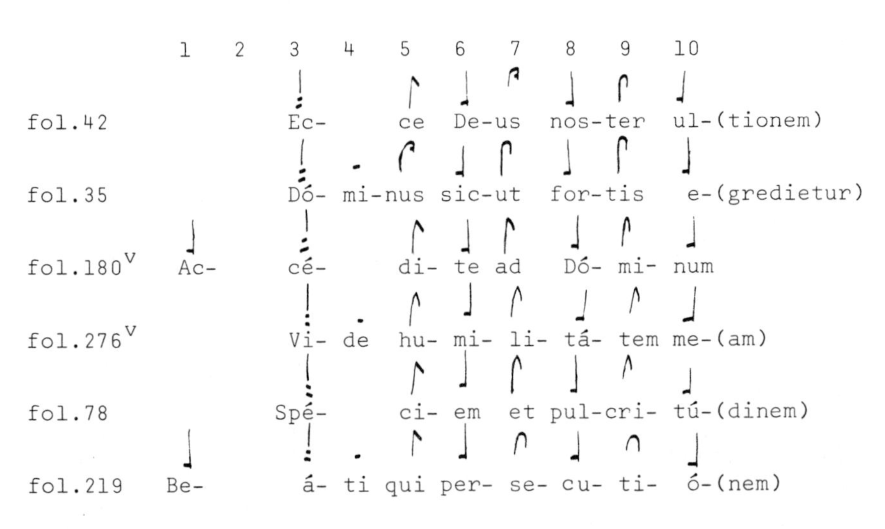

among the pieces which Wagner studied. On the other hand, his tones I, II, and III are unica. Of course, he had not studied *AL* when he made this classification ("Untersuchungen ...," p. 104).

[12] See the examples and discussion by Dom Paolo Ferretti, O.S.B., *Esthétique Grégorienne*, (Paris, 1938).

Once again, the limits within which the melody may be modified are clear. Only three pieces include so much as an extra punctum in column 4.[13]

One further modification of this formula may serve to place accents under a podatus instead of a clivis. When the syllable in column 8 is followed immediately by an accented syllable, or when it is separated from the mediant by three or fewer syllables, podatus 8 and clivis 9 are contracted to form a torculus. This contraction governs an accent in column 10 only when the preceding accent has been placed in column 6. Otherwise, accents falling in column 10 are governed by punctum 4. Unless followed immediately by the mediant, the torculus is followed by podatus 10 and, if necessary, a number of puncta. Upwards of ten pieces, however, make this contraction for no apparent reason, the second syllable after the torculus bearing an accent which could have been placed in column 10.

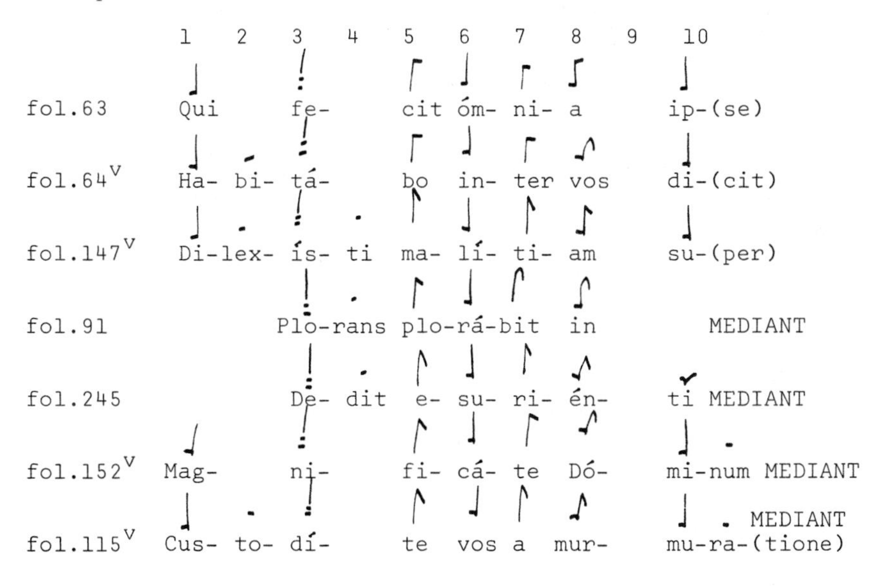

[13] fol. 113v *VR Pauperem nolite*, fol. 161v *VR Oculus adulteri*, and fol. 220v *VR Oleum recondite*. In all three pieces, the puncta bear the final two syllables of a word accented on the antepenultimate syllable and followed by a

The only additional alteration of this intonation results from the shortness of some texts. When column 6 is separated from the mediant by only one or two syllables, clivis 7 and clivis 9 may be contracted as follows:

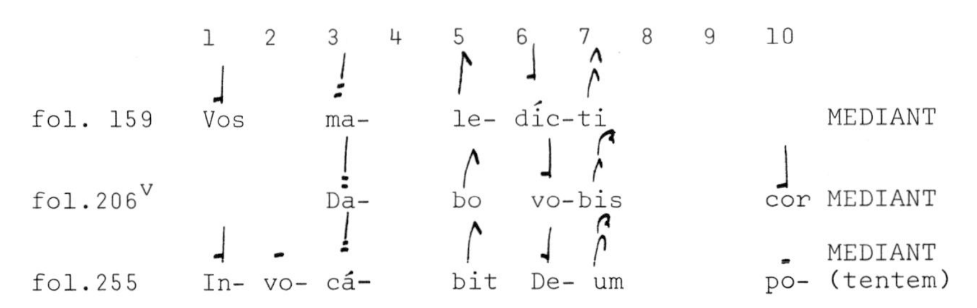

Where there are two syllables between column 6 and the mediant, however, there is no apparent reason for preferring the treatment of the last two examples to that of *VR Plorans plorabit,* shown in the preceding examples.

In the majority of cases, the text accentuation is straightforward. Thus, problems in the adaptation of the melodies according to the foregoing principles rarely arise. Nevertheless, some cases have characteristics which require special comment. This intonation formula, as well as that of tone B, has, built into it, a series of accents on alternate syllables. This reflects a certain period in the development of Latin in which polysyllabic words tended to acquire secondary accents on alternate syllables preceding and following the primary accent.[14] It also reflects the fact that two accented syllables normally cannot occur successively. A monosyllable, however, may bear a logical accent and thus, if it is followed by another accented syllable, disrupt the even flow of primary and secondary accents. These intonations cannot always accommodate such

---

word which accents the second syllable. But they could equally well be handled like *VR Accedite ad Dominum* in the examples above.

[14] Ferretti, *Esthétique,* p. 6.

situations in the text, e.g., fol. 260^v *VR Stetit rêx ânte altare* (tone B). As in this example, such occurrences may occasion a violation of the clivis rule. In any case, the presence of a monosyllable gives rise to a certain flexibility in adapting the melody. Texts such as *VR Tu es enim Christus* (fol. 77) and *VR Hic est filius meus* (fol. 80^v) receive the treatment they do because of their sense, even though one might consider their first accents to fall on the third syllable. The criterion of logical accent also affects the treatment of some introductory bisyllabic words, both syllables of which may be treated as merely anticipatory to the primary accent of the following word, e.g., fol. 125^v *VR Numquid ôculi*, fol. 48 *Quia hostendîsti* (tone B), and fol. 269 *VR Propter fratres* (tone B).

Non-Latin proper names may also appear to contradict the normal accentuation of the melody. Nevertheless, medieval practice often accented the final syllables of such names which were not declined in Latin,[15] thus, fol. 45 *VR Audi me Iacôb* and fol. 59^v *VR Et tu Bethlêm* (both tone B). This treatment accords with modern Spanish pronunciation. Mozarabic sources, however, do not always agree on this matter, manuscript *A30* accenting both *Bethlem* and *Iacob* on the first syllable. *Iherusalem*, furthermore, seems to be accented always on the penultimate syllable, e.g., fol. 66^v *VR Lauda Iherusalem* (tone B), even though it too is accented on the final syllable in the vernacular.

Finally, the Latin language underwent changes in the Middle Ages which affected pronunciation and account for other peculiarities in the application of the Mozarabic psalm tones.[16]

[15] Peter Wagner, *Einführung in die Gregorianischen Melodien* (Hildesheim, 1962), III, 39, 126, 288. First edn., 3 vols., Leipzig, 1911-1921.

[16] See M. C. Díaz y Díaz, "El latín de la liturgia hispánica," *Estudios sobre la Liturgia Mozárabe*, ed. Juan Francisco Rivera Recio (Toledo, Spain, 1965), pp. 55-87.

The third conjugation became progressively less important, many of its verbs being transferred to the second or fourth conjugations. Thus, the present imperative active of *plaudo, plaudĕre* appears in *AL* as *plaudēte,* transferred to the second conjugation (fol. 30 *VR Omnes gentes plaudēte,* a common text), and in *A30* as *plaudíte,* transferred to the fourth conjugation (*A30* fol. 5^v^ and elsewhere *VR Omnes gentes plaudíte).* Similarly, *quáerite,* from the third conjugation *quaero, quaerĕre,* becomes *queríte* on *AL* fol. 115 *VR Queríte Dominum. Erípe* is almost always accented as on fol. 135^v^ *VR Erípe me de inimicis.* A student of the language might say whether this too results from a shift in conjugation or perhaps a levelling tendency, associated with the rise of the vernacular, to accent words on the penultimate syllable. Orthography also causes difficulty with the accentuation at times, e.g., fol. 225^v^ *VR Felix qui suscepit,* which doubtless should be *súscipit,* as in *BM45* fol. 58^v^, instead of the perfect tense *suscépit.* As Professor Díaz y Díaz notes, a careful and thorough study of such linguistic phenomena in peninsular sources remains to be made. It is to be hoped that musicology will be of aid in such a study.

In tone A, those syllables, if any, occurring in the first half of the verse between the intonation and the mediant are borne by puncta.[17] The mediant is then a one-accent tonic formula. Where the final accent of the first half of the verse falls on the penultimate syllable, the mediant invariably consists of two elements as follows:

---

[17] In only three pieces is this series of puncta interrupted by so much as a single podatus.

2 1

fol.197v Dominus Ihesus Christus qui est testis fi-dé- lis

fol.236v Liverabo te de manu pessi- mó- rum

fol.195v Pertransierunt quasi ná- bes

fol.208v Ego rogabo pa- trem

If the final accent falls on the antepenultimate syllable, the torculus is divided into a podatus and a clivis. In short texts, however, this podatus may be contracted with podatus 10 of the intonation. Thus, if there are only three or fewer syllables between podatus 6 of the intonation and the accent-bearing antepenultimate syllable of the first half of the verse, the mediant assumes the form shown in the first three examples below. Otherwise, the form is that of the last three examples.[18]

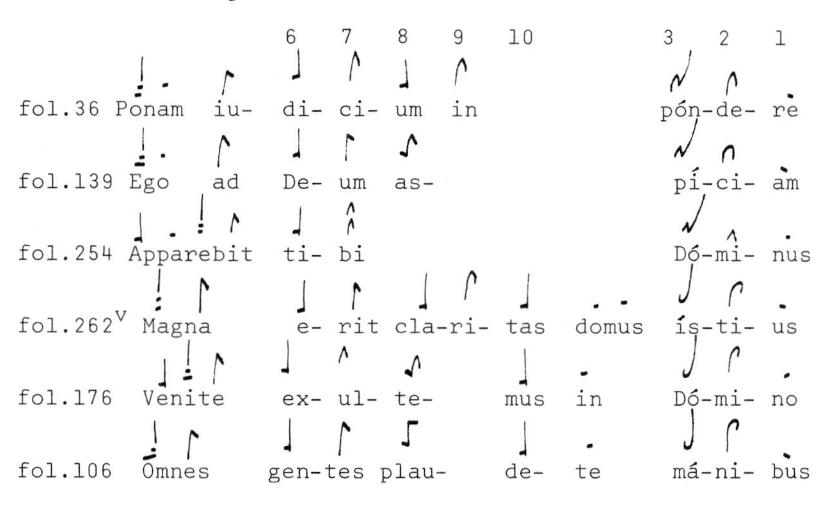

[18] The formula shown in the first three examples is that of Wagner's tone VIc, and in his scheme it may be joined to either of two formulas for the second half of a verse. What-

In its simplest and most common form, tone A consists of two parts, corresponding to the bipartite structure of the accompanying text. We have seen that both the intonation and the cadence of the first part are adjusted to the accents of the text. The second part, however, has fixed formulas for both the intonation and the cadence in this simple form. Elements of these formulas may be suppressed or contracted only in cases of a reduced number of syllables in the text. The intonation consists of a scandicus and a clivis applied mechanically to the first two syllables of text. The cadence consists of six elements plus an anticipatory punctum applied mechanically to the last seven syllables of text. The following examples illustrate the treatment accorded texts of varying lengths.

1 2 A 6 5 4 3 2 1

fol.74 VR Quid retribuam...

cá- li- cem sa- lu- tá- ris ac- cí- pi- am

fol.145 VR Qui custodiebant...

con-sí- lium fecé-runt in ú- num di- cén-tes

fol.211 VR Mulier fortis...

et án- nos vi- te íl- li- us

fol.255[V] VR Ad te lebamus... qui á- bi- tas in cae-lis

fol.158 VR Suscitatur... con-tra-dí- cens mi-ci

fol.254 VR Propter veritatem... et ius- tí- ti-am

---

ever the name, it should be noted that it results simply from the application of the first half of tone A (his VIa) to a short text, despite the two exceptions in *AL* which might have been handled with the normal three element mediant (fol. 248[V] *VR Vos sancti* and fol. 249 *Beati omnes*). The first half of tone C bears a strong resemblance to that of tone A, but we shall see that it is treated differently with respect to the texts.

The complete formula for the second half in this simple form thus consists of nine elements, all syllables in excess of this number being borne by puncta. If there are only eight syllables, the clivis of the intonation is suppressed,[19] if seven, the scandicus is also suppressed, and so on.

Six pieces substitute a podatus for punctum 2 of the cadence.[20] This variant apparently has nothing to do with the texts, for two of them (*VR Vide humilitatem*, on foll. 276^v and 294^v, and *VR Deus in nomine*, on fol. 122^v) appear elsewhere without it. Nor does this variant appear in either *Sant* or *Sal*. Finally, there are six pieces in which the podatus has been erased and replaced by a punctum.[21] Thus, this podatus seems to be a peculiarity of the original scribe in *AL* and one regarded by the reviser of *AL* as a mistake at least half of the time. The reviser once again shows himself to incline toward the readings of *Sant* or *Sal* where these differ from *AL*. With only one exception, *Sal* gives the form h for punctum 2 of the cadence. In *AL* this form occurs in this position only three times by the original scribe,[22] but eight times by the reviser. Only twice was the erased podatus replaced by the simpler punctum.

Some texts are divided into three or even four parts according to their sense or grammatical construction. In such cases, the psalm tones reflect the construction of the texts by including secondary intonations and mediants. These

---

[19] This clivis is occasionally replaced by a punctum in texts of nine syllables.

[20] Fol.125^v *VR Numquid oculi*, fol. 127^v *VR Vide humilitatem*, fol. 240 *VR Descendit cum illis*, fol. 255 *VR Invocabit Deum*, fol. 275^v *VR Deus in nomine*, and fol. 280 *VR Dominus mortificat*.

[21] Fol. 63^v *VR Deus pacis*, fol. 73^v *VR Ego Dominus*, fol. 80^v *VR Hic est filius*, fol. 150 *VR Amici mei*, fol. 262^v *VR Magna erit*, and fol. 290^v *VR Ponam sanctuarium*.

[22] Fol. 36 *VR Ponam iudicium*, fol. 77 *VR Tu es enim Christus*, and fol. 90 *VR Beati qui persequutionem*.

melodic formulas are occasionally applied to texts in which the sense of the subdivision is not clear. But when such texts appear more than once, they invariably receive the same treatment. Given such a division, the melodic formulas are applied with great consistency. In tone A, the first part is always left intact as described above, what follows being divided into two or three subsections if necessary. When there are three subsections, the last one is treated exactly like the second part of the two-part melody described above. When there are two subsections, the second intonation described above is replaced. But the final cadence remains the same in all cases.

The formula applied to the first subsection depends on the number of syllables preceding the final accent of that portion of text. Three or four such syllables require the following formula in which the final accent is adjusted to fall under a scandicus. The final syllable may be borne by either a podatus or a punctum.

fol.219 VR Beati qui persecutionem... prop-ter ius-tí-ti-am

fol.184[v] VR Ego dormibi... et re- sur-réx- i

fol.194 VR Laudem dicite... om-nes ser-vi e- ius

If there are five or more syllables preceding the final accent of this subsection, the formula is altered and expanded as follows:

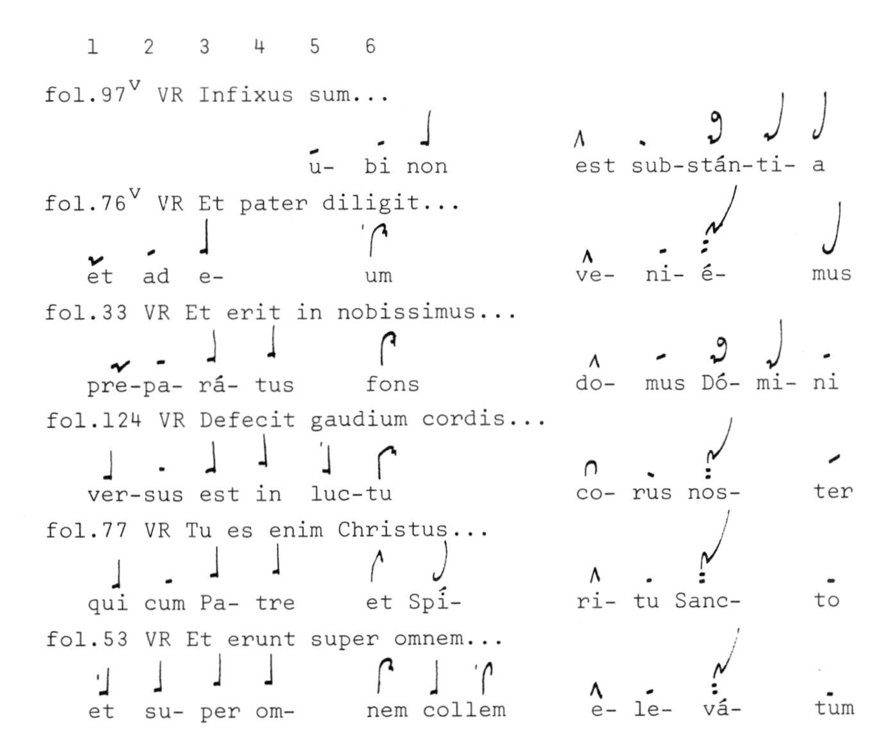

The cadence is adjusted to the final accent, but is preceded by a clivis and a punctum which are mechanically applied. When more than three syllables precede this clivis, the intonation is adjusted for accent by placing a podatus in column 2 if necessary. The clivis in column 6 never bears an accent. Instead, it may be followed by an accent-bearing podatus. Lengthy texts may require additional podati and clives between column 6 and the final clivis. Once again, the final syllable may appear under either a punctum or a podatus.

If there are three subsections, the first invariably ends with a podatus, the second beginning with a punctum and a torculus applied mechanically to the first two syllables. A podatus follows if the third syllable is accented. Only four pieces are divided into three subsections in this way, and in all of them, the final accent happens to fall on the penultimate syllable. Thus, the available examples offer no check on whether the cadence is adjustable.

fol.63^{v} VR Deus pacis...

ánima et cor-pus si- nè que-rél-la

fol.97^{v} VR Infixus sum...

devéni in al- ti- tú- di- ne ma- ris

fol.180 VR Et non egebunt...

quóniam Dóminus De- us in- lú- mi- nat e- os

fol.229 VR Quum intenderes...

extendísti ma- num tu- am

If there are only two subsections, the first may end with either a punctum or a podatus, the intonation of the second being determined accordingly. A punctum ending results in a final subsection treated like the unsubdivided second part of this tone described above. A podatus ending results in an intonation for the final subsection in which a punctum and a torculus are mechanically applied to the first two syllables. The torculus is at times followed by a podatus, but this has no relation to the accent. The final cadence for the psalm tone is, of course, the same regardless of the number of subsections preceding.

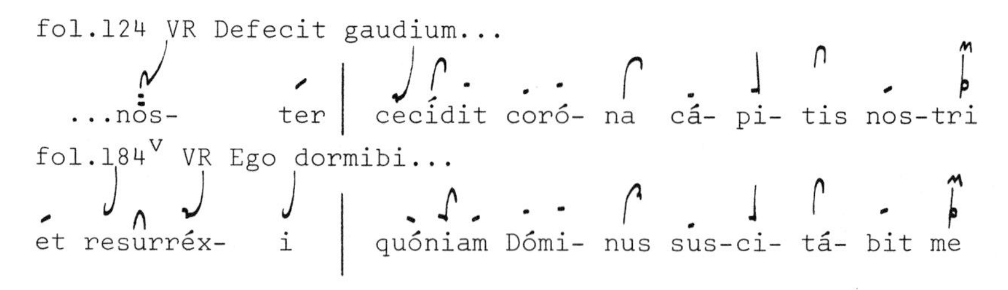

The reasons governing the choice of podatus or punctum

for the final syllable of the first of two subsections are not apparent. Nevertheless, such reasons seem to have existed, for on two occasions, the reviser has substituted a podatus for a punctum, revising the following intonation accordingly (fol. 76^v *VR Et pater diligit* and fol. 186 *VR Et undecim discipuli*).

We may now characterize tone A as follows:

1. The structure is basically bipartite. But the second part may consist of two or three subsections. The formula for the unsubdivided second part may be preserved intact at the end in such cases, although its intonation is often replaced.

2. The intonation for the first part is always adjusted for the text accent. The intonation for the second part, or its final subsection if it is divided, is never adjusted. The intonations for subsections, other than the last, vary in this regard.

3. All mediants are adjusted to the final accent of their texts.

4. The final cadence consists of six elements, mechanically applied to the last six syllables of text, preceded by an anticipatory punctum.

Tone B

There are 227 respond verses in *AL* notated with tone B. Thus, it is by far the most common of the seven tones. Its intonation clearly resembles that of tone A, but the following examples will illustrate some of its peculiarities.

	1	2	3	4	5	6	7	8	9	10	11
fol.56			Ec-		ce	De-	us		nos-	ter	ul-(tionem)
fol.82v	Os-		tén-		de	no-	bis		Dó-	mi-	ne
fol.86v	In-	ve-	né-	runt	pu-	é-	rum		cum	Ma-	ri-(a)
fol.116v	De		sanc-		tu-	á-	ri-	o	tu-	o	Dó-(mine)
fol.224v	In-		plé-	tus	es	qua-	si		flu-	men	sa-(pientia)
fol.223v	Os		ius-		ti	me-	di-		tá-	bi-	tur
fol.247v	Be-		á-	ti	qui	per-	se-		quu-	ti-	ó-(nem)
fol.251v			Ho-		mo	is-	te	in	vi-	ta	su-(a)

The scandicus of column 6 is the most obvious difference between this intonation and the intonation of tone A. This scandicus never appears in an intonation associated with the formulas of the second half of tone A. The other principal difference with the intonation of tone A lies in the punctum of column 8. In tone A, accents may be adjusted to fall on the final podatus by means of contracting the preceding podatus and clivis into a torculus. In tone B, however, punctum 8 serves this purpose. This punctum never appears in tone A. Compare, for example, the settings of the following text in tones A and B.

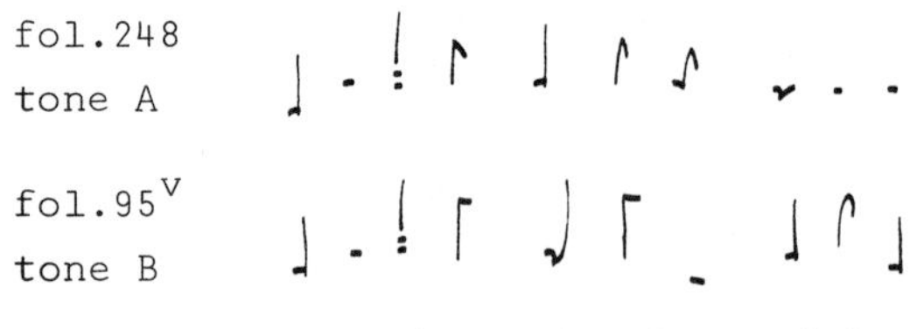

Clamabérunt iusti et Dóminus

Although the function of the contraction in tone A is assumed by the punctum in tone B, a similar contraction of elements 9 and 10 in tone B is also made at times. However, this contraction results primarily from the shortness of some texts. Only rarely is it made if there are as many as six syllables separating column 6 from the mediant, regardless of the accent pattern. But texts with as few as five syllables between column 6 and the mediant are occasionally set by the complete formula, as in the last of the examples below.

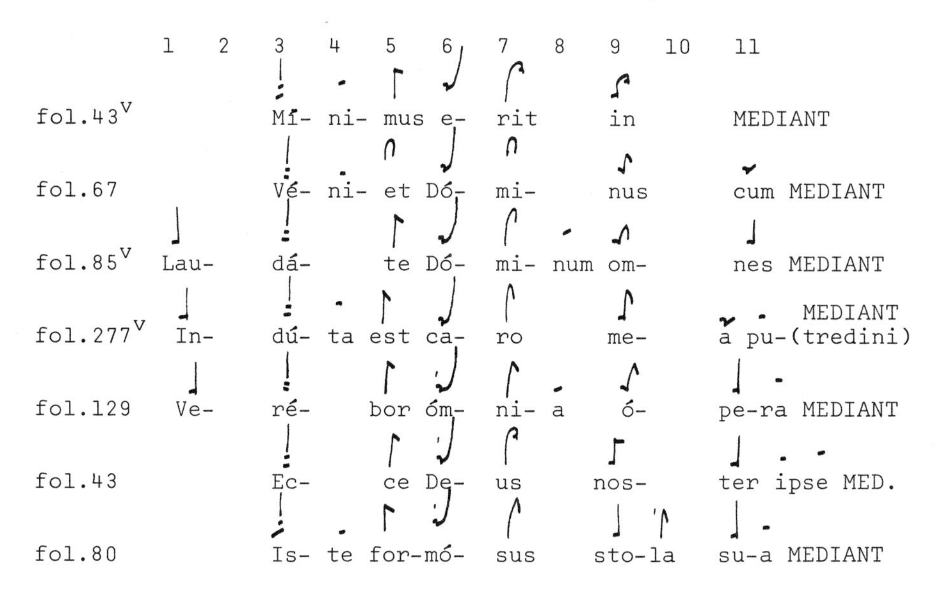

Still shorter texts may bring about more fundamental alterations in the intonation. Scandicus 6 may be omitted, and clivis 10 may bear an accent as a result. Although a torculus in column 9 may bear the accent instead, the only real exceptions to the clivis rule are found among pieces in which scandicus 6 is omitted.

	1	2	3	4	5	6	7	8	9	10	11
fol.66^v	Pa-		rá-		te					vi-	am
fol.87			E-	go	sum				al-		fa
fol.113^v			Tá-	cu-	i					sem-	per

When scandicus 6 appears, it is always followed by clivis 7 and podatus (or torculus) 9. Thus, texts with as many as four syllables between column 3 and the mediant need not eliminate scandicus 6 unless the third of these syllables is accented, as in the last two examples above. Nevertheless, it is eliminated in a few pieces that have five such syllables.

Thus, the intonation for tone B, like that for tone A, is clearly tailored to the structure of the text. But only certain alterations of the formula are allowed. Puncta may be inserted for the purpose of regulating accents at only three points and, in general, only one punctum at each of these. Furthermore, the functions of these three puncta are differentiated. The punctum of column 2 governs the placing of the first accent even if that accent is placed after column 4. Similarly, if an accent falls in column 3, the punctum of column 4 governs the placing of the following accent even if it falls after column 8. Finally, when elements of the formula must be suppressed, a priority of the elements or groups of elements is always observed.

Like tone A, tone B generally assumes a simple bipartite form. The mediant is adjusted to the final accent of the first part of the text as in the examples below. Note that if podatus 11 is omitted from the intonation, it is contracted with the first element of the mediant, as in the last two examples.

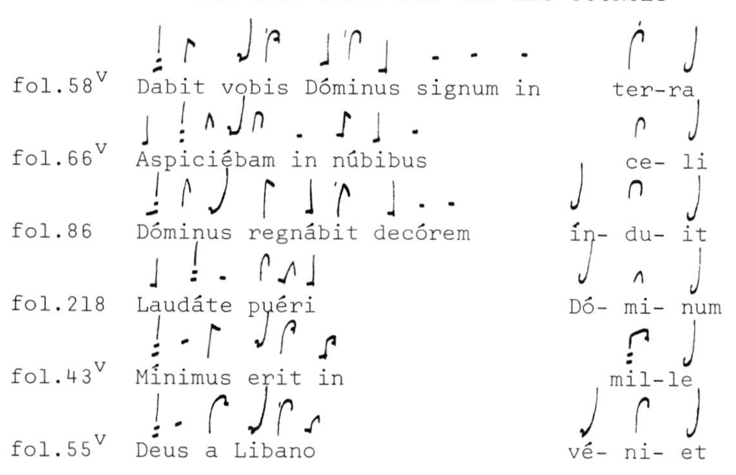

However, there may be more than one division in the text. In such cases, tone B, as opposed to tone A, subdivides in the first part of the melody, but this first part may be divided only into two subsections. If further subdivisions are necessary, the second part may also be divided. The secondary mediant inserted in the first part of tone B is adjusted to the final accent of the text phrase. Here again, a contraction may be made with podatus 11 of the intonation.

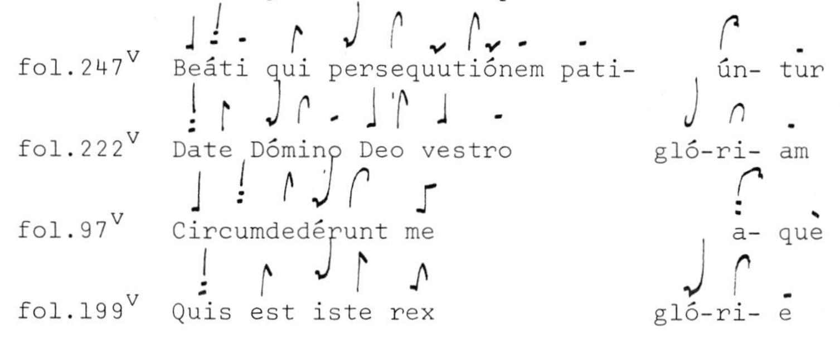

When the first part is subdivided, the mediant which ends it (that is, the cadence for the second subsection) takes a form slightly different from that described above. The following examples illustrate the way in which it is adjusted to the final accent of the text in such cases.

fol.199^{v} VR Quis est iste rex glorie | Dominus vir-tú- tum

fol.222^{v} VR Date Domino Deo vestro gloriam|...tene- brés- cat

fol.97^{v} VR Circumdederunt me aque | usque ad á- ni-mam

fol.247^{v} VR Beati qui persequutionem... | ...ius- tí-ti-am

The remainder of the second subsection depends on the number of syllables of text to be set. If there are five or fewer syllables preceding the mediant, the formula is that shown in the examples below.

fol.183 VR Christus surgens a mortuis | iam non móritur

fol.45 VR Audi me Iacob et Israhel | quem e- go vo- co

fol.48 VR Quia hostendisti mici... | mul-tas et ma- las

fol.91^{v} VR Deducant oculi mei lacrimas | per di- em et noc-tem

fol.71 VR Ecce Deus noster iste est | expec-tá- bi- mus e- um

The podatus and the clivis of this formula are never separated, and the clivis is never followed by more than one punctum. Thus, accents cannot always be adjusted to fall under the podatus, although they frequently are, as in the second and third examples.

If there are six or more syllables preceding the mediant in the second subsection, a clivis and a punctum are applied mechanically to the last two. The intonation for this subsection is then adjusted for the first accent of the text and takes the form shown in the following examples.

		1	2	3	4	5
fol.208	VR Spiritus sanctus...		et	im-	plé-	vit...
fol.109ᵛ	VR Maledicta dies...		di-	es	in	qua...
fol.127	VR Peregrinus ego...	re-	mít-	te	mi-	ci...

If only one syllable separates column 5 from the final clivis preceding the mediant, that syllable is borne by a podatus. If there are more syllables intervening and the second is accented, it may be borne by a podatus. Otherwise, syllables falling between column 5 and the final clivis are generally borne by an uninterrupted series of up to ten puncta.

The form assumed by the intonation of the second part of tone B depends on the length of the text in question. If there are seven or more syllables, the intonation consists of a punctum and three podati applied mechanically to the first four. If there are fewer than seven, this intonation is contracted to a four note scandicus which is placed over the first syllable.[23] Syllables falling between the intonation and the final cadence are borne only by puncta in all but seven pieces. Four of these introduce a single podatus at some point or other. The other three make subdivisions as follows.

---

[23] Four pieces, fol. 97^{v} *VR Circumdederunt me,* fol. 110 *VR Quiescite agere,* fol. 230^{v} and 239 *VR Fulgebunt iusti,* make the contraction even though they have seven syllable texts. In the last two of these, the four element intonation was erased and replaced by the contraction. The same text appears a third time on fol. 249 with the four element intonation. A handful of other pieces lack either the punctum or the final podatus for no apparent reason.

fol.152 VR Et alias abeo...

et il- las me op- pór-tet ad- dú- ci | ut sit...

fol.241^{v} VR Extendit super...

et ef- fú- dit in funda- mén-to al- tá-ris | odórem...

fol.103^{v} VR Quocumque ligaberis...

et quo-cúm-que sol- vé-ris super terram | erunt...

The final cadence consists, without exception, of two elements applied to the last two syllables mechanically. The following examples illustrate the treatment of the entire second part of the tone.

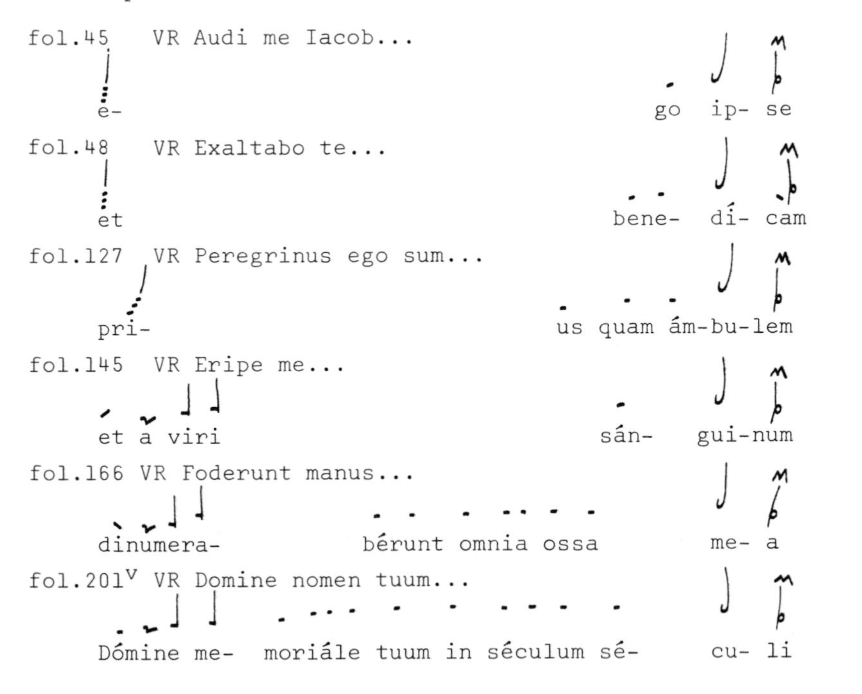

In summary, tone B may be described as follows.

1. The structure is basically bipartite. The first part

may be divided into two subsections. Only rarely is the second part divided.

2. The intonation for the first part is always adjusted for the text accent. The intonation for the second part is never adjusted for accent, although it may be contracted to a single figure for short texts. The secondary intonation which is at times inserted into the first part is adjusted for the accent.

3. All mediants are adjusted to the final accent of their texts.

4. The final cadence consists of two elements mechanically applied to the last two syllables of text.

Tone C

Only one respond verse in *AL* appears with the notation for tone C (fol. 276^{v} *VR Domine non sum dignus*). For other examples, we must turn to the night office in manuscripts *Sant* and *Sal* where the complete formula for this tone is associated with five pieces. In *Sal*, each of these pieces is given twice. Thus, we have in this source ten examples of the notation for this tone.

The intonation, as suggested above, bears a very strong resemblance to that of tone A. In fact, it is in some cases identical. But an examination of melodies the second parts of which clearly belong to tone C suggests that the intonations have certain peculiarities as well. These peculiarities have to do with the ways in which the formula is altered to accommodate different texts. First, pieces in which the second syllable bears the first accent may begin with a punctum. In tone A, all three of the León sources begin such pieces with a podatus. Second, two of the six different pieces with this melody omit clivis 7 following podatus 6. This happens only once in all of the examples of tone A (*AL* fol. 254^{v} *VR Recordatus sum*). Third, clivis 9 is followed directly by the mediant in one case. This too happens only once among all of the examples of tone A. Finally, *Sal* gives the first scandicus the form [neume] seven out of ten times, a form which never appears in this position either in tone A or tone B. The complete first parts of all six pieces are given below, the first five taken from *Sal* and the last from *AL*.

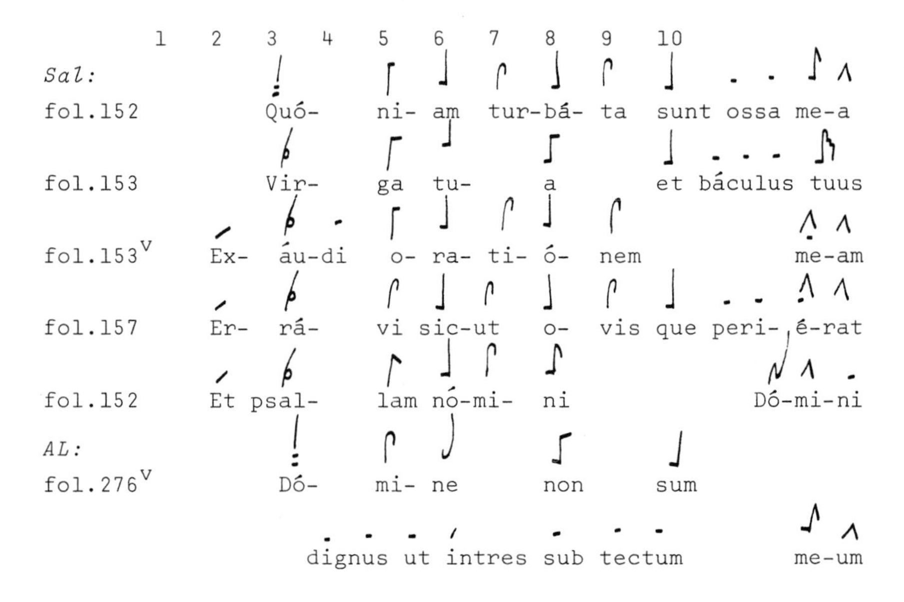

The mediant is adjusted to the final accent of the text, and where this falls on the penultimate syllable, the melodic formula employed is one not found in any examples of tone A. In one piece, however, the final accent falls on the antepenultimate syllable of a rather short text. Here the mediant takes the same form as that found with similar texts in tone A.

The second part of tone C resembles none of the other tones. Its intonation consists of a single podatus placed over the first syllable if that is accented and over the second syllable in all other cases. The final cadence consists of three elements applied mechanically to the last three syllables, although in one piece the first two elements are contracted.

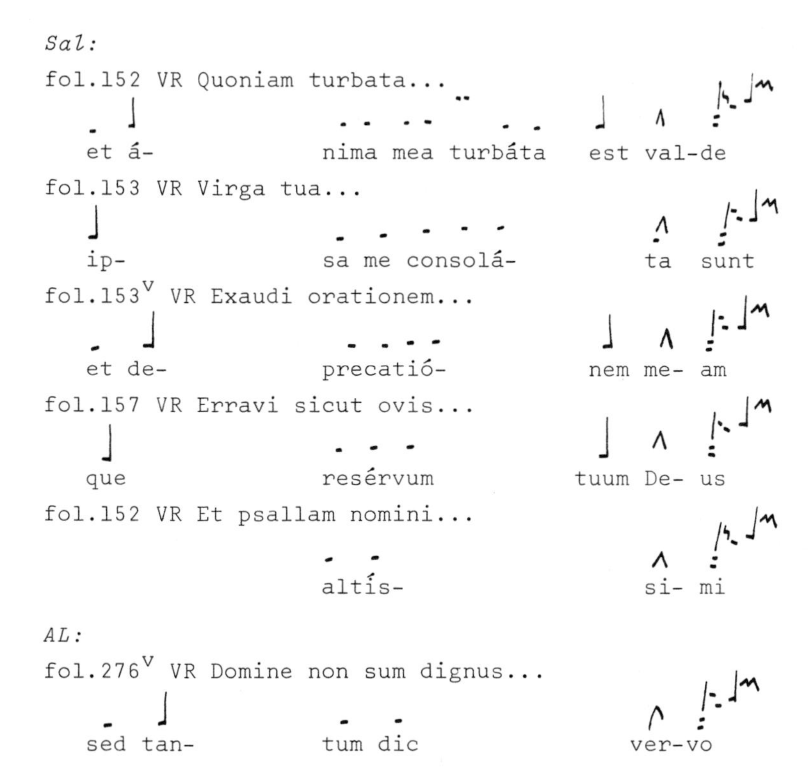

The second half of tone C appears with one more verse in both *Sant* and *Sal*, but in this case with an intonation for the first half which is unique. The piece in question is *RS Domine Deus virtutum VR Quam amabilia.*[24] The first half of the refrain is exactly the same in both text and music as the second half of the verse. Thus, on fol. 157 of *Sal*, the second half of the verse is not copied, a repetition of the entire refrain being indicated instead. On fol. 167v, the entire verse is written out, and only the second part of the refrain is repeated. This might somehow account for the

[24] Wagner makes this his tone II, saying that the absence of other examples indicates that it is in one of the less common modes. "Untersuchungen...," p. 93.

peculiar intonation except that, on fol. 157, the refrain *Vibit anima mea* has the same melody, and its verse, *Erravi sicut ovis*, is treated with the normal intonation shown above.[25] This suggests, first of all, that the melody for *VR Quam amabilia* is in the same mode as tone C, and second, that the second part of a tone may be more important than the intonation in establishing relationships among tones. Thus, despite the similarity between some of the intonations for tone C and those for tone A, pieces ending with the second part of tone C are best regarded as belonging together.

Tone C, then, has the following characteristics:

1. The structure is bipartite.
2. The intonation for the first part is adjusted for accent, as is the single podatus which comprises the intonation for the second part.
3. The mediant is adjusted to the final accent of its text.
4. The final cadence consists of three elements mechanically applied to the last three syllables of text.

Tone D

Tone D appears twenty-three times in *AL*, but only once in *Sant* and *Sal*. The one piece common to all three sources (*AL* fol. 295 *VR Qui das salutem*, see figure 1) has a middle portion which differs from the other examples in *AL*. Furthermore, this piece is the only one to appear with the melody for tone D in any of the Rioja sources, other concordances with *AL* in these sources giving tone B instead.[26] Thus,

---

[25] Fol. 157 of *Sal*, with both of the pieces in question, appears in plate 9 of *El Canto Mozárabe* by Rojo and Prado.

[26] Only once does a piece appearing in *AL* with tone D appear in another source with a tone other than tone B: *VR Tu es Deus* on fol. 119^v of *A30* which appears with tone A. The melody for the refrain and the point at which the repetition of the refrain is to begin agree with *AL*.

except for this one piece from the night office,[27] tone D is peculiar to *AL*. Its formal design clearly resembles that of the tones already discussed, but its modal relationship to tone B cannot be determined.

The underlaying of text for the intonation follows principles much like those at work in tones A and B, as the following examples show.

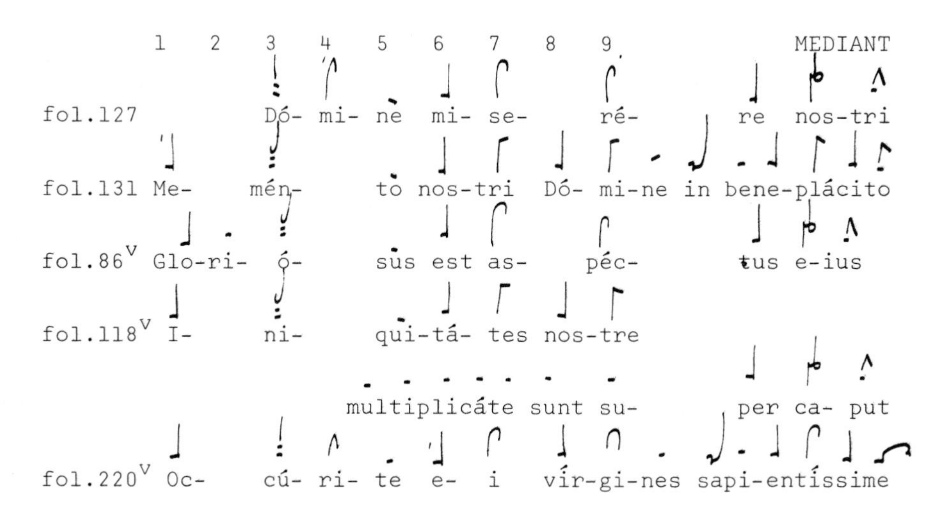

The first accent is placed in column 3 if it falls on one of the first three syllables, otherwise in column 6. The placing of this accent is regulated by columns 1 and 2, the punctum of column 2 appearing only after the podatus of column 1. If the first accent is placed in column 3, the placing of the second is regulated by clivis 4. Punctum 5 is a fixed element in the formula. The clivis rule applies except when podatus 8 is suppressed, in which case clivis 9 may bear an accent. There is no great consistency in the suppression of podatus 8, but it most often takes place in short texts such as the first and third examples above.

---

[27] *AL* gives it along with five other responds under the rubric *ITEM RESPONSURIA AD NOCTURNOS DOMINICALES* on fol. 295.

The mediant is adjusted to the final accent of the text, although it differs from the mediant in the tones already discussed in that it consists of three elements when the accent is on the penultimate syllable and four elements when the accent is on the antepenultimate syllable. The four element form is evidently derived from the three element form by division of the middle element.

The following are examples of the second part of tone D.

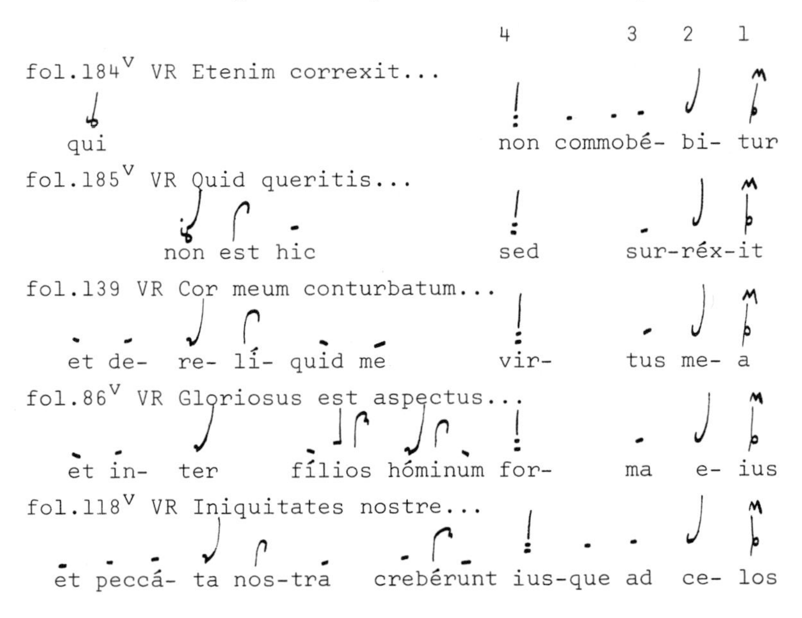

Although the intonations for this second part generally resemble each other, it is not possible to formulate very simple principles for their behavior. If there is only one syllable preceding the cadence, it is always borne by a podatus, as in the first example above. Otherwise, the intonation is usually built around a scandicus and a clivis. The number of puncta preceding and following these two figures does not seem to depend on the accent pattern of the text.

The final cadence consists of four elements, the last

three of which are applied to the last three syllables of the text. Element 4 may be adjusted to bear an accent by inserting as many as two puncta between it and punctum 3.

Thus, tone D, may be described as follows:

1. The structure is bipartite.

2. The intonation for the first part is adjusted to the text accent. The intonation for the second part is not treated consistently with regard to accent.

3. The mediant is adjusted to the final accent of its text. It consists of three elements when the accent is on the penultimate syllable. This becomes a four element formula by division of the middle element when the accent is on the antepenultimate syllable.

4. The final cadence consists of four elements, the last three of which are mechanically applied to the last three syllables of text. The first element may be adjusted to bear an accent through the insertion of one or two puncta between it and the following element.

Tone E

Figure 1 gives the five examples of this tone appearing in *AL* plus the one example in *Sant* and *Sal*. Once again, the single piece appearing in the night office differs from those for the secular office even though all are members of the same family. In *Sant* and *Sal*, the intonation for tone E is very much like that for the one example of tone D, also shown in figure 1. But these tones are clearly differentiated in *AL*. Here the first scandicus for tone E is always of the three note type.[28] For purposes of adjusting the accent, it may be preceded by a single punctum. And the clivis following this first scandicus is a fixed part of the formula instead of an optional one.

---

[28] Four of the examples in *AL* have an erasure at this point, but the original notation is not visible.

Figure 1

Tone D:
AL fol.295 Qui das salutem regibus et liveras David

Tone E:

AL: 1 2 3 4 5 6 7 8

fol.50ᵛ In- tro-dúx-it me in cellam vi- ná- ri- am

fol.50ᵛ Per vi- cos et pla- té- as que- sí- bi

fol.129 Pec-cá- bi- mus cum pá- tri- bus nos- tris

fol.185 Dix- it Ihe-sus dis-cí- pu- lis su- is

fol.203ᵛ Ti- bi de- re- líc-tus est pau-per

Sal:

fol.168 De- us Is- ra- hel ip- se davit vir-tú- tum

Figure 1

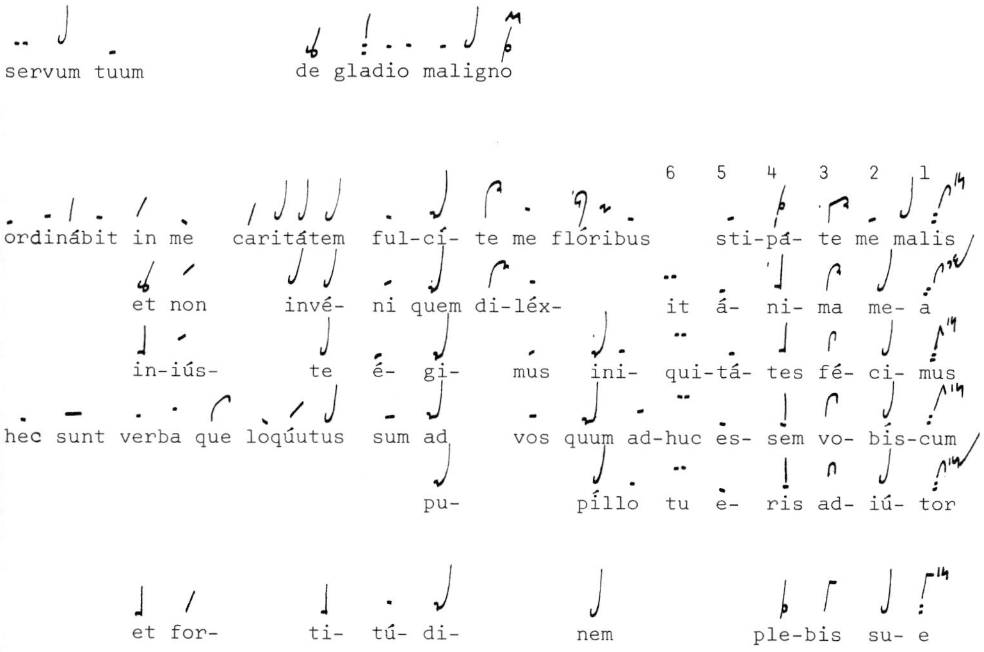

servum tuum   de gladio maligno

6 5 4 3 2 1

ordinábit in me caritátem ful-cí- te me flóribus sti-pá- te me malis

et non invé- ni quem di-léx- it á- ni- ma me- a

in-iús- te é- gi- mus ini- qui-tá- tes fé- ci- mus

hec sunt verba que loqúutus sum ad vos quum ad-huc es- sem vo- bís-cum

pu- píllo tu e- ris ad- iú- tor

et for- ti- tú- di- nem ple-bis su- e

Figure 2

Tone F:

AL:

fol.41	O bo- na crux que decórem et pulcritúdinem	de membris
fol.80	Iu-cun-ditá- tem fecísti cum servo tuo Dó-mi-ne	
fol.130	Mi-se- ré- bi-tur nostri Dó- minus	et abstérget
fol.141v	A me ip- so ánima me-a turbá-ta est	
fol.162	Filius quidem hó- mi- nis vadit	
fol.279v	Ne iras- cá- ris Dó-mi-ne satis	
fol.204	Conver- tá- tur vir a via sua ma- la	et ab iniquitáte

Sal:

fol.151	Cus- tó- di nos Dómine ut pupíllam ó- cu-li	sub umbra
fol.151v	Vi- dé- te ne quando adgraventur corda vestra	in crápu-
fol.153	Cus- tó- di nos Dómine ut pupíllam ó- cu-li	sub umbra [?]
fol.154v	Spe- rá- te in eum omnis conventus ple-vis mee	et ef-

Figure 2

		6 5 4 3 2 1
Dómini suscepísti	diu desideráta	sol- lí- ci-te a- má- ta
	secúndum	ver- bum tuum in pa- ce
iniustí-tias nostras	et dimérget in prófundum maris ómni-	a pec- cá- ta nos- tra
		prop- té- re- a
		sicut scrip-tum est de e- o
	et ne	ul- tra me- mi- né- ris
que est in manu sua	et revertátur Deus	a fu- ró- re i- re su- e
alá- rum tuárum		pró- te- ge nos
la et e- bri-etáte		et in curis huius mun- di
alá- rum tuárum		pró- te- ge nos
fún-di-te co-ram illo		cor- da ves- tra

Figure 3

Tone G: 1 2 3 4 5 6 7 8 9 10

AL:

fol.85 A- pe- ri- én- tur por-te tu- e iú- gi- ter

fol.111ᵛ Con-ver- tí- mi- ni ad me et salvi é- ri- tis

fol.137ᵛ Qui-a tri- bu- lá- ti- o próx-i- ma est

fol.140ᵛ Prop-ter in- no-cén- ti- am au- tem me- am

fol.146 Prop-ter no- men tu- um Dó- mi- ne vivificábis me in equi-

fol.204 Con-vér-te nos De- us sa- lu- tá-ris nos-ter

fol.217ᵛ Haec lo-qúu- tus sum vo-bis ut in me pacem

fol.221 Au- dí- te me di- ví- ni fruc-tus et quasi rosa

fol.238ᵛ Con-sum-má- tus in bre-bi explévit témpora longa

Sal:

fol.151 Gló-ri- a et ho- nor Pa- tri et Fí- li- o et Spíri-

Figure 3

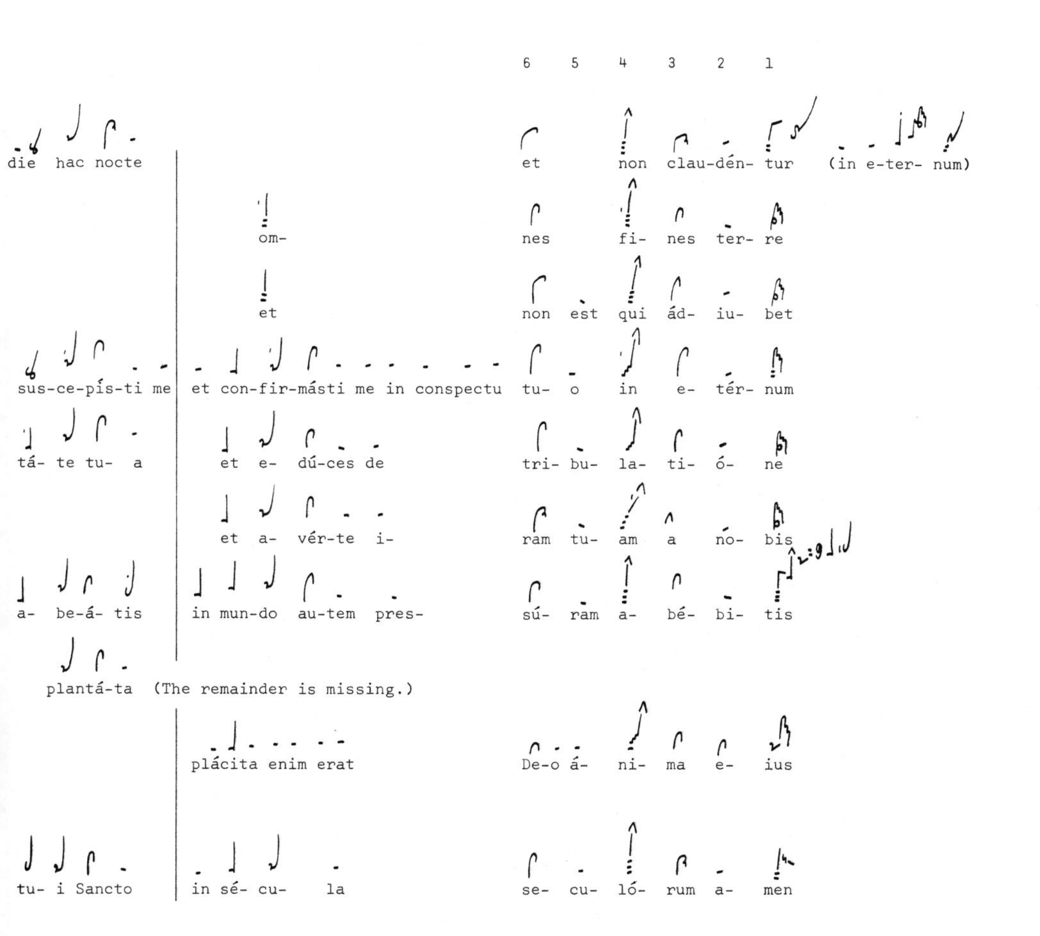
6 5 4 3 2 1
die hac nocte
et non clau-dén- tur (in e-ter- num)
om-
nes fi- nes ter- re
et
non est qui ád- iu- bet
sus-ce-pís-ti me
et con-fir-másti me in conspectu
tu- o in e- tér- num
tá- te tu- a
et e- dú-ces de
tri- bu- la- ti- ó- ne
et a- vér-te i-
ram tu- am a no- bis
a- be-á- tis
in mun-do au-tem pres-
sú- ram a- bé- bi- tis
plantá-ta (The remainder is missing.)
plácita enim erat
De-o á- ni- ma e- ius
tu- i Sancto
in sé- cu- la
se- cu- ló- rum a- men

The remainder of tone E is not subject to confusion with any of the other tones, but there is some disagreement among the examples. The mediant in the example from *Sal* differs from all of the other examples. The first example from *AL*, *VR Introduxit me*, also stands apart in this respect. Suffice it to say, however, that this piece does resemble the reading of *A30*. The last four pieces from *AL* form something of a homogeneous group, and from them a few generalizations about this tone may be made.

1. The structure is bipartite, although two of the pieces, *VR Peccabimus cum patribus* and *VR Dixit Ihesus*, might be said to subdivide in the second part. The former text is always divided in a similar fashion in other tones.

2. The intonation for the first part is adjusted to the text accent. No two intonations for the second part are exactly alike.

3. The mediant consists of two elements apparently adjusted to the final accent of the text.

4. The final cadence consists of six elements mechanically applied to the last six syllables of text.

Tone F

Figure 2 gives all seven of the pieces in *AL* which belong to tone F as well as the four complete examples of this tone in *Sal*.[29] *VR O bona crux* is clearly a case apart, of which more will be said later. But the remaining pieces, despite differences among those in *AL*, suggest the following outline for this tone.

1. The structure is basically bipartite, although subdivision of the second part is common.

2. The intonation for the first part consists of only three elements which are adjusted to the text accent by the insertion of puncta between the first and second. The

---

[29] Both *Sant* and *Sal* include two pieces which give only the first part of the formula, the texts being quite short. The two verses *Custodi nos* shown in figure 2 have different refrains.

intonations for the remaining parts vary among the examples.

3. The first mediant, as given in *Sal*, consists of three elements applied mechanically. In *AL*, there appear to be four elements, but the examples differ on this point. The second mediant consists of four elements, and all texts accent the penultimate syllable.

4. In *AL*, the final cadence consists of six elements applied to the last six syllables of text. In only one text in *Sal* is the final subsection longer than four syllables. In this one case, elements 2 and 3 are divided to accommodate the additional syllables.

Tone G

There are nine examples of tone G in *AL* and one in *Sal*, all of which are given in figure 3. Except for *VR Consummatus in brebi*, which is notated after the Rioja tradition, these pieces show consistent application of the melody to the various texts. If the first accent falls on the first or second syllable, it is borne by element 2, otherwise by element 4. This adjustment is made by punctum 1. Podati 4, 5, and 6 may all bear accents, and punctum 8 serves to place an accent in column 9. If there are any syllables between podatus 10 and the mediant, they are borne by puncta. As in other tones, short texts may result in the contraction or suppression of elements in the intonation. The mediant consists of two elements when the text accents the penultimate syllable. When the antepenultimate syllable is accented, the first element, a torculus, is divided into a podatus and a clivis.

The second part of the tone may be subdivided. The mediant ending the first subsection consists primarily of a scandicus and a clivis adjusted so that the latter bears an accent. To this end, one or two puncta may follow the clivis. Syllables preceding the mediant are arranged under a series of alternating puncta, podati, and clives, so that accents will fall under the podati, much as in tones A and B. In its fullest form, the second subsection begins with a podatus, a scandicus, and a clivis, all adjusted so that the clivis will bear the accent. The final cadence then consists of six elements mechanically applied to the last six syllables of the text, syllables between the intonation and the cadence being borne by puncta. For texts without enough syllables to accommodate the entire formula, punctum 5 of the cadence may be suppressed, and the intonation may be suppressed or consist of a single scandicus.

Thus, the characteristics of tone G are as follows:

1. The structure is basically bipartite, although the second part may be subdivided.

2. The intonation for the first part is adjusted to the text accent as are the intonations in the second part.

3. The mediant for the first part is adjusted to the final accent of the text as is the secondary mediant in the second part.

4. When there is a sufficient number of syllables in the text, the final cadence consists of six elements mechanically applied to the last six syllables.

Of the entire repertory of responds in *AL*, only seven have verses with tones different from the seven just described:

fol.40^{v} RS Iam securus VR O bona crux
II Salve crux
fol.196 RS Isti sunt lapides VR In die illa
fol.227 RS Sapientia Domini VR Quoniam observaberunt
fol.227^{v} RS Laetati sunt parvuli VR Lignum vite
fol.251 RS Vir iste in populo VR Vir iste conservabit
fol.251 RS Ex quo honorabi te VR Dedi te plebi
fol.291^{v} RS Magnus Dominus VR Et sapientie

It is not surprising that there should be such pieces; for the same thing happens among the Gregorian responds, especially for feasts introduced in the Middle Ages.[30] Two

---

30 Ferretti, *Esthétique*, p. 257.

of these pieces, though not pertaining to a feast of late origin, do belong to a set of pieces apparently composed together sometime after 711--that is, after the bulk of the Mozarabic rite was already set. The two pieces are *RS Sapientia Domini* and *RS Laetati sunt parvuli,* and they belong to Matins for the feast of Saints Iustus and Pastor. This service begins on fol. 226^{v} of *AL* with three *antiphonae de concordes* which, as Dom Brou notes,[31] have rather longer texts and more elaborate melodies than is the norm for such pieces. The first *missa* of three antiphons and a respond is then indicated by text incipits alone, a marginal note giving reference to another feast where these pieces may be found complete. Our two responds are found among the following *missae.* A look at this series of pieces beginning on fol. 227 shows that they relate to each other in a way which does not generally obtain on other feasts. In each of the first three *missae,* the three antiphons are clearly cut from the same stock. And in the first two *missae,* this similarity extends to the responds as well--the two responds which concern us here. Furthermore, the final melisma, representing about fourteen notes, of both the refrain and the verse of *RS Laetati sunt parvuli* occurs at the end of antiphons in two other *missae.* Finally, two of the antiphons in the last *missa* (fol. 228^{v}) relate to the melody of the *antiphonae de concordes.* These similarities certainly suggest that the pieces were composed to form a single group.

A comparison of *AL* with the *Oracional Visigótico* of Verona[32] suggests in turn that this group of pieces came into the liturgy after 711. The *Oracional* gives not only prayers

---

[31] "Notes de paléographie musicale mozarabe," *Anuario Musical,* VII (1952), p. 65, n. 37.

[32] Ed. José Vives, *Monumenta Hispaniae Sacra, Serie Litúrgica,* Vol. I (Barcelona, 1946).

for services throughout the year, but also incipits for the antiphons and responds accompanying the prayers. The close correspondence between these incipits and the repertory of *AL* has led to the conclusion that *AL* presents the liturgy essentially as it existed at the time of the Moorish invasion of the peninsula in 711, the latest possible date for the *Oracional*.[33] For the feast of Saints Iustus and Pastor, the *Oracional* gives only the incipits appearing first in *AL*, referring like the latter to the order of service *In Die Allisionis Infantum*. The pieces for the *missae* which are written out in full in *AL* for Matins on the feast of Saints Iustus and Pastor appear nowhere in the *Oracional*.[34]

RS Iam securus also appears to be part of a *missa* composed some time after the date of the *Oracional*. However, in this case the pieces composing the *missa* do not appear to be related melodically. We have already noted that the melody for

---

[33] "L'Antiphonaire wisigothique et l'antiphonaire grégorien du VIII siècle," *Anuario Musical*, V (1950), 3-6. Also the same author's "Le joyau des antiphonaires latins," *Archivos Leoneses*, VIII, No. 15 (1954), 11-13.

[34] A similar situation appears for the feast of St. Felix, the music for which is given in *AL* beginning on fol. 224. For Matins on this feast, *AL* gives a total of five *missae* excluding a final *missa* for the feast of the Maccabees which is joined to that of St. Felix. In both the fourth and the fifth *missae*, the three antiphons are based on a single melody. None of the other *missae* has this feature. In the *Oracional*, there are incipits for the pieces of the first two *missae* together with the appropriate prayers. Then there are four prayers without incipits, and these are followed by three prayers for the Maccabees. Neither do incipits for the pieces of the fourth and fifth *missae* appear anywhere in the *Oracional*, nor is there a sufficient number of prayers for this feast to account for the number of pieces in *AL*. The four prayers which are without incipits for antiphons or responds do not relate in the normal way to any of the texts of the third, fourth or fifth *missae* in *AL*. Hence, the fourth and fifth *missae*, and probably the third, too, were almost certainly composed as an afterthought to the first two and after the year 711.

VR O bona crux bears a slight resemblance to tone F; but the second verse, *Salve crux,* has quite an extended melody which resembles none of the tones employed elsewhere. In *AL,* this respond is part of the third *missa* at Matins on the feast of St. Andrew, but in the *Oracional,* incipits and prayers are given only for the first two *missae.*

A simpler case is that of *RS Isti sunt lapides.* It belongs to the feast of St. Torquatus which does not figure in the *Oracional* at all. This feast does, however, appear in the Mozarabic prayer book of the British Museum (Add. MS 30852) with incipits for all of the antiphons and responds in *AL.* Since the British Museum manuscript is from the 9th century, the office for St. Torquatus would seem to have been composed during the 8th or 9th centuries.[35]

The remaining three pieces in *AL* with unique verse melodies come from either the common of saints or the pieces for ordinary Sundays. The *Oracional,* however, contains almost exclusively the proper of time and of the saints. Thus, it is of no assistance in determining whether these three pieces are late compositions. *RS Magnus Dominus,* in any case, has for its verse a melody which begins exactly as does tone B. It is also the only one of these seven pieces aside from *RS Iam securus* which appears with notation in another source--*Sant*--where it is assigned to Nocturns on Sundays instead of Matins on Sundays as in *AL.* The tone for *RS Vir iste in populo* also might be related to tone B, but it clearly differs from all of the other examples.

From the night office, there are four pieces which are unrelated to any of the tones described above. They are given here with folio references to *Sant.*[36]

---

[35] Vives, *Oracional*, pp. xxvi-xxvii.

[36] The first two are Wagner's types I and III respectively. The other two are not among the pieces he studied.

fol.212 RS Per diem clamavi VR Media nocte surgebam
fol.218 RS Adiutorium nostrum VR Laqueus contritus
II Gloria et honor patri
fol.224 RS Quis michi det VR Quis michi tribuat
fol.224v RS Qui est enim Domine VR Nec fortitudo

Before turning to the Rioja tradition and its sources, we should make special note of three more pieces from *AL:*
fol.195v RS Hec dicit Dominus pertransibunt VR Volabunt
fol.238v RS Homo iste custodivit VR Consummatus in brebi
fol.254v RS Haec dicit Dominus dilectione VR Recordatus

These three pieces are notated after the Rioja tradition, the first and third belonging to tone A, the second belonging to tone G. The third offers an instructive comparison, for it is copied two times in succession. The first time, the verse follows the León tradition, the second time the Rioja tradition. The melody for the refrain in the two instances is clearly the same, although here too there are notational variants which must occasionally represent differences in pitch content. The study of isolated pieces which happen to occur twice in a single source, or at most, once in each of several different sources casts, at first glance anyway, little light on the significance of what appear to be matters of notational detail. But the respond verses present a controlled situation in which a great number of examples may be marshalled to determine whether these differences represent anything more than accidents of a sort. We shall see that the respond verses can serve as a tool for relating groups of manuscripts. Once these relationships are established, a detailed study of individual pieces, such as the respond refrains, can be undertaken. It should be possible to attribute additional notational characteristics to the groups of manuscripts and thus to see how the refrains as well as the verses of the three pieces just cited relate to the Rioja tradition. It should also be possible to determine whether certain recurring melodic units appear exclusively in refrains assigned to a particular tone and thus have a kind of modal significance.

CHAPTER III

THE RIOJA TRADITION AND ITS SOURCES

If one considers the number of manuscripts that must have been required for the ongoing worship of the Christian Church throughout the Spanish peninsula up to the end of the 11th century, the number of manuscripts for the Mozarabic rite which have survived is minimal. The centers from which manuscripts have been preserved are even fewer in number. This situation has led to the naming of the two principal branches of the Mozarabic notation--the northern and the Toledan. Within the sources containing the northern notation, this situation has suggested the names "León" and "Rioja" for the two traditions which concern us here. The danger in such a procedure is that it may assume the surviving sources to be representative of all that have ever existed. The Mozarabic sources simply will not bear the weight of such an assumption. The terms "León" and "Rioja" may characterize more aptly an historical accident having to do with the preservation of manuscripts from the 11th century to the present than a general state of affairs in the Spanish Church before the 11th century. We just have no way of knowing what musical traditions were operative over most of Spain. But as regards León and the Rioja, the relationship of the musical sources does have historical parallels. The sources transmitting what we have called the Rioja tradition come from two centers in the Rioja itself and one in Castile just to the west. We shall see that there are also non-musical reasons for linking the Rioja with this part of Castile and for distinguishing the ecclesiastical traditions of this region from those of León.

Sources from the Rioja proper

A30, an antiphoner from San Millán de la Cogolla, has suffered greatly at the hands of men as well as the elements and now lies badly mutilated in Madrid. Nevertheless, it contains more respond verses with notation than any of the other northern sources after *AL*. It also serves well for comparison with *AL*, since its format, except for the inclusion of prayers accompanying the antiphons and responds, is the same.

A few examples of the intonation for tone A taken from this manuscript will show some of the peculiarities of the Rioja tradition. The top line shows the full formula as it is found in *AL*.

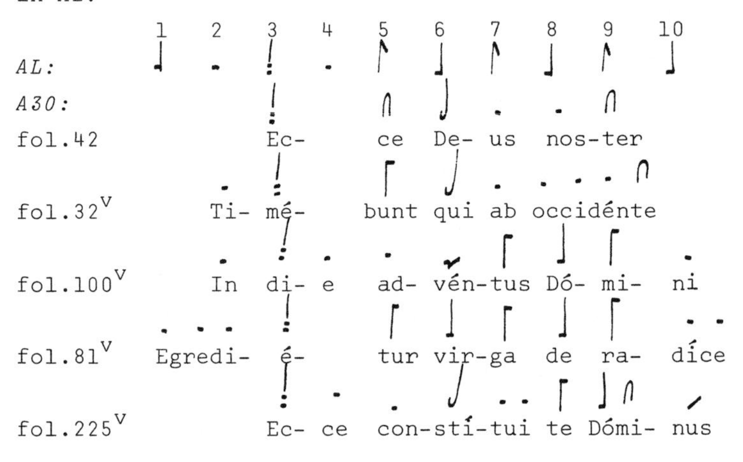

The first accent is placed in column 3, which may be preceded by as many as three puncta for this purpose. Podatus 1 of the *AL* formula never appears. If there is only one syllable between columns 3 and 6, it is borne by a clivis. If there are two, the clivis is divided into two puncta. Following podatus 6, the only constant element of the formula is clivis 9, which never bears an accented syllable. Clivis 7 and podatus 8 are lacking in ten out of twenty-two pieces with texts long enough to accommodate them. When they do appear, they are not treated consistently, for puncta may precede or follow clivis 7, or both. This suggests that these two elements were not originally part of the formula in the Rioja tradition. Thus, they may be regarded as representing a tendency toward more elaborate formulas of the León type. The same may be said of podatus 10, which never appears in *A30*.

The mediant follows the same principle as in *AL*, being adjusted to the final accent of the text. But the form is slightly different from that in *AL* when the text is short and when the accent is on the antepenultimate syllable.

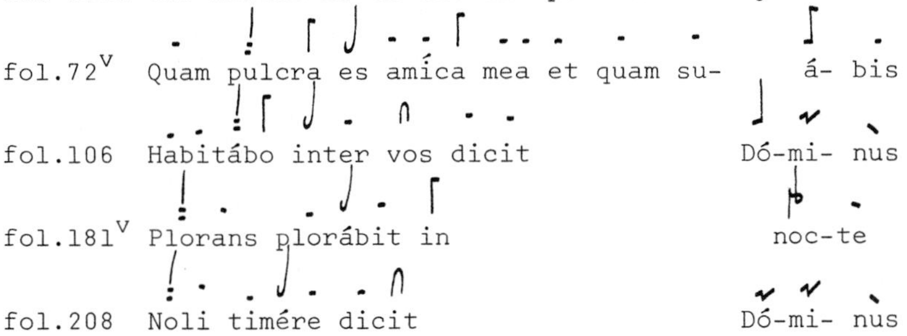

Note that, whereas in *AL* the torculus of this mediant is never combined with other elements to form a more complex figure, here the mediant takes the form shown in the third example whenever there is not at least one punctum between it and clivis 9 of the intonation.

As in *AL*, the second part of tone A may be subdivided. Normally, however, the intonation is a single element placed over the first syllable, and all remaining syllables before the cadence are borne by puncta. The final cadence consists of six elements applied mechanically to the last six syllables of the text and is usually preceded by a punctum even at the expense of the intonation. Thus, the design is the same as that in *AL*, but the elements differ in part.

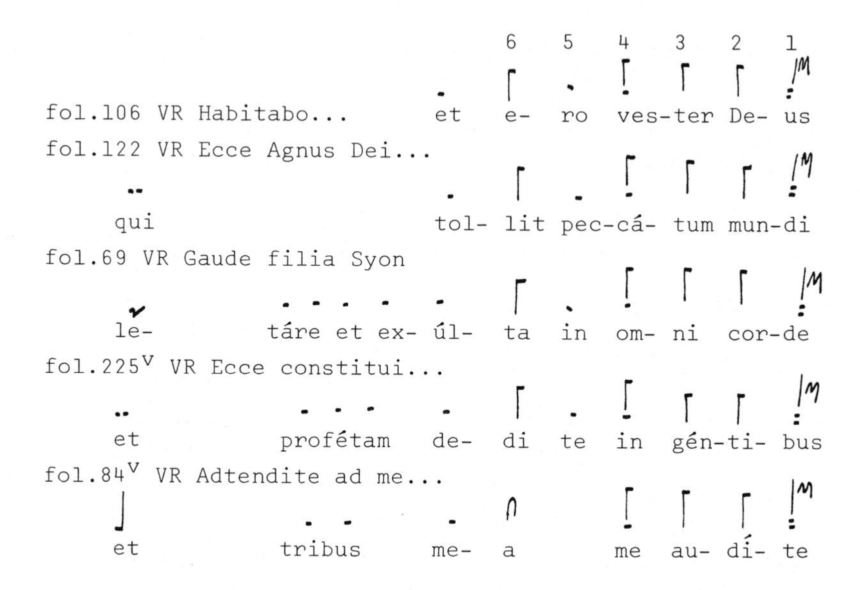

The three figures used for the intonation are used indiscriminately, and only once does the scandicus-clivis formula of *AL* appear. Except for occasional omissions of punctum 5, the cadence, including column 1, is subject to little or no variation.

When the second part of the tone is subdivided, the outline is that of *AL*. That is, the final subsection, if there are three, takes the form just described for the second part of the tone without subdivisions. The same is true of the final subsection, if there are only two, when the first ends with a punctum. Nevertheless, the melodies which fill in this outline differ from those of *AL*. The following examples give the notation from both *AL* and *A30*.

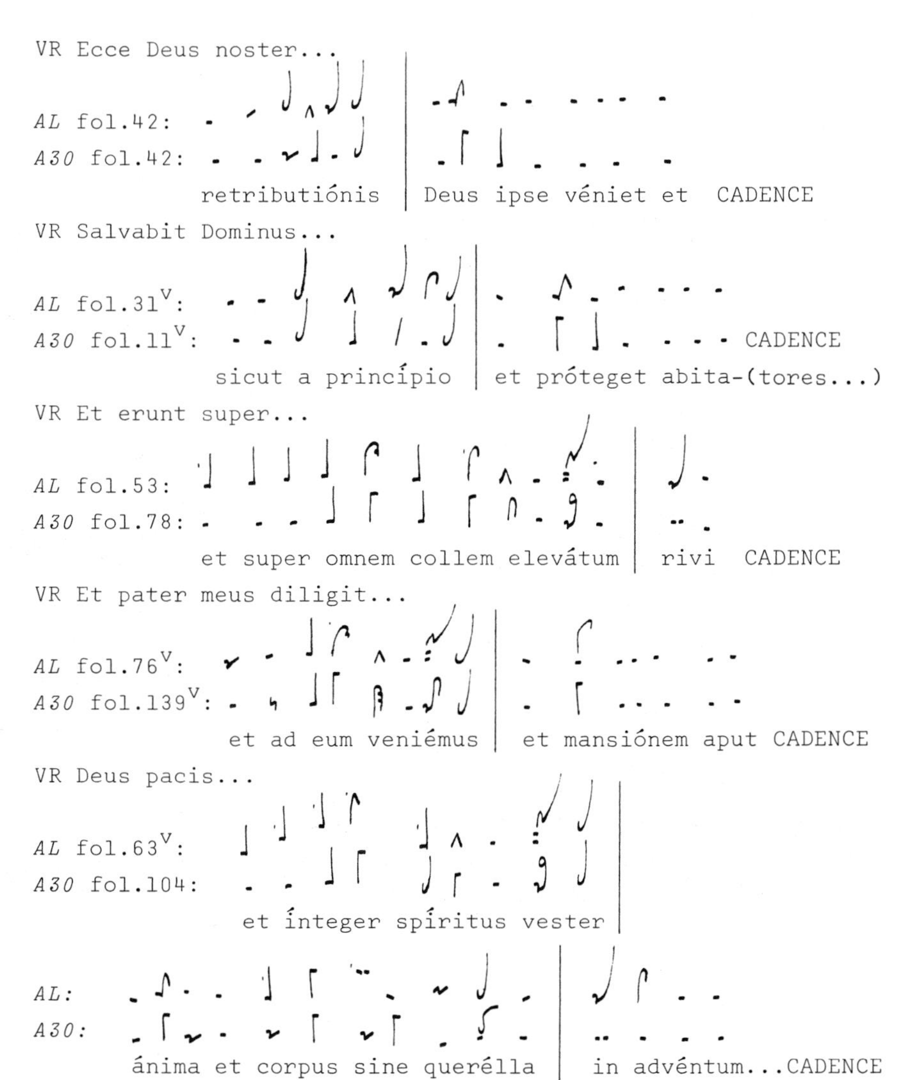

As with tone A, a comparison of the formulas for tone B in *AL* and *A30* gives the impression that *A30* is a simplified version of *AL*. Compare the following examples from *A30* with the complete formula for the intonation as found in *AL*.

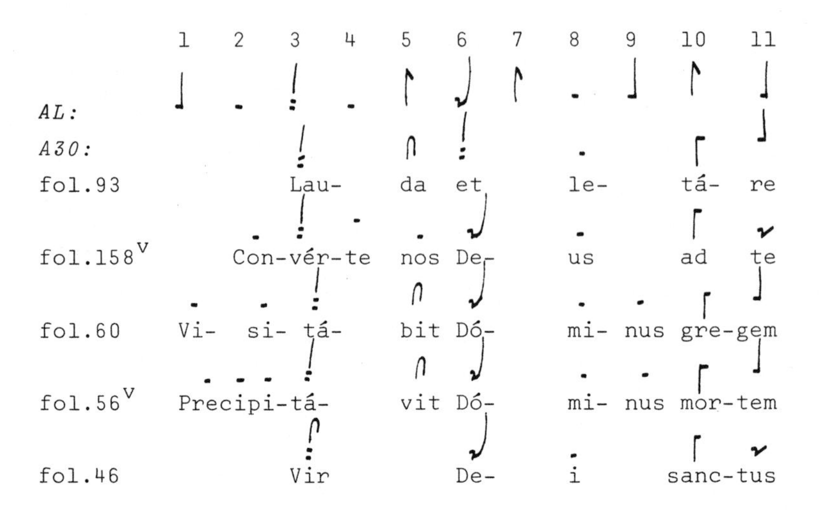

Once again, scandicus 3 is preceded only by puncta, of which there may be as many as three. If there are two syllables between columns 3 and 6, clivis 5 is divided into two puncta. Clivis 7 is never part of the formula in *A30* nor is podatus 9. However, clivis 10 and podatus 11 are invariable except in short texts. It is clivis 10 which bears accents falling after column 6, and to this end it may be preceded by up to three puncta. Thus, the clivis rule which is so scrupulously observed in *AL* is not operative in *A30*. Note, however, that the problem created by monosyllables in *AL* may be solved in *A30* by the contraction of elements 3 and 5.

The remainder of the first part of tone B, whether or not it is subdivided, has virtually the same form in *AL* and *A30*. The first four examples below show the mediant, as it appears in *A30*, when the first part of tone B is not subdivided. They may be compared with the examples from *AL* on page 29 above. The remaining examples illustrate the treatment of subdivided texts in both sources.

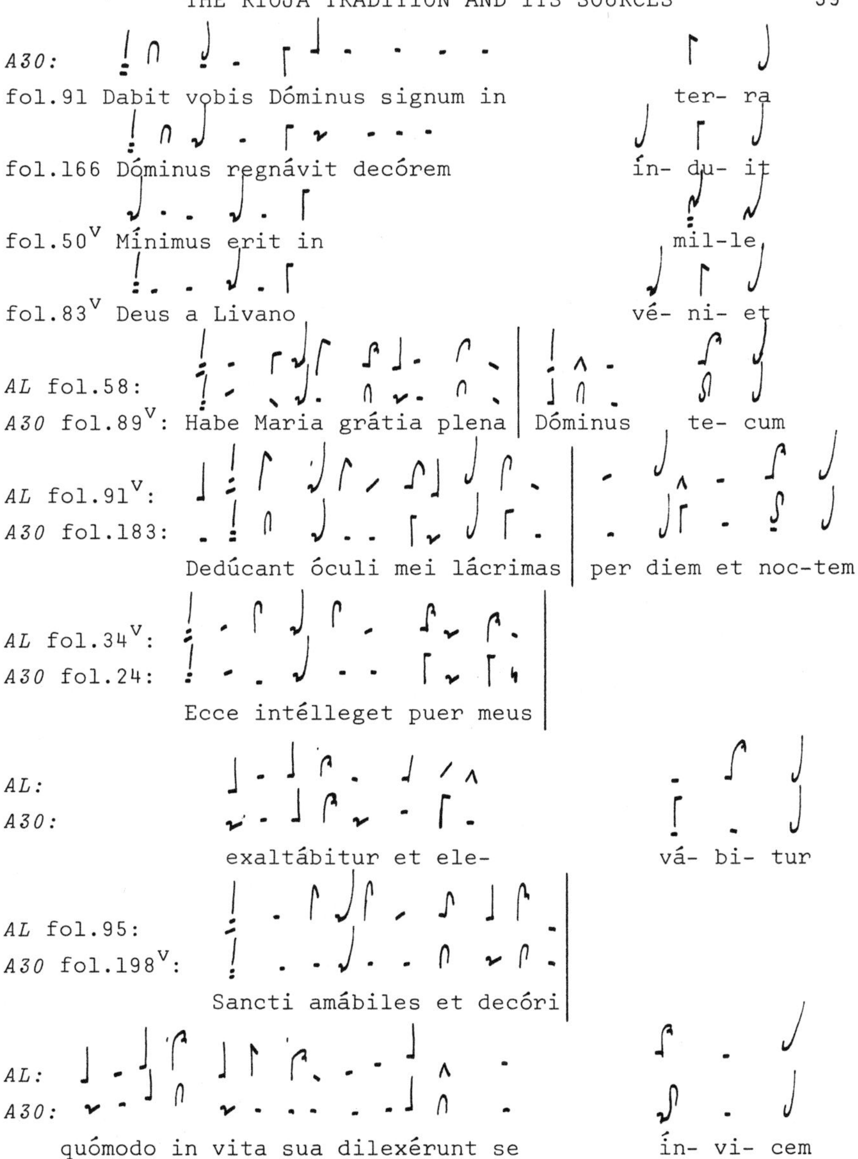

For the second part of tone B, three different intonations are used in *A30*, the choice apparently depending on the length of the text and the accent pattern.

A30:

fol.61 VR Exaltabo te...

et bene- dí- cam

fol.182 VR Defecerunt oculi...

quan- do consolavé- ris me

fol.83v VR Deus a Livano...

et sanctus a monte opaco et con- dén-so

fol.78v VR Humiliata est...

e- dé-sit in terra venter nos-ter

fol.121 VR Hic est dies...

exultémus et letémur in e- o

fol.132 VR Dum lapidaretur Stefanus

génibus pósi- tis orábat di- cens

The first of these, a four note scandicus, is used for short texts, but also occasionally for longer texts in which the first syllable is accented. It would appear to be a contraction of the following type which consists of two puncta and a podatus. This three element type is usually associated with texts accenting the second and fourth syllables. The four element type--a clivis, two puncta, and a podatus--usually appears with texts accenting the third or the first and third syllables. However, it is sometimes preceded by a punctum, apparently designed to bring the accent under the third element. Since these various possibilities in the texts are not mutually exclusive, there is frequently no apparent reason for preferring one form over another.

The final cadence consists of two elements applied to the last two syllables of text as in *AL*. But the first of these, instead of being a podatus, is a virga. The second is always the one shown in the examples above.

There are only six respond verses in *A30* with melodies other than tones A and B, all of which appear in figure 4. *A30* lacks tones C and D altogether, but the remaining tones may be compared with the readings of *AL* in figures 1, 2 and 3. With such a reduced number of examples, we can only note a few of the differences which also turn up in other sources for the Rioja tradition. In general, the formulas of *A30* are simpler than those of *AL*, a punctum or a virga often taking the place of a podatus as in the final cadences of tones E and F and the intonation of tone G. The final cadence of tone G differs from the reading of *AL* in substituting a clivis for a punctum as the penultimate element. In this respect, it is reminiscent of the final cadence for tone A.

Because of the numbers of examples involved, tones A and B must form the principal basis for comparison of the sources. In turn, *A30* can supply the standard for these tones in the Rioja tradition. But within this tradition, each manuscript may have its own notational characteristics. Observing these will help to determine which are the most stable elements of the tones and which of the apparently equivalent notational symbols have different functions.

The notation of *A30* is distinguished primarily by the preponderance of the right angle clivis ( ). In tone A, the last two clives of the final cadence almost always take this form as does clivis 5 of the intonation. However, if the rounded clives ( ) are used in the cadence, clivis 5 is rounded as well. Clivis 9, on the other hand, alternates regularly between these forms. Podatus 6 is relatively stable in that it is almost always of the rounded type ( ), this type never appearing in column 8. Scandicus 3 is also quite constant, taking the form in every case but one. In tone B, however, this scandicus occasionally appears as or . In both tones, the scandicus of the final figure is with only a few cases of . Clivis 5 in tone B is rounded in every case but one where it is of the acute type ( ),

Figure 4

Tone E:

A30:	1 2 3 4 5 6 7 8
fol.67v	In- tro-dúx-it me rex in cellam vi- ná- ri- am
fol.67v	Per vi- cos et pla- té- as quesívi

Tone F:

A30:	
fol.46v	O bona crux que decórem et pulcritúdinem
fol.46v	Gló-ri- a et honor Patri et Fílio
fol.150	Iocunditátem fecísti cum servo tuo Dómine

Tone G:	1 2 3 4 5 6 7 8 9 10
A30:	
fol.193	O- le- um recóndi- te in va- sis ves-tris

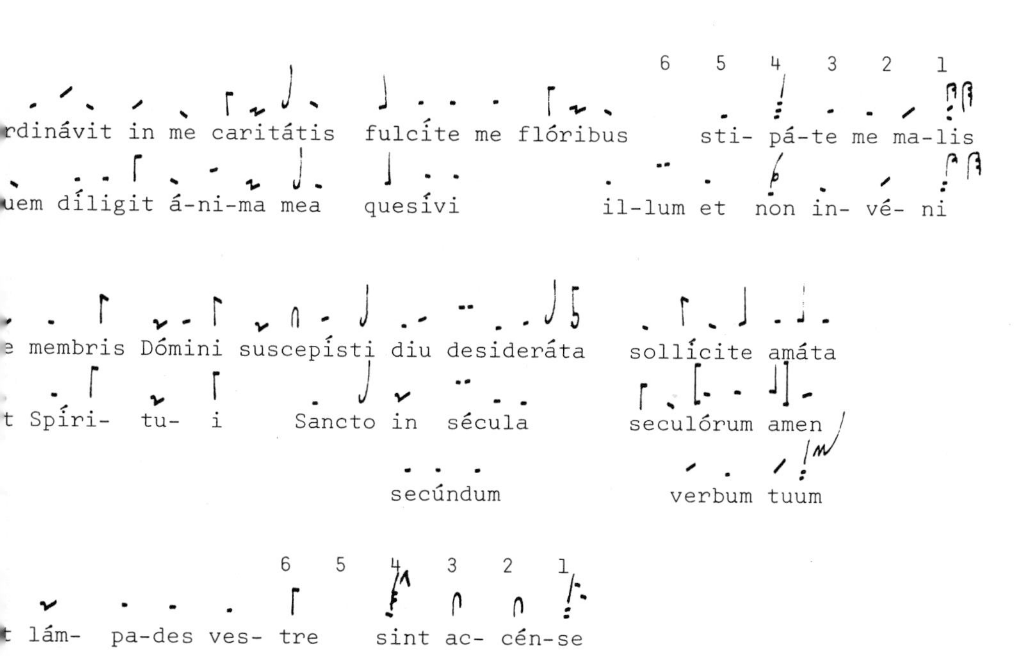
6 5 4 3 2 1
rdinávit in me caritátis fulcíte me flóribus sti- pá-te me ma-lis
uem díligit á-ni-ma mea quesívi il-lum et non in- vé- ni
e membris Dómini suscepísti diu desideráta sollícite amáta
t Spíri- tu- i Sancto in sécula seculórum amen
secúndum verbum tuum
6 5 4 3 2 1
t lám- pa-des ves- tre sint ac- cén-se

whereas clivis 10 and the clivis of the mediant are almost always of the right angle type. Thus, the two tones are frequently differentiated in what appear to be matters of notational detail.

The notation of *A30* also shows signs of incipient diastematicism. The dry point line which runs through almost all of the notation in this manuscript clearly has no fixed function, as a comparison of respond verses with the same tone readily shows. The manuscript was simply ruled uniformly; and for reasons of space, texts with notation were copied on alternate lines, the neumes falling on the blank lines. Nevertheless, the impulse toward diastematicism is clear in the treatment of clivis 5 in both tones A and B. When this clivis is divided into two puncta, the first is invariably written higher than the second. The final cadence of tone B shows a similar effect. The penultimate figure is almost always a virga, but even when it can scarcely be distinguished from the preceding puncta in size, it is written somewhat above them. In considering the pieces in *A56* which appear in Aquitanian notation, we shall see that the penultimate figure does, in fact, represent a pitch higher than that of the preceding puncta.

A56, the *Liber Ordinum* of San Millán, contains only five respond verses with Mozarabic notation, three with tone B and two with tone G. But these five pieces place the manuscript firmly within the Rioja tradition. In tone B, scandicus 3 is preceded only by puncta, clivis 7 and podatus 9 are never present, the intonation for the second part is once two puncta plus a podatus, and the penultimate element of the final cadence is always a virga. In tone G, element 5 of the intonation is a punctum, the intonation for the second part is simply one or two podati, and the penultimate element of the final cadence is a clivis. The notation differs from *A30*, however, in that all clives are of the acute type (Λ), and the final scandicus of tone B is always of the type [neume] . The final figure of tone G takes the form [neume] instead of [neume] or [neume] .

The fame of this manuscript derives primarily from the pieces in it with Aquitanian notation. In all of these pieces, the new notation was written over the erasures of the Mozarabic notation. The original notation was erased in several other pieces as well which were unfortunately left blank. The twenty or so pieces with Aquitanian notation are the only ones from the entire Mozarabic repertory which can be transcribed into modern notation with any certainty. Among them are two respond verses, one giving the melody of tone B and another the melody of tone G. The following transcriptions modify those given by Rojo and Prado, especially in the first part of *VR Propter nomen*. The Mozarabic notation is given in parallel after *Silos 4*.

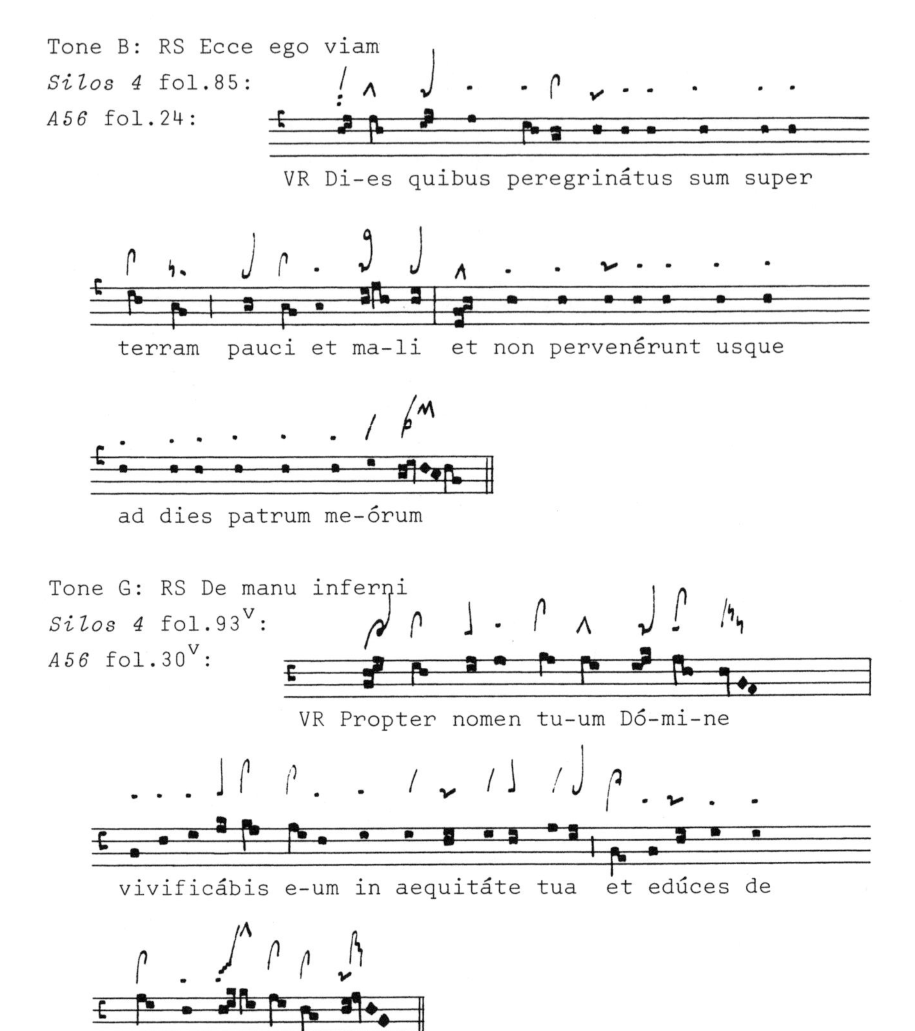

Despite the occasional discrepancies with the *Silos 4* reading, the Aquitanian notation clearly transcribes the melodies of the Rioja tradition. Note, for example, the absence of clivis 7 and podatus 9 in the intonation of tone B. The intonation for the second part of tone B is the one element type associated only with short texts in the León sources, and the penultimate element of the final cadence is a single note one step above the preceding puncta, corresponding in the Mozarabic notation to a virga instead of a podatus. The Aquitanian transcription of tone G follows the reading of *Silos 4* quite closely, and a comparison of the *AL* reading in figure 3 readily shows the differences between the two traditions.

Silos 4, also a *Liber Ordinum,* contains a note by the copyist which tells us that the manuscript was copied at San Prudencio de Laturce and thus belongs to the Rioja proper. It is not entirely free of León symptoms, but the eleven respond verses with notation show that it belongs in a group with the San Millán manuscripts.

The only examples of tone A are provided by a single piece, *RS Requiem eternam VR Aperiat tibi,* which is copied on fol. 87^{v} and again on fol. 106. The first time, it follows the León tradition, as may be seen in plate 6 of the book by Rojo and Prado. The single syllable preceding scandicus 3 of the intonation is borne by a podatus. Clivis 7 is present, podatus 8 and clivis 9 are contracted to form a torculus, and podatus 10 is present. The intonation for the second part consists of a scandicus and a clivis, and although the final cadence does not follow the León version exactly, the resemblance to the León version is stronger than to the Rioja version. On fol. 106, the refrain is virtually identical, but the verse differs in just the way that the other Rioja sources differ from *AL*. The syllable preceding scandicus 3 is borne by a punctum, scandicus 3 and podatus 6 are separated by two puncta instead of a punctum plus clivis 5, and although clivis 7 and podatus 8 are present, podatus 10 is missing. The mediant for the first part and the intonation and final cadence for the second part reproduce the Rioja versions exactly.

The remaining pieces, six examples of tone B and three examples of tone G, show none of the peculiarities of the León tradition. Instead, they resemble the readings of *A56* even in matters of detail. *Silos 4* does, however, employ two types of clivis: the rounded and the acute. In tone B, clivis 5 is always acute, whereas clivis 10 and the clivis of the mediant are usually rounded. Thus, *Silos 4* distinguishes between these various positions in the tone just as does *A30*, but it does so with different symbols. An example of tone B may be found in plate 6 given by Rojo and Prado, and examples of tone B and tone G are given above with the transcriptions from *A56*.

Sources from Santo Domingo de Silos

The Silos sources vary greatly in quality. Some have musical notation throughout supplied by a single hand, but others lack notation for many pieces, such notation as there is being the work of different hands of varying elegance. *BM51*, as regards the respond verses, has the most consistent notation. Being a source for the night office, it also offers examples of all seven tones.

This manuscript clearly transmits the Rioja tradition. Nevertheless, the examples of tone A contained in it show a slightly greater tendency toward an elaborate version of the León type than do the examples in *A30*. We have seen that in *A30* clivis 7 and podatus 8 are lacking from the intonation in about half of the cases. In *BM51*, there are eleven pieces with texts long enough to accommodate the complete formula, and these two elements are lacking from only two. Even so, they are not stable elements of the formula here, as they are in the León manuscripts. Clivis 7 may be separated from scandicus 6 as well as from podatus 8 by puncta. This is never the case in the León manuscripts. One piece in this manuscript, fol. 163 *VR Et ne nocturnis*, is notated after the León tradition in all details, including the absence of the final figure . But in all other respects, *BM51* belongs to the Rioja group.

This manuscript contains more examples of tone C than any of the other Rioja sources. For comparison with the readings of *Sal* on pages 34 and 35 above, all five examples of this tone appearing in *BM51* are given below.

Tone C First Part

	1	2	3	4	5	6	7	8	9	10	
fol.174			Quó-		ni-	am	turbáta		sunt	ossa	me-a
fol.175			Vir-		ga	tu-	a	et	bá-	culus	tuus
fol.175		Ex-	áu-	di	o-	ra-	ti-	ó-	nem		me-am
fol.176v		Er-	rá-		bi	sic-ut		o-	vis	que	perié-rat
fol.189		Qui	re-		gis	S-rahel		in-			tén-de

Tone C Second Part

fol.174 VR Quoniam turbata...

et á- nima mea turbáta est val-de

fol.175 VR Virga tua...

ip- sa me consolá- ta sunt

fol.175 VR Exaudi orationem...

et de- precatiónem me- am

fol.176v VR Errabi sicut ovis...

que resérvum tuum De- us

fol.189 VR Qui regis Srahel...

qui de- dúcis velut ovem Yo- sep

Note that, once again, the Rioja version is simpler than the León version. The final cadence consists of two elements instead of three, and the intonation for the second part is a virga instead of a podatus.

Similar considerations apply with respect to tones D, E, F, and G, examples of which are given in figure 5. The one example of tone D, it will be recalled, is unique to the night office and even within *AL* differs from the other examples of this tone.

The notation of *BM51* represents both greater consistency and a levelling tendency in the function of various symbols over the notation of *A30*. For example, the torculus for the mediant of tone A always takes the form ⁂ in *BM51*, whereas in *A30* it may appear in any one of five different forms. Nor are the three forms of the three note scandicus ever interchanged in *BM51*. In tone B, scandicus 3 is always ⁝ , scandicus 6 is always ✓ , and the scandicus of the final cadence is always / . With the clivis, however, there is a tendency toward uniformity, all clives being acute except in some examples of the final cadence for tone A.

The notation of *BM45* is rather less elegant in appearance than that of *BM51*; and although it clearly embodies the Rioja tradition, it shows a greater number of León symptoms. In tone A, for example, clivis 7 is present in nine out of ten cases, and in eight of these, podatus 8 is present as well. In tone B, an occasional piece includes podatus 9, an element not found in any of the Rioja sources discussed up to now. The use of the virga also shows a tendency to bring the formulas into line with the León versions. We have seen that a virga in the Rioja tradition often corresponds to a podatus in the León tradition. In *BM45*, the virga is more common than in other sources, and it often appears in positions filled in the León sources by a podatus and in other Rioja sources by a punctum. Thus, occasionally a syllable preceding scandicus 3 in tone B is borne by a virga. Similarly, the intonation for the second part of tone B, which in Rioja sources may take the form ..✓ , may appear in this manuscript in the form ./✓/ , thus approaching the form.✓JJ of *AL*.

The most obvious peculiarity of the notation for the tones

in this manuscript is the final figure of tones A and B, which takes the form instead of . But the forms of the podatus used in various positions are perhaps more significant. As in all of the Rioja sources, podatus 6 of tone A is of the round type ( ), as are the podati for the mediants of tone B. All of the remaining podati of tones A and B, with the exception of a single example of tone A, take the form . In other sources from both traditions, podati 8 and 10 of tone A and 9 and 11 of tone B alternate regularly between the forms and . Thus, *BM45* may present the notation at a state before these two forms of the podatus became distinct. Viewing these two as descendants of the single form of *BM45* accounts for the fact that other sources do not consistently make a distinction between and , whereas they do generally distinguish between both of these and the rounded type ( ). This manuscript dates from the 10th century or perhaps even from the first part of the 11th, and thus it is no older than several other sources without this peculiarity. Nevertheless, there is perhaps another sign of archaism in the use of intermittent notation. Puncta are frequently omitted from all of the tones appearing here.

Silos 3 contains examples of tones A, B, C, and G, and it follows the Rioja tradition quite closely. In only one of the six examples of tone A do both clivis 7 and podatus 8 appear. In tone B, one piece has a podatus instead of a virga for the penultimate element of the final cadence, but in all other details, this piece, as well as the other examples, adhere to the Rioja tradition. One example of tone C shows tendencies toward the León type in its intonation, but all three examples of tone G lie wholly within the Rioja tradition. This manuscript shares with a few other Silos sources the peculiar form for the scandicus of the final element in tones A and B. It also includes the clivis , which apparently corresponds to the found in the León sources. The clivis , of which there are only a few instances, does

Figure 5

Tone D:
BM51 fol. 170v Qui das salutem regibus et liveras David

Tone E: 1 2 3 4 5 6 7 8
BM51:
fol. 176 De- us Is- ra- hel ip- se dabit vir-tu- tem

Tone F:
BM51:
fol. 166v Cus- tó- di nos Dómine ut pupíllam ó- cu- li

fol. 170 Ne iras-cá-ris Dó- mi-ne ni-mis

fol. 175v Spe- rá- te in eum omnis convéntus ple- bis mee

Tone G: 1 2 3 4 5 6 7 8 9 10
BM51:
fol. 166v O- le- um recóndi- te in va- sis ves-tris

ervum tuum de gladio maligno

t for- ti-tú-di-nem 6 5 4 3 2 1 ple- bi su- e

ub umbra alá- rum tu-á-rum 6 5 4 3 2 1 pró- te- ge nos

t ne ul- tra me- mi- né- ris

t ef- fúndite coram illo cor-da ves-tra

6 5 4 3 2 1

t lám- pa-des ves- tre sint ac- cén-se

not occur in the respond verses of any of the other sources in northern notation.

Silos 7 contains the order of service for monastic hours around the clock, but only five of the many responds for which the texts are complete have musical notation. There are two examples of tone A, both of which include clivis 7 and podatus 8 (the latter contracted with clivis 9 in one case), but otherwise give the Rioja version. Of the three examples of tone B, two give the Rioja version without León symptoms. The other follows the León tradition in all details, but is probably an addition by a later hand. The ink is of the same color in all pieces. Nevertheless, puncta are almost always omitted from the other pieces, but here they are always provided and are slightly elongated by comparison. And scandicus 6 of the other two pieces is written , whereas here it is written . However many hands are involved, four of the five verses with notation belong to the Rioja tradition.

In discussing the manuscripts preserved at Silos, Fray Justo Pérez de Urbel and Walter M. Whitehill note that the script of *Silos 5* differs greatly from that of other products of the Silos scriptorium in lacking their elegance.[37] The musical notation, too, presents a rather cruder aspect. There are only seven respond verses with notation, and none of these is complete. But these seven pieces show a strong influence of the León tradition. In fact, it is difficult to say which of the two traditions these seven pieces as a group represent. Four of them begin with a podatus preceding scandicus 3, the other three employing a punctum or leaving the syllables preceding scandicus 3 blank. The two examples of tone A both include clivis 7 and podati 8 and 10. But only one of these has any notation for the final cadence, and it belongs to the Rioja tradition. Notation is given

---

[37] "Los manuscritos de Santo Domingo de Silos," *Boletín de la Real Academia de la Historia*, XCV (1929), 539.

only twice for the final cadence of tone B, and both times it includes a podatus for the penultimate element as in the León tradition. Yet another piece gives, for the second part of tone B, the four element intonation beginning with a clivis which is found only in the Rioja tradition. Thus, *Silos 5* is perhaps described best as a mixed source. With paleographic evidence in support, we might conjecture that it is not from Silos--perhaps from farther west toward León.

Silos 6 consists of two parts which did not originally belong together. The first thirty-seven folios are paper, and the remainder are parchment. In a recent article, Dom Ismael Fernández de la Cuesta discusses the several hands which have provided the musical notation. He distinguishes two hands in the paper portion and three hands in the parchment, two of the latter apparently being the same as the two hands supplying the notation on paper. The first hand in the parchment notates only a few pieces completely, but supplies the melismata plus an occasional neume for pieces throughout the parchment portion. The second hand completed a number of these pieces and supplied notation for a number of pieces in the paper portion. This hand is readily distinguished by the color of the ink, the notation of the first hand being the same color as that of the text. The third hand appears in still a third color completing pieces in both sections of the manuscript, but often erasing and altering the notation of the preceding hands.[38]

Altogether, there are twelve respond verses with notation, some of them with notation by both the first and second hands. The first hand is found in only three of these pieces, and twice it has supplied a podatus for the final cadence of tone B, suggesting the León tradition. Otherwise, what it has

---

[38] Ismael Fernández de la Cuesta, O.S.B., "El 'Breviarium Gothicum' de Silos," *Miscelánea en memoria de Dom Mario Férotin, Hispania Sacra*, XVII (1964), 393-494. See esp. pp. 400f.

supplied suggests neither one tradition nor the other. The second hand clearly follows the León tradition. The third hand supplies notation for only two verses, but just as clearly follows the Rioja tradition. It is a much more graceful hand, furthermore, which recalls the notation of *BM51* or *A56*. Thus *Silos 6*, too, is in a sense a mixed source. However, the last hand to intervene in it sought to bring it into the Rioja tradition not only by making his own additions, but also by "correcting" the work of his predecessors.

CHAPTER IV

THE NORTHERN FRAGMENTS CONTAINING RESPOND VERSES

Unfortunately, not all of the fragments of otherwise lost Mozarabic manuscripts contain even a part of a respond verse with notation, and thus we are at a loss to relate them to the more complete sources by this means. However, there are four fragments which come from places other than Toledo and which contain enough of at least one respond verse to allow us to assign them to one of the two traditions. There is also manuscript *A60* which is not primarily a musical manuscript, but does contain a few pieces with notation, among them three respond verses.

BN11556 is a single folio, from an antiphoner, used in the binding of a later manuscript from the monastery of San Zoilo de Carrión, just to the east of the city of León along the route of St. James. Plates VI and VII in Dom Brou's "Notes de paléographie musicale mozarabe" (1952) reproduce the two sides of this folio; and from these reproductions, it may be seen that the fragment contains part of a single respond verse on what is the recto in its present orientation in the binding. Unfortunately, the photograph cuts off part of the notation for this verse. Thus, it is transcribed here after the original with the notation for the same piece from *AL* in parallel.

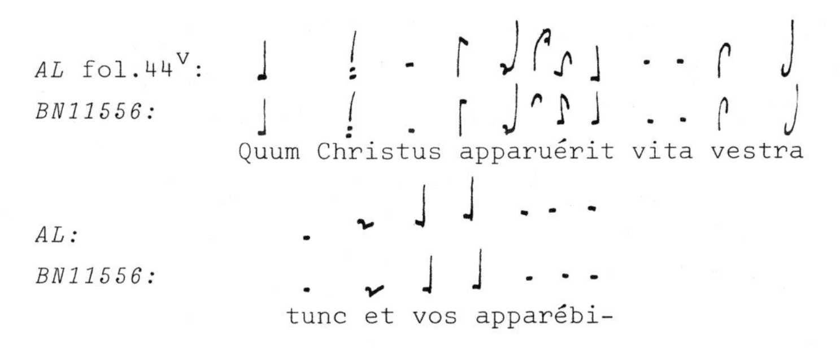

The agreement between the fragment and *AL* could scarcely be closer, and thus the fragment may be grouped with the sources for the León tradition. As Dom Brou pointed out (in his article "Le joyau...," p. 81), this fragment has another strong tie with *AL* in its use of scriptural references, in the margins, for the texts.

A photograph of the fragment *LF-5* is given by Clyde Waring Brockett, Jr., in his "Antiphons, Responsories, and Other Chants of the Mozarabic Rite" (p. 54). Although this single leaf appears to be badly stained, enough of *RS In hoc cognovi VR Propter innocentiam autem* is legible to allow us to assign this fragment to the León tradition. The reading of tone G for the verse accords quite closely with that for the same piece in *AL*, particularly in presenting podati 5 and 6 of the intonation. Thus, as Brockett suggests, the fragment may have been copied in León, where it is still preserved.

The fragment *Calz* is of unknown origin, but is now preserved in the Cathedral of Santo Domingo de la Calzada, which lies in the Rioja. It is the second of the fragments described by María Luisa Povés in her article "Los fragmentos de códices visigóticos de la catedral de Santo Domingo de la Calzada."[39] The fragment consists of two folios, of which a photograph is given of fol. 2^{r}. Unfortunately, the two respond verses are badly out of focus. But examination of the original confirms that one is an example of tone B and the other an example of tone C. Both follow the Rioja tradition. In tone B, the first syllable is borne by a punctum, clivis 7 and podatus 9 are missing, the second intonation is a four note scandicus despite the length of the text, and the penultimate figure of the final cadence is a virga instead of a podatus. The example of tone C is less clear, but clivis 7 and podatus 8 are missing, the second intonation appears to be a virga instead of a podatus, and the final cadence consists of two elements instead of three, despite the length

---

[39] *Revista de Archivos, Bibliotecas y Museos*, LVIII (1952), 517-520.

of the text. Thus, wherever this fragment was copied, it follows the tradition embodied in other manuscripts known to have been copied in the region of its present home.

SJP consists of eight folios of an antiphoner from the Aragonese monastery San Juan de la Peña in the mountains to the north of the Ebro. Dom Brou published a transcription of the text together with fourteen photographs in *Hispania Sacra* (Vol. V, No. 9 [1952]). Despite the poor condition of these few folios, the photographs reveal that they follow the Rioja tradition in the notation of their respond verses. There are eight verses in all, of which one is wholly illegible. Of the remaining seven verses, one presents tone B and the others tone A. There is no doubt about the example of tone B, *VR Germinate iusti* on fol. 8. The examples of tone A vary greatly with respect to legibility; but in all of them, it is at least possible to determine that they employ, for the final cadence, the formula of the Rioja tradition.

In *A60*, a manuscript from San Millán de la Cogolla, a second hand made use of a few blank folios to insert antiphons and responds for the office *De Letanias Apostolicas*.[40] In all, there are three respond verses with notation, tones B, F, and G being represented. Both text and music are in a rather crude hand which differs greatly from those of other San Millán sources. But in all three tones, the Rioja tradition is followed. Puncta are generally omitted, but the more important figures, including the virgae of the final cadences in tones B and F, appear and leave no room for doubt.

---

[40] Adalberto Franquesa, O.S.B., "El códice emilianense 60 y sus piezas litúrgicas," *Hispania Sacra,* XII (1959), 423-444.

CHAPTER V

THE TOLEDO SOURCES

The name of Toledo is generally given to a group of sources with little in common. For example, some are provided with northern notation instead of Toledan notation. And by no means all of the manuscripts with Toledan notation were definitely copied in Toledo. In short, the Toledo sources owe their name to the fact that all, at some time or other, passed into the hands of the various churches in Toledo. The greatest concentration is still to be found in the cathedral, although time has seen some of its holdings transferred to the Biblioteca Nacional in Madrid and others lost from sight altogether. The surviving Toledo manuscripts transmit three separate traditions for the pieces under study: one in the manuscripts with northern notation and two in the manuscripts with Toledan notation.

Of the several manuscripts described by Dom Brou under the heading "Manuscrits de Tolède notés en 'notation du nord,'"[41] only two have respond verses with notation. *BN10001* includes one such piece on the verso of the first of the two folios used in the binding. This is given in plate II of Dom Brou's article, and in it the Rioja tradition may be readily recognized. Except for the use of a scandicus instead of a podatus in position 6 of the intonation, the melody is that of tone A, the same tone employed for this respond in both *AL* and *A30*. *BN13060*, the Palomares copy, includes twelve respond verses with northern notation, one of which may be seen in plate VI of Dom Brou's article. Here again, the Rioja tradition is followed, and one is not even inclined to question the accuracy of the copyist very frequently. There are eleven examples of tone B and one of tone A.

The manuscripts in Toledan notation may be divided into two groups on both liturgical and musical grounds. *BN10110*,

---

[41] "Notes de paléographie musicale mozarabe," *Anuario Musical*, X (1955), 29.

T35.5, and *MSC* embody, together with the printed Breviary prepared under Cardinal Cisneros, a liturgical tradition which differs from that of all remaining manuscripts, both northern and Toledan.[42] It is not surprising, therefore, that these three manuscripts should also transmit a different tradition for the responsorial psalm tones. But even the manuscripts in Toledan notation which agree liturgically with the northern sources transmit their own tradition for these psalm tones. The differences between this tradition and both the León and Rioja traditions are more than can be accounted for by the differences between Toledan and northern notation. Thus, while the refrains in the two notations may reasonably be regarded as the same, the melodies for the verses clearly are not the same. Nor does the number of tones and their distribution among the refrains in these manuscripts correspond at all to the number and distribution of tones in the northern manuscripts.

T35.4 contains fifty-four respond verses with notation and is thus the most complete of the manuscripts with Toledan notation transmitting the liturgy found in the manuscripts of the north. Two tones account for all but one of these pieces, and they will be identified here with the letters L and M.

Tone L

The structure of this tone is bipartite, and it appears forty-two times in *T35.4*. The following examples show the first part.

---

[42] See José M.[a] Martín Patino, S. J., "El breviarium mozárabe de Ortíz: Su valor documental para la historia del oficio catedralicio hispánico," *Miscelánea Comillas*, XL (1963), 205-297.

1 2 3 4

fol.13 An- ge- lus Domini dixit muli- é- ri- bus

fol.11 Lau- dá- te Dó- minum omnes gen- tes

fol.117v Dis-ru- pís- ti vincula me- a

fol.74v Ap- pa- ru- é- runt illis dispertite

lingue tamquam ig- nis

The intonation consists of three elements which may be preceded by a punctum in order to adjust the accent. These three elements are never separated, and only the first and third may bear an accent. Thus, if the first accent falls on the first or second syllable, it is placed in column 2. If it falls on the third or fourth syllable, it is placed in column 4. The mediant is adjusted to the final accent of the first part of the text by dividing the torculus when this accent is on the antepenultimate syllable. All syllables between the intonation and the mediant are borne by puncta or are left without notation.

The following examples show the second part of the tone in its simplest form.

fol.58 VR Quis est iste rex...

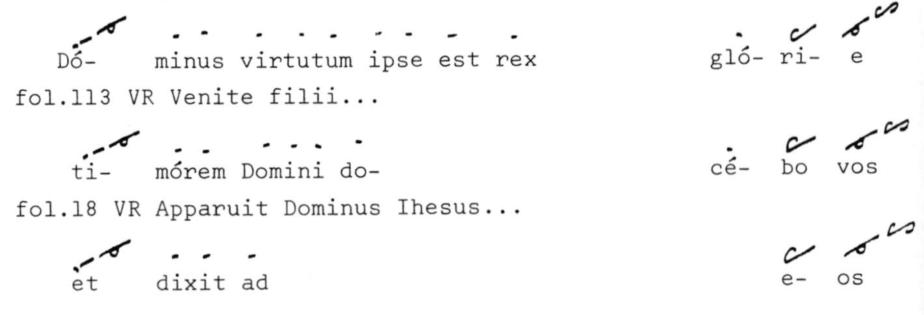

Dó- minus virtutum ipse est rex gló- ri- e

fol.113 VR Venite filii...

ti- mórem Domini do- cé- bo vos

fol.18 VR Apparuit Dominus Ihesus...

et dixit ad e- os

The intonation consists of a single element applied without

regard for the accent, and the final cadence consists of two elements also applied without regard for the accent.[43]

This second part of the tone, unlike the first part, may be subdivided. If so, the secondary mediant of the music always corresponds to some mark of punctuation in the text, either . or ./ . These same marks are used to divide all texts into their two basic parts whether or not the notation has been supplied. The second subsection of the second part is treated after the fashion of the second part when this is without subdivisions. The first subsection is treated as follows.

fol.13 VR Angelus Domini dixit...

quid queritis biventem cum mór- tu- is.

fol.73 VR Spiritus Sanctus descendit...

et implevit do- mum il- lam.

The single element of the intonation is the same as that for the second part when it is without subdivisions. The mediant consists of three elements applied mechanically, although twice a punctum is placed between the first and second for no apparent reason.

Tone M

As opposed to the forty-two examples of tone L, there are only eleven examples of tone M in *T35.4*. But these eleven examples provide a clear outline for the tone.

1 2 3 4

fol.9^{v} Christus sur- gens a mortuis iam non mó- ri- tur

fol.121^{v} Cla-má- vi ad te Domine Deus me- us

---

[43] The final cadence of *VR Laudate Dominum* on fol. 11 is the sole exception to this principle.

The available pieces show that the first accent is placed in column 2 if it falls on the first or second syllable. The mediant for the first part is then adjusted to the final accent of the text, as in the pieces shown above.

The intonation for the second part of this tone consists of a single element applied mechanically to the first syllable of text, and the final cadence is applied mechanically to the last four syllables. The following are examples, there being none which give any further subdivisions.

fol.43 VR Volabunt in navibus

ét mare pariter pre-da- bún-tur

fol.52 VR Dominus Ihesus Christus qui est testis...

ip- se dilexit nos et labit nos a pec- cá- tis nos-tris

T33.3 belongs to the same liturgical tradition as *T35.4* and the northern manuscripts, and it contains certain of the daytime hours. Unfortunately, it is in very poor condition, but it does include ten respond verses with enough notation to permit us to relate it to the other sources. There are one example of tone L and six examples of tone M. The melodies are the same as those in *T35.4*, except that one example of tone M shows a subdivision in the second part. It is given here in its entirety.

fol.7v Defecit gaudium cordis nostri.

versus est in luctu corus noster. cecidit corona capitis nostri:

As with other examples of what must have been the two most common tones in this manuscript, the notation here is not complete. But the text has been marked clearly to show the divisions. We may take the absence of mediant and intonation at the first division to mean that "the usual ones" found in *T35.4* are called for.

The remaining three verses in *T33.3* appear to represent a third tone (N). That the notation for them should be relatively complete suggests that this was not a common tone. Perhaps it was found only among monastic hours. It bears a certain resemblance to tone D as found in *AL*. Nevertheless, only one of these three pieces is found outside of *T33.3*, and it appears in *AL* with a different text for the verse and with the melody of tone B. All three examples are given below.

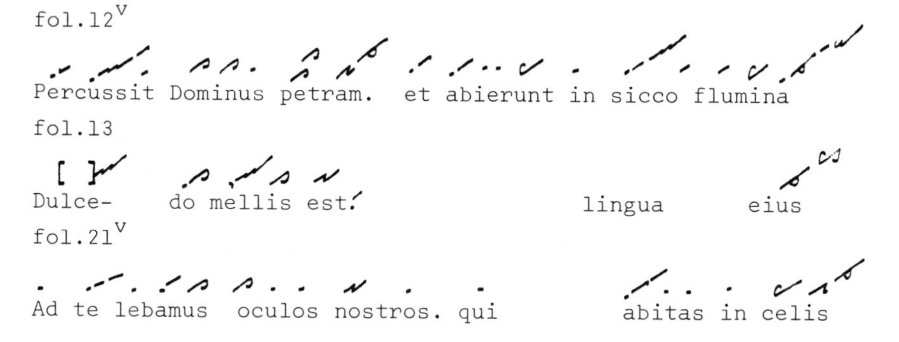

T35.7 also belongs to the liturgical tradition of the northern manuscripts. Musically, it appears to belong with the two manuscripts we have just discussed. However, only seven respond verses were provided with notation, and this was done by a second hand, writing very lightly. One of these pieces definitely represents tone L, and another definitely represents tone M. The other five pieces do not resemble, to any significant extent, tones found in other manuscripts. Two of them might be related to one of the tones appearing in the manuscripts of the other liturgical tradition to be discussed below. But the relationship is far from being one of identity.

Photographs of the fragment *Cinc* were published by Eric Werner in the *Miscelánea en homenaje a Monseñor Higinio*

Anglés (Barcelona, 1958-61), II, 985-991. The only notation for a respond verse which is legible is part of that for *VR Invocabit Dominum potentem* (p. 986), and the final cadence is clearly that of tone M.

BN10110 and *T35.5* complement one another, and they provide all of the hours and Masses to be said during Lent in public worship. Together, the two manuscripts are analogous to that portion of *AL* which corresponds to Lent. However, the order of service for the various hours, the distribution of texts among the services, and the days on which Mass is to be said in these two manuscripts differ from the practice of all other surviving sources. About a third of the texts for respond refrains in *BN10110* have concordances in *AL*, but the verse is the same in only one case. Although most of the concordances are assigned to Lent in *AL* too, in no case does a text belong to the same service in both manuscripts. The melodies for a number of the refrains could reasonably be regarded as being related in the two manuscripts. But the melodies for the verses are clearly different in all cases. *BN10110* provides us with a total of ninety-nine respond verses with notation. Thus, we may be reasonably sure of gaining a complete view of the responsorial psalm tones for the office corresponding to this liturgical tradition. In *T35.5* there are only nine respond verses with notation, but the melodies are the same as those in *BN10110*. The fragment *MSC* contains a single respond verse with notation, and it is an example of the most common tone in *BN10110*.

In this tradition, there are four separate tones (to be designated here with the letters H, I, J, and K), the first of which accounts for fifty-eight pieces--somewhat more than half of the total. This tone is also treated with much the greatest consistency.

Tone H

The structure of the tone is bipartite, and its components are quite simple. The first intonation consists of only two elements in addition to the puncta which bear all syllables preceding the first accented syllable. The second of these elements varies, for no apparent reason, between the two shown in the examples below. The first two elements may be contracted, but they are never separated by another figure. They are adjusted so that the first will bear the first accented syllable of the text and may be preceded by as many as three puncta for this purpose. The mediant ending the first part of the tone is adjusted to the final accent of the appropriate part of the text. The syllable preceding this accent is always borne by a podatus. The following element is divided into two puncta if the accent is on the antepenultimate syllable. The following examples show the entire first part of the tone.

fol.47 Fác- ti sumus quasi in prin-cí- pi- o

fol.46 Peccá- bi- mus in conspec- tu tu- o

fol.35v Flagellá- bit nos ab iniquitati- bus nos-tris

fol.100 Venatió- ne ceperunt me quasi

avem inimici me- i gra-tis

If the second part is to be subdivided, the first subsection takes the form shown in the following examples. The first syllable is borne by a podatus, the two syllables preceding the final accent are borne by a torculus and a podatus respectively, and the final accent and following syllable (or syllables) are borne by puncta.

fol.52^{v} VR Ne avertas faciem...

a pu- e- ro tu- o

fol.110^{v} VR Locutus est Dominus...

dis- cipulis su- is di- cens

fol.67 VR Da filios...

et deduc eos in ma- nu glá-dii

The final subsection takes the same form as does the second part when it is not subdivided. All syllables preceding the final cadence are borne by puncta. The scandicus of the final cadence is adjusted to the text accent on the condition that it not be separated from the final element by more than three or less than two puncta. If the accent cannot be brought under the scandicus while fulfilling this condition, the number of puncta following is chosen so that the accent will not be placed adjacent to the scandicus.

fol.49 VR Salba plebem...

et benedic heredi- tá- tem tu- am

fol.31^{v} VR Peccavimus cum patribus...

iniqui- tá- tes fé- ci- mus

fol.52^{v} VR Ne avertas faciem...

quoniam tribulor velóci- ter ex- áu- di me

fol.48^{v} VR Inter vestibolum...

ministri Dómi- ni di- cén-tes

Tone I

BN10110 contains twenty examples of this tone, but the melodies vary enough from one example to the next to make abstractions difficult. The examples in figure 6 suggest the more stable features. Even the basic design of the tone is not clear in many pieces. Nevertheless, it may be regarded as bipartite if we consider the first example in figure 6 and compare it with the others. The first intonation consists, apart from anticipatory puncta, of three elements, the middle of which may be divided into two puncta. Either or both of the first and third elements may bear an accent, but the placing of accents is not consistent here or elsewhere in the tone. Aside from the first intonation, only the final cadence shows much stability. But the final element may be either one of two figures, and there is no ready way of determining how many puncta should separate it from the preceding scandicus.

Tone J

There are thirteen examples of tone J in *BN10110*, and once again, they are not in close agreement with one another. The examples in figure 6 are, in this sense, representative of the whole collection. The structure seems to be bipartite, although many examples introduce elements which suggest that the final cadence consists of six elements. But only the last of these elements is common to all thirteen pieces. In neither the intonation nor the cadence are accents treated consistently.

Tone K

There are only eight examples of tone K in *BN10110*, and perhaps for that reason this tone appears to receive slightly more consistent treatment than tones I and J. The design is bipartite, although all but one of the eight examples appear to make additional subdivisions. The first intonation consists of two elements which are never separated. They are adjusted, through the use of anticipatory puncta, so that the first bears the first accent of the text. The mediant ending the first part is usually adjusted to the final accent of the text, as in the first three examples of this tone in figure 6. But there are exceptions such as the fourth example. The

Figure 6

BN10110:

Tone I:

fol.59 Dix- é- runt ve- ní- te mittamus lignum in pa- ne e- ius ‖

fol.23v Dex- pecx- ís- tis omne consili- um me- um

fol.32v Qué- ri- te Dó- mi- num

fol.63 Tu au- tem Dó- mine Deus ex- er- ci- tuum ‖ omnium regum terre qui sedes super cherubin

Tone J:

fol.3 Ve- ní- te ex- ultémus in Dó- mi- no ‖

fol.12 Non men- ti- é- mini ín- vi- cem

fol.21v De- us in nó- mine tu- o sal-vos nos fac

fol.55 Ef- fún- de frá- mea et con- clú- de ‖ adversus eos qui me perse- cun- tur

Tone K:

fol.97 Po- su- é- runt me in lacu inferi- ó- ri- ‖

fol.97v In lá- bi- is suis indulcat ini- mí- cus ut subvertat amicum suum in fo- be- am

fol.21 Con-ver-tí- mi- ni et agite peni- tén- ci- am ab omnibus iniquita- ti- bus ves- tris

fol.33 Qua-re in per- pé- tu- um ‖ o- bli- bis- ce- ris nos- tri

Figure 6

et in crepationes meas ne- glex- is- tis
dum inve- ni- ri po- test
aperi oculos tuos et vi- de

et erradamus eum de terra vi- ben- ti- um
vocabi enim vos et re- mis- tis
invocate eum dum pro- pe est
in- clina au- rem tu- am

iubilemus Deo sal- ba- to- ri nostro
nec decipiat unusquisque proxi-mum suum
et in virtute tua li- be-ra nos
et dic a- ni- me mee

in tenebris et in um- bra mor- tis
ex multa enim loquella temtavit eum et de- ri- det
et non erit vobis in ruina i- ni- qui- tas
derelinques nos in longitudi- ne di- e- rum

second part of the tone (or the final subsection if the second part has been subdivided) consists of puncta up until the final cadence. The cadence should probably be applied mechanically to the last four syllables of text, but the alignment of the notation with the text leaves room for doubt in some cases.

CHAPTER VI

THE ORIGINS AND RELATIONSHIP OF THE TRADITIONS

The existence of more than one practice in the music of the Mozarabic Church is not without literary testimony. In the third prologue to *AL*,[44] the poet praises the divine music contained in the manuscript and the holy men who composed it, but bewails the state to which the music has fallen in his own day. He describes the ancient psalmody sung with three choirs and says that, "at that time," the church preserved the chant correctly. But "now" the church is wide of the mark and sings the chant in several different ways.

> Tunc omnesque ordines eclesia recte tenebat
> nunc proculque ditant adhuic viventibus.
> Disparesque modos nunc te eclesia canet
> finitam habentes hanc artem prefulgidam.

Aside from claiming that the manuscript in which he writes preserves the true ancient form, the poet tells us nothing about the nature of the *dispares modos* or their origins.

If we consider the northern sources, it is not hard to believe that the two traditions we have distinguished here descended from a single archetype. For one thing, most of the elements of the Rioja tradition, other than puncta and virgae, are common to both. For another, the elements common to both are the most stable with respect to notation. For example, the first scandicus in tones A and B is almost always of the form [neume] in both traditions, whereas the second scandicus of tone B is almost always of the form [neume].

---

[44] *Antifonario Visigótico Mozárabe de la Catedral de León*, ed. Dom Louis Brou and Dr. José Vives, *Monumenta Hispaniae Sacra, Serie Litúrgica*, Vol. V, 1 (Barcelona-Madrid, 1959), p. 4ff.

Similarly, the podati of the mediant in tone B are almost always rounded in both traditions. On the other hand, the elements which are not always common to both traditions--e.g., the clives and podati of the intonations for tones A and B--show the least notational stability.

If we are to take the word of the poet, we must regard the Rioja tradition as the decadent form of the Leonese. Unfortunately, the chronology of the sources is of no help in deciding this. The two traditions evidently existed contemporaneously, and there is no way of establishing which is the more ancient. *AL* dates from the 10th century, along with the earliest Rioja sources; and *Sant* dates from the middle of the 11th century along with the latest Rioja sources. We are thus obliged to turn to questions of style, and here we must proceed fundamentally on assumption. There is no way of establishing logically that the simple form must have preceded the complex or that inconsistency preceded consistency. But this seems more likely, our poet to the contrary. The formulas of *AL* are the more elaborate, as is its notation in sheer numbers of symbols. In most respects, the formulas of *AL* could be derived from those of the Rioja sources by simple addition of notes, and even the number of tones employed in the León tradition represents an addition to the system at work in the Rioja tradition. All of this, taken with the fact that the elements common to both traditions are treated with consistency in both, while some which are consistent in León are quite inconsistently treated in the Rioja, suggests that both traditions represent elaborations of an earlier form, but that the Rioja tradition represents less of an evolution of this archetype and stands, therefore, closer to it.

The most obvious thing about the two northern traditions is their geographical distribution. All of the sources known to proceed from the province of León transmit a single tradition. All of those known to proceed from the Rioja, as well as the fragment from San Juan de la Peña (neighboring to the north of the Ebro river) and most of the sources from Silos (just over the mountains to the west in Castile), transmit another tradition. But how can we account for differing traditions in two regions which are so intimately connected during just the period which produced our sources?

One possibility is that what we have called the León tradition is an import from the south--from lands still controlled by the Moslems in the 10th and 11th centuries. Andalusian immigration to León began as soon as Alfonso III had consolidated his kingdom to some extent, and many of the monasteries founded on the Leonese plain at the end of the 9th and beginning of the 10th centuries were populated by monks from Andalucía.[45] The monastery of San Zoilo de Carrión, from which the fragment *BN11556* proceeds, was founded during the first half of the 11th century by monks from San Zoilo de Córdoba, and thus the antiphoner of which only part of one folio has survived may have been copied in the south.[46] *AL* itself shows signs of having been copied from a model of Toledan or perhaps even Andalusian provenance.[47] But whatever the origins of their models, both *AL* and *Sant* are evidently products of the kingdom of León.

A more likely explanation for the two northern traditions is suggested by the nature of the repopulation of Castile and the Rioja immediately following their reconquest. Both of these regions were reconquered under the aegis of the kings of León, although in the case of the Rioja, there was an alliance with the rulers of Navarre granting them dominion over this territory. And in both of these regions, the principal instrument of repopulation and consolidation was the monastery. This made the Rioja, during the 10th century,

---

[45] Fray Justo Pérez de Urbel, *Historia del Condado de Castilla* (Madrid, 1944), I, 335.

[46] Jaime Moll Roqueta, "Nuevos hallazgos de manuscritos mozárabes con neumas musicales," *Anuario Musical,* V (1950), 12.

[47] Fray Justo Pérez de Urbel, "Antifonario de León: El escritor y la época," *Archivos Leoneses,* VIII, No. 15 (1954), 135ff.

one of the most brilliant centers of learning in northern Spain.[48] But the strongest influence on the reorganization of monastic life in Castile and, as a result, in the Rioja, came from neither León nor from Navarre. It came from Galicia.[49] Charles Bishko has shown that various types of pacta between abbot and monks provided the organizing principle for the monasteries founded in Castile during the reconquest period, and that from here this pactualism was carried into the Rioja by the first monastic colonizers. He has also noted that pactualism can only have come from Galicia and that it is wholly absent from León--indeed, from all of the rest of Spain as well save eastern Asturias. Since the first evidence for pactualism in Castile comes at the same time that Alfonso I is known to have repopulated these lands and depopulated the homeland of pactualism south of the Miño river in Galicia (ca. 750), Bishko concludes that it must have been Gallegan monks who colonized Castile.[50] Almost two centuries later, the Gallegan heritage was transplanted to Riojan soil by the Castilian founders of monasteries such as San Millán de la Cogolla, San Martín de Albelda, and the latter's dependency San Prudencio de Laturce. At about the same time, it even spread into parts of Navarre above the Ebro.

We are without musical sources antedating the depopulation of Galicia and thus without musical evidence for a connection

---

[48] Fray Justo Pérez de Urbel, "La reconquista de la Rioja y su colonización espiritual en el siglo X," *Estudios Dedicados a Menéndez Pidal* (Madrid, 1950), I, 495-534.

[49] Charles Julian Bishko, "Gallegan Pactual Monasticism in the Repopulation of Castile," *Estudios Dedicados a Menéndez Pidal* (Madrid, 1951), II, 513-553. Also the same author's "Salvus of Albelda and Frontier Monasticism in Tenth-Century Navarre," *Speculum*, XIII, No. 4 (1948), 559-590.

[50] "Gallegan Pactual Monasticism..." p. 524.

between this region and Castile or the Rioja.[51] But we have seen that the Silos sources give evidence of a close connection between Castile and the Rioja. Thus, bearing in mind the way in which pactual monasticism links Castile and the Rioja to each other and the two of these to Galicia at the exclusion of León, we may suppose that the tradition for the responsorial psalm tones which came to rest in the Rioja had its beginnings in Galicia. Springing from a community of monasteries which, by the middle of the 7th century, had already begun to distinguish itself from the rest of the peninsula in its manner of organizing monastic life, this tradition must have been carried eastward in some form or other by Gallegan monks when they were forced to abandon their homeland and settle again on the eastern fringe of the Leonese kingdom in what soon after became known as Castile. There it continued to form part of a practice different from that of León. In the 10th century, this practice followed the advancing Christian armies into the Rioja. But in the following century, both it and the practice of León bowed to the practice of Rome.

---

[51] "It looks very much as if pactual monasticism never effectively re-established itself in Galicia after the eighth century,...partly because most monastic colonizers, in the repopulation of the western zone of the Peninsula, propagated the Visigothic tradition [associated with León], but also because the chief center of pactual monasticism shifted to the eastern marchlands of the Asturo-Leonese state." Bishko, *Ibid.* p. 517. One would thus expect Galician musical sources from after the 8th century to embody the León tradition. Escorial MS a I 13 is a miscellany copied in Galicia in 902, and Brockett copies the single musical item appearing in it ("Antiphons, Responsories, and Other Chants of the Mozarabic Rite," p. 51). This piece, *RS Egredietur Dominus de Samaria VR Ecce veniet in nubibus,* appears in the lower margin of the manuscript across the opening from fol. 196^{v} to 197. Hence, the date and provenance of the manuscript need not apply to the musical notation. But Brockett's copy shows clearly that the verse is set with an example of tone B from the León tradition. This is apparently the only surviving source known to have originated in Galicia which contains notation.

What then of the Toledo sources? Are we now obliged to account for the existence of two distinct liturgical traditions and three distinct musical traditions within a single city or province? Not entirely, for there is no reason to believe that northern notation was ever in use generally in Toledo. In a detailed study of *BN10001*, Mons. Enciso has suggested that this manuscript was copied in the region of León. More to the point, he has noted that the verso of the second of the two folios used in the binding is written in a hand which differs from the style of most southern manuscripts and approaches the Castilian school.[52] As for the manuscript of which Palomares made a copy, we know only that it belonged at one time to the cathedral of Toledo. But the same is true of *BN10001*, and we have just seen that it probably was not copied in Toledo. The only other manuscript in northern notation which has been associated with Toledo is 35.6 of the Biblioteca Capitular. There is no reason to believe that this manuscript was copied in Toledo either. It was, however, probably copied in a place where northern notation was in general use, for the few pieces which are provided with notation (among them no respond verses) are the work of several different hands.[53]

Of the manuscripts with Toledan notation, only one is of known origin.[54] This is *BN10110*, the work of a presbyter of

---

[52] Mons. Jesús Enciso, "El breviario mozárabe de la Biblioteca Nacional," *Estudios Bíblicos*, Vol. II, Cauderno 2 (1943), 195. Dom Brou evidently did not know this study when he wrote of this manuscript in *Anuario Musical*, X (1955), 30-31.

[53] One of the possibilities suggested by Dom Brou is that such a manuscript might be the work of a visitor to Toledo from the north. *Ibid.* p. 31.

[54] For example, Agustín Millares Carlo writes, concerning Toledo Cathedral MSS 35.3 and 35.4, that "we know they proceed from the Mozarabic parish of St. Eulalia, but it cannot be said with certainty that they were copied there." *Los códices visigóticos de la catedral toledana: Cuestiones cronológicas y de procedencia* (Madrid, 1935), p. 43.

the parish church of Saints Justa and Rufina in Toledo. Thus, the variant liturgical tradition of this manuscript and *T35.5* is definitely tied to Toledo. Father Martín Patino is of the opinion that this tradition is not a regional peculiarity growing out of a common stock with the liturgy of the northern manuscripts. Instead, he believes it to be an early state of the liturgy of which the northern manuscripts embody a reform. Of course, the fact that *BN10110* was copied in the 11th century indicates that this earlier state was kept alive along with the reformed version.[55] But with our present information, we cannot be certain that it was kept alive only in Toledo or that it was kept alive in Toledo to the exclusion of the reformed version. Whatever its history, its music for the pieces we have been studying shows almost no contact with that of the remaining manuscripts--both those with northern notation and those with Toledan notation.

The manuscripts with Toledan notation and with the liturgy of the northern manuscripts lend themselves more readily, of course, to comparison with the northern manuscripts from a musical point of view. In the abstract, tone L of these manuscripts, though simpler, might even be identified with tone B of the northern manuscripts. Certainly the second parts of these two tones could scarcely be more similar. Tone M is not so easily identified with any of the tones found in the northern manuscripts. But its basic design, the intonation beginning with a scandicus of a sort, the final cadence, including the same final element as that of tone L--all of these recall features of the tones in the northern manuscripts, especially those of the Rioja. If we compare *T35.4* with *AL*, however, the relationship of tones L and M to the tones of the northern manuscripts becomes more problematical. There are forty-nine concordances between these two manuscripts,

---

[55] Martín Patino, "El breviarum...," p. 297.

and although the texts for the verses differ in seven cases, the refrains are the same in both text and music in all forty-nine. The difference between the two notations naturally accounts for variants in the melodies of the refrains, but the placing of the melismata, as well as more detailed notational characteristics, makes it clear that the two manuscripts transmit the same repertory. The distribution of tones is as follows:

T35.4		*AL*	
Tone L	40	Tone A	14
		Tone B	21
		Tone D	3
		Tone E	1
		unica	1
		Total	40
Tone M	8	Tone A	7
		Tone B	1
		Total	8

One piece has a unique melody in each of the two manuscripts.

It is evident that tone L is not equivalent in function to tone B or any other northern tone, nor by the same token is tone M. It seems unlikely, therefore, that the assignment of tones to these refrains depended on any well-defined concept of mode. If the concept of mode existed at all, it must have been sufficiently flexible to allow two quite different interpretations of it with respect to the same body of melodies. Once we are inclined to doubt the existence of a well-defined modal system, we need not be surprised to find only two tones in *T35.4* instead of seven or eight.

The existence of two systems of tones in two groups of manuscripts which share a single repertory of melodies for the refrains of the responds suggests that the written tradition for the latter very much antedates that for the tones. The tones, being simple and common melodies, must have been transmitted orally well after the northern and Toledan notations had become separate written traditions. By the time they were written down in these two notations, the melodies themselves and the criteria for assigning them to the refrains had taken on very different features in the communities using the different notations. If we ask how the two musical traditions remained separate while following a single liturgy, we can perhaps find the answer in the Moslem domination of Spain. This one liturgy, whether or not a reform of an earlier liturgy, must have been largely set by the time of the invasion of the peninsula in 711, as we have seen in connection with the *Oracional* of Verona. Musical notation can only have been in its very beginnings at this time, if that. Thus, the two notations must have become recognizable as such after the Moslems were well in control of the greater part of the peninsula. What we now know as the northern notation is the product of Christian Spain--either lands never taken by the Moslems, such as the kingdom of Asturias, or lands recaptured by the Christians, such as León and Castile. Toledan notation is probably Mozarabic properly so called--that is, the product of Christians living under Moslem political rule. Between the lands using these two notations lay a frontier at times sealed with scorched earth. Christians emigrating from the south and fleeing Moslem domination could account for the copying of an occasional manuscript with Toledan notation in the north, as with the body of *BN10001*. At the same time, Christian northern Spain was open to the influences of the rest of the Christian world. Perhaps it is to these influences that we should attribute the more elaborate character of responsorial psalmody in the north.

APPENDIX

The following tables list alphabetically by refrain and by verse the responds appearing in the manuscripts named on pages 6 and 7 above with the following exceptions: the pieces without notation in *Silos 7* and *T35.7* are omitted. For each piece, the folio number is given in the appropriate columns for its sources, followed by the letter designating the tone for the verse. The letter X is used for unique melodies, and sn (*sine notis*) indicates that the verse is either without notation or that only the incipit is given. The Biblical sources for the texts are supplied in parentheses and are taken, for the most part, from the index to the text of *AL* published by Dom Louis Brou and José Vives. However, I have made no attempt to indicate whether the Biblical citation is the source for all of the text in question. Frequently, the source for the first phrase of a text could not be found, while sources for subsequent phrases could.

A single refrain appearing with different verses in different sources is not repeated in the list, each of the verses being listed below it. Thus, the repetition of a refrain text indicates a different melody from the one preceding in all cases except those involving *BN10110*, *T35.5*, and *MSC*. All pieces in these manuscripts have been listed separately even though some of the texts which they have in common with *AL* might be regarded as having common melodies.

Wherever possible, the spellings of the manuscripts have been preserved for both texts and liturgical assignments. For purposes of alphabetization, however, it has been necessary to correct some of the more common inconsistencies: the substitution of *v* for *b* and vice versa, the omission or unnecessary addition of *h*, and the use of *e* for *ae*. Letters supplied by me are enclosed in square brackets, superfluous letters are enclosed in parentheses, and *v*'s or *b*'s which have been substituted are underscored. These changes have been made only where a difference in the alphabetical order is implied.

Abbreviations

Books of the Bible:

Abd	Abdias
Act	Actus Apostolorum
Agg	Aggaeus
Am	Amos
Apoc	Apocalypsis B. Ioannis Apostoli
Bar	Baruch
Cant	Canticum Canticorum
Col	Epistola B. Pauli ad Colossenses
Cor	Epistola B. Pauli ad Corinthos
Dan	Daniel
Deut	Deuteronomium
Eccli	Ecclesiasticus
Eph	Epistola B. Pauli ad Ephesios
Esd	Esdrae
Esth	Esther
Ex	Exodus
Ez	Ezechiel
Gal	Epistola B. Pauli ad Galatas
Gen	Genesis
Hab	Habacuc
Heb	Epistola B. Pauli ad Hebraeos
Ier	Ieremias
Io	Evangelium secundum Ioannem
I Io	Epistola I B. Ioannis
Iob	
Ioel	
Ion	Ionas
Is	Isaias
Iud	Iudices
Iudith	
Lc	Evangelium secundum Lucam
Lev	Leviticus
Mach	Machabaeorum

Mal	Malachias
Mc	Evangelium secundum Marcum
Mich	Michea
Mt	Evangelium secundum Matthaeum
Num	Numeri
Or Man	Oratio Manassae regis Iuda
Os	Osee
Par	Paralipomenon
Petr	Epistola B. Petri
Phi	Epistola B. Pauli ad Philippenses
Phil	Epistola B. Pauli ad Philemonem
Prov	Proverbia
Ps	Psalmi
Reg	Regum
Rom	Epistola B. Pauli ad Romanos
Sap	Sapientia
Soph	Sophonias
The	Epistola B. Pauli ad Thessalonicenses
Thr	Threni, id est Lamentationes Ieremiae
Tob	Tobias
Zach	Zacharias

Passio In *AL*, often *de passione sua*, referring to the passion of the saint in question. See José Vives, "Fuentes hagiográficas del antifonario de León," *Archivos Leoneses*, VIII, No. 15 (1954), 288-299.

Liturgical Assignments:

Adsum S Mariae -- Officium in Adsuntio sancte Marie

Adv -- Adventus Domini. The ferial office is interspersed with that for the saints and is not assigned to specific days.

Adv ad tert -- Responsuria de Adventu Domini dicende ad tertiam per singulos dies a sancti Aciscli usque in diem Nativitatis Domini.

Allis Infant -- Officium in diem Allisionis Infantum

Apparit Dni -- Officium in diem Apparitionis Domini

Carnes Toll -- Officium in Carnes Tollendas

Cat S Petri -- Officium in diem Catedrae sancti Petri

Circumcis Dni -- Officium in diem Circumcisionis Domini

conm corp defunct -- Ordo ad conmendandum corpus defunctum infra domum

conm corp parv -- Ordo ad corpus parvuli conmendandum

conm pres -- Ordo in conmendatione presbiteri

consecr nov sep -- Ordo ad consecrandum nobum sepulcrum

conversorum -- Ordo conversorum conversarumque

decoll S Iohannis -- Officium in decollatione sancti Iohannis

defunct aep -- Officium de defunctorum aepiscoporum

defunct sacerd -- Officium de defunctorum sacerdotum

defunctis -- Officium de defunctis generalis

Dom -- Dominico

Dom ante intr XLme -- Officium in Dominico ante introitu Quadragesime

Dom de Med -- Officium de Mediante die festo

Dom post Vic -- Officium in subsequenti Dominico post Vicesimam. Also referred to as Lazaro and Ovile Ovium.

fer -- feria

fin hominis die -- Ordo in finem hominis die

Lazaro -- Sunday preceding Ramos Palmarum. In *AL*: Officium in subsequenti Dominico post Vicesimam.

let apost -- Officium de Letanias apostolicas

let can -- Officium de Letanias canonicas

let de clade -- Responsuria de Letanias de clade dicendi

let pro plubia -- Responsuria de Letanias pro plubia postulanda

mat -- ad matutinum

med noct -- ad medium noctis

Nat Dni -- Officium in diem Nativitatis Domini

nat S Iohannis -- Officium in nativitate sancti Iohannis Babtiste

nocturnos et mat ora diei Dom -- Responsuria Dominicales ad nocturnos et matutinum sive in ora diei

non -- ad nonam

oct pasc -- octabas Paschae

ordin episcopi -- Officium in ordinatione episcopi

ord nat regis -- Officium in ordinatione sive in natalicio regis

penitentie -- Ordo penitentie

quot -- de quotidiano

reconcil penit -- Ordo ad reconciliandum penitentem

Res Dni -- Officium de Resurrectione Domini de XV^{m} diebus collectum usque ad Ascensione Domini. The number of the day in this series is indicated by an Arabic numeral.

rest bas -- Officium de restauratione baselice

S Emiliani -- Officium in diem sancti Emiliani presbiteri et confessoris

S Engrat et com -- Officium in diem sanctae Engratiae et Comitum

SS Faust, Ianuar, et Martial -- Officium in diem sanctorum Faustus, Ianuarus, et Martialis

SS general -- Officium de sanctis generalibus

S Hieronimi pres -- Officium in diem sancti Hieronimi presviteri

S Iac frat Dni -- Officium in diem sancti Iacobi fratris Domini

S Martini vigil -- Officium in diem sancti Martini Aepiscopi. Ad vigilias quando vita sancti Martini legitur

SS Simon et Iud apost -- Officium in diem sanctorum Simonis et Iudae Apostolorum

SS Vinc, Sav, et Cris -- Officium in diem sanctorum Vincenti, Savine, et Cristetis

S Vincenti laev -- Officium in diem sancti Vincenti laevite

sabb -- sabbato

sacr bas -- Officium de sacratione baselice

sacr S Martini -- Officium in diem sacrationis sancti Martini

sext -- ad sextam

super sepulcrum -- Ordo super sepulcrum quando clamore proclamatur

tert -- ad tertiam

Tradit Dni -- de Traditione Domini

trans corp S Satornini aep -- Officium in translationis corporis sancti Satornini Aepiscopi

unius virg confess -- Officium unius virginis confessoris

unoq Dom -- Officium de quotidiano Dominicale. Antiphone per unoquoque Dominico ad matutinum

vesp Ascension -- in vespera Ascensionis Domini

vesp Nat Dni -- in vespera Nativitatis Domini

XLma -- Quadragesima. The Sundays in Lent are given in *AL* as follows:

Officium in Carnes Tollendas
Officium in Primo Dominico Quadragesime
Officium in II° Dominico Quadragesime
Officium de Mediante die festo
Officium in subsequenti Dominico post Vicesimam
Ordo psallendi in Ramos Palmarum

In the tables, the week following each of these six Sundays is designated in order by an Arabic numeral.

The feria is designated by a Roman numeral.

	AL
A laqueo lingue libera me (Eccli 51:3-5)	
VR Eripe me de inimicis meis Deus meus (Ps 58:2)	135 A
VR A me ipso anima mea	
RS Quare tristis es anima mea	
VR A parte regis clamabatur	
RS Quumque Iulianus letaretur	
Ab homine iniquo et doloso (Ps 42:1-2)	
VR Eripe me de operantibus (Ps 58:3)	145 B
VR Abominati sunt me consiliari	
RS Omnes amici mei inluserunt	
Abundantia frugum erit in omnem (?)	
VR Et erunt super omnem montem (Is 30:25)	52^{v} A
(H)abundaverunt iniquitates nostre (Or Man 9-10)	
VR Iniquitates nostre multiplicate sunt (Or Man 9-10)	118^{v} D
VR Peccabimus cum patribus (Ps 105:6)	
VR Abundaverunt iniquitates nostre	
RS Ne abstuleris Domine misericordiam	
VR Accedite ad Dominum	
RS Si consurrexistis Christo	
Acceperunt prudentes oleum (Mt 25:4,6)	
VR Date nomini eius (Eccli 39:20)	
VR Oleum recondite in vasis (Mt ?)	220^{v} A
Ad adiubandum me festina (Ps 69:2,6)	
VR Deus in adiutorium (Ps 69:2)	

A30	Silos	*BN10110*	Other Sources	Liturgical Assignment
				XLma 4 II sext
				XLma 5 II mat
78 A				post Dom III Adv mat
				XLma 2 II tert
	6 96^{v} C			Dom V quot mat
	BM51 166^{v} B			med noct de virginibus
	BM45 43 A			SS Iuste et Rufine mat
				SS Iustae et Rufinae mat
			Sal 150^{v} A	med noct
	3 142^{v} A			de virginibus mat
	6 27^{v} A			"
	BM51 176 B			nocturnos fer VI
			Sant 218 B	"

VR Ad odorem aque germinabit
    RS Alleluia erit tamquam
VR Ad te lebamus oculos
    RS Exurge Domine miserere nobis
    RS Miserator Domine miserere
    RS Miserere quia Deus es misericors
VR Ad te lebamus oculos
    RS Qui respicis in terram
    RS Salus nostra in manu tua
    RS Subveni Domine quia conturbatur
    RS Virtus nostra Domine
VR Adduxit eos in montem
    RS Sanctis ab altissimo conceditur
Adesit Domino Deo suo (IV Reg 18:6-7)
    VR In lege Domini congregabit (Eccli 46:17,22) 236 B

VR Adhesit Domino Deo suo
    RS Iste homo in professione sua
VR Adiciet Dominus super vos
    RS Benedictio Domini super vos
Adiutor et liberator meus es tu (Ps 39:18)
    VR Exaudi orationem meam (Ps 38:13)

Adiutorium nostrum in nomine Domini (Ps 123:8)
    VR Laqueus contritus est (Ps 123:7)

A30	Silos	*BN10110*	Other Sources	Liturgical Assignment
			Sal	
			156 B	"
			170 B	nocturnos in Lazaro
				decoll S Iohannis mat
			Sant	
			217 C	nocturnos fer IV
			Sal	
			153^{v} C	"
			169^{v} C	nocturnos in Lazaro
	BM51 175 C			nocturnos fer IV
			Calz	
			2 C	

AL

II Gloria et honor Patri

VR Adiutorium nostrum
    RS Auxilium meum a Domino
Adiuva Domine sperantes in te (?)
    VR Adiuba nos Deus (Ps 78:9)
    VR Deus in nomine tuo salvos nos fac (Ps 53:3) 294v A

Adiuva nos Deus (Ps 78:9)
    VR Et propter honorem nominis (Ps 78:9) 242 A
VR Adiuva nos Deus
    RS Adiuva Domine sperantes in te
    RS Ne memineris Deus iniquitates
    RS Propitius esto peccatis
VR Adorabo ad templum sanctum
    RS In conspectu angelorum psallam
Adprendite disciplina nequando (Ps 2:12)
    VR Servite Domino in timore (Ps 2:11)

Adtende Domine ad me (Ier 18:19-20)
    VR Tu autem Domine exercituum (IV Reg 19:15-16)
Adtende et abscultabi (Ier 8:6)
    VR Quare adversus est populus iste (Ier 8:5)
Adtende Israhel et audi (Bar 3:9; Is 59:21)
    VR Effundam super vos aquam (Ez 36:25) 208 A

VR Adtende popule meus
    RS Audi popule meus vocem

A30	Silos	*BN10110*	Other Sources	Liturgical Assignment
	BM51 176^v X		*Sant* 218 X	nocturnos sabb
			Sal 157 X	"
			170 X	nocturnos in Lazaro
				nocturnos et mat ora diei Dom
				let can mat
	BM51 173^v B		*Sant* 216^v B	nocturnos fer II
			Sal 175 B	"
			167^v B	nocturnos in Dom II XLmae
		62^v I		XLma 4 V mat
		26^v H		XLma 2 IV tert
			T35.4 73^v L	Pentecost mat

RS Audite audite me populele meus	
RS Ponite verba Domini in cordibus	
VR Adtendite ad me populele	
RS Sapientiam suam Deus revelabit	
RS Convertimini ad me omnis congregatio	
Adversum me exercebantur (Ps 68:13,8)	
VR Eripe me Domine de manu peccatoris (Ps 70:4)	150^{v} A
VR Adversum me exercebantur	
RS Deus Israhel propter te sustinui	
[A]Edificabit Dominus in celo ascensum (Am 9:6)	
VR Qui operit celum nubibus (Ps 146:8)	200 A
Alienigena non transibit (Ioel 3:17-18)	
VR Montes exultabunt ante faciem (Ps 97:8)	46 A
Alleluia absterget Deus (Apoc 21:4)	
VR Et videbunt faciem eius (Apoc 22:4)	180 sn
II Et non egebunt lumine (Apoc 22:5)	180 A
Alleluia deduc me per semitam (Ps 118:35)	
VR Legem pone mihi Domine (Ps 118:33)	295 B
Alleluia egredietur dominator (Mich 5:2,5,4,18,19)	
VR Ecce Deus noster ultionem adducit (Is 35:4)	42 A
Alleluia emittit Dominus ex Syon (Ps 109:2)	
VR Egredietur virga de radice (Is 11:1)	54^{v} A
Alleluia erit tamquam (Ps 1:3)	
VR Ad odorem aque germinabit (Iob 14:9)	197 A
VR Quod ad humorem (Ier 17:8)	
Alleluia in labiis iusti (Eccli 21:19-20)	
VR De ore iusti procedunt mella (Cant 4:11)	234^{v} B
Alleluia in omni loco oculi Dei (Prov 15:3-4)	

A30	Silos	*BN10110*	Other Sources	Liturgical Assignment
				XLma 5 VI sext
			T35.4 59 M	Ascension mat
				Dom III Adv mat
				Res Dni 1 mat
			T35.4 6 L	"
	BM51 170 B		*Sant* 216 B	nocturnos Dom
			Sal 165 B	"
41^{v} A			*T33.3* 30^{v} sn	Dom II Adv mat
81^{v} A				Dom IV Adv mat
				S Crucis mat
			T35.4 51^{v} L	"
	BM45 110^{v} B			S Cipriani Aep mat

	AL
VR De ore prudenti procedunt mella (Cant 4:11)	293 B
Alleluia iudicia iudicium (Ps 118:154)	
VR Vide humilitatem (Ps 24:18)	
Alleluia laudabo te Domine semper (?)	
VR Exaltabo te Domine rex meus (Ps 144:1)	290v B
VR Disrupisti vincula mea (Ps 115:17)	
Alleluia misericordia mea alleluia (Ps 143:2)	
VR Diligam te Domine virtus mea (Ps 17:2)	295 B
Alleluia nunc agnovi quia voluisti me (Ps 40:12-13)	
VR Dedisti mici protectionem (Ps 17:36)	234v sn
Alleluia spiritum meum dedi (Is 59:20-21)	
VR Ego rogabo Patrem et dabit (Io 14:16)	208v A
Alleluia vide humilitatem meam (Ps 24:18)	
VR Viam iniquitatis amobe a me (Ps 118:29)	295 B
Amara facta est vita nostra (?)	
VR Inter vestibolum et altare (Ioel 2:17)	256 D
Amen amen dico vobis quia qui verbum (Io 5:24)	
VR Ego sum resurrectio (Io 11:25)	
VR Si quis sermonem meum (Io 8:52)	
II Amen dico vobis quia venit hora (Io 5:25)	
Amen amen dico vobis quodcumque (Io 14:12-14)	
VR Dabo vobis cor nobum (Ez 36:26)	206v A
VR Amen dico vobis quia venit hora	
RS Amen amen dico vobis quia qui verbum	
VR Amici mei adversum me	
RS Multiplicati sunt super capillos	

A30	Silos	*BN10110*	Other Sources	Liturgical Assignment
				unoq Dom mat
	BM51 170^{v} B			nocturnos Dom
				unoq Dom mat
	6 118bis B			Dom VII quot mat
			T35.4 117^{v} L	"
	BM51 170 B		*Sal* 166 B	nocturnos Dom
				S Cipriani Aep mat
			T35.4 74 L	Pentecost mat
	BM51 170 B		*Sant* 216 B	nocturnos Dom
			Sal 165^{v} B	"
				let de clade
	7 18^{v} B			defunctis mat
	BM51 197^{v} B			defunct sacerd mat
	BM51 197^{v} B			"
				let apost sabb mat

AL

Angelus Domini dixit mulieribus (Mt 28:5-7)
  VR Ego dormibi et quiebi (Ps 3:6) — 184v A

VR Angelus Domini dixit mulieribus
  RS Nolite timere vos scio quia
Angelus Domini loquutus est (Lc 2:10-12)
  VR Pastores erant in regione eadem (Lc 2:8) — 69v B

Angelus Domini venit ad Mariam (Lc 1:26,35)
  VR Abe Maria gratia plena (Lc 1:28) — 58 B
Anima mea cessa iam peccare (?)
  VR Quare tristis es anima mea (Ps 41:6)

Anima mea desiderat te Deus (Is 26:9)
  VR Sicut cerbus desiderat ad fontes (Ps 41:2)
Animam meam dilectam tradidi (Ier 12:7-9,11)
  VR Posuerunt me in lacu (Ps 87:7)
Animam meam dilectam tradidi (Ier 12:7-9,11)
  VR Quum mici molesti essent (Ps 34:13) — 146 B
VR Annuit oculo digito loquitur
  RS Sagitta vulnerans lingua inimici
Aperi Domine oculos tuos (Dan 9:18)
  VR Domine Deus virtutum convertere (Ps 79:15)
VR Aperi manuum tuam
  RS Tu Domine virtutum cum tranquillitate
VR Aperiat tibi
  RS Requiem eternam
VR Aperientur porte tue iugiter
  RS Iherusalem erit tibi Dominus lux
  RS Surge inluminare Iherusalem
VR Aperuerunt contra me inimici
  RS Tradiderunt me in manus impiorum
VR Aperuerunt in me ora sua
  RS Ecce nunc cithara

A30	Silos	*BN10110*	Other Sources	Liturgical Assignment
			T35.4 12 L	Res Dni 12 mat
118 B			*T35.7* 58^{v} X	Nat Dni mat
89^{v} B				S Mariae mat
			Sant 213 A	med noct
			212^{v} F	med noct
		97 K		XLma 6 II tert
				XLma 5 III tert
		1^{v} H		XLma 1 II mat

	AL
Apparebit claritas Domini (Is 19:20)	
VR Ecce Deus noster ultionem adducit (Is 35:4)	56 B
VR Apparebit tibi Dominus	
RS Gaude filia Syon quoniam veniet	
VR Apparuerunt illis dispertite	
RS Spiritus Sanctus de caelo descendit	
VR Apparuit Dominus Ihesus	
RS Una sabbatorum cum sero	
Aput te laus mea est Alleluia (Ps 21:26)	
VR Quid retribuam Domino (Ps 115:12)	
Aspice Domine quia factus sum (Thr 1:11,13-14,16,20)	
VR Infirmatus est in paupertate (Ps 30:11-12)	166 B
II Foderunt manus meas (Ps 21:17)	166 B
VR Aspiciebam in nubibus celi	
RS Regem Dominum exercituum	
Aspiciebam in visu noctis (Dan 7:13-14)	
VR Ecce quasi filius hominis (Dan 7:13)	67v B
Audi dilecta mea propera (Cant 2:10,12)	
VR Gaude filia Syon letare (Soph 3:14)	51 A
VR Audi me Iacob et Israhel	
RS Ego sum Dominus Deus vester	
Audi popule meus vocem Dei (Deut 28:2,11)	
VR Declina a malo et fac bonum (Ps 36:27)	289 B
VR Audi popule meus vocem meam	

---

* VR missing.

A30	Silos	*BN10110*	Other Sources	Liturgical Assignment
85^{v}*			*T33.3* 30^{v} sn	post Dom IV Adv mat
			T35.4 140^{v} L	Dom XIII quot mat
				XLma 6 VI mat
				"
				Adv ad tert
69 A				S Eolalie mat
				unoq Dom mat
	BM51 201 B			Dom I quot mat
	6 45^{v} B		*T35.4* 84 L	"

	AL
RS Pepercit Dominus populo suo	
Audite audite me popule meus (Is 51:4-5)	
VR Adtende popule meus (Ps 77:1)	52 B
VR Audite me divini fructus	
RS Clamor factus est	
Audite me rectores (Eccli 33:19; Is 44:8; Lev 26:5)	
VR Convertimini et agite (Ez 18:30)	
Audite me rectores (Eccli 33:19; Is 44:8; Lev 26:5)	
VR Si volueritis et audieritis (Is 1:19)	112^{v} B
VR Audite obsecro omnes	
RS Domine qui consoletur	
Auxiliabo puero meo (Is 42:1)	
VR Ecce intelleget puer meus (Is 52:13)	34^{v} B
VR Auxiliabo puero meo	
RS Qui diligit me diligitur	
VR Auxiliator meus es tu	
RS Iste homo supplicabat	
Auxilium meum a Domino (Ps 120:2)	
VR Levabi oculos meos ad montes (Ps 120:1)	295 B
VR Adiutorium nostrum	
VR Ave Maria gratia plena	
RS Angelus Domini venit ad Mariam	
Averte Domine iram tuam (Ps 84:5-6)	
VR Mitiga Domine omnem iram (Ps 84:4)	
Beati misericordes quia ipsis (Mt 5:7-8)	
VR Beati qui esuriunt (Mt 5:6)	179 A
VR Beati mundo corde	
RS Isti sunt qui non polluerunt	
Beati oculi qui vident (Mt 13:16-17; Lc 10:20; 22:28)	

A30	Silos	*BN10110*	Other Sources	Liturgical Assignment
				post Dom III Adv mat
		21 K		XLma 2 II mat
				XLma 1 IV tert
24 B				S Clementi Aep mat
				nocturnos et mat ora diei Dom
	BM51 171 B			nocturnos Dom
			T33.3 30^{v} sn	nonam Dom
		7^{v} H		XLma 1 III sext
				[S Engrat et com] mat

	AL
VR Esuribi et dedistis (Mt 25:35)	218^{v} B
VR Beati omnes qui timent	
RS Qui diligunt te Domine sicut sol	
VR Beati qui esuriunt	
RS Beati misericordes quia ipsis	
VR Beati qui habitant in domo	
RS Super muros tuos Iherusalem	
VR Beati qui persequutionem	
RS Beati servi illi	
RS Beati sunt sancti qui laberunt	
RS Iulianus invenit gratiam coram Domino	
RS Sanctis ab altissimo dicebitur	
RS Venite benedicti patris mei	
RS Via veritas et vita	
Beati qui sperant in Domino (?)	
VR Multe tribulationes iustorum (Ps 33:20)	219^{v} B
Beati servi illi (Lc 12:37)	
VR Beati qui persequutionem (Mt 5:10)	29^{v} A
Beati sunt sancti qui laberunt (Apoc 22:14)	
VR Beati qui persequutionem (Mt 5:10)	247^{v} B
VR Beatus vir qui timet	
RS Iustus iustificetur et sanctus	
Benedicam Domino in omni tempore (Ps 33:2)	
VR In Domino laudabitur (Ps 33:3)	
VR Benedicti erunt qui hedificaverunt te	

* VR missing.

A30	Silos	*BN10110*	Other Sources	Liturgical Assignment
				SS Simon et Iud apost mat
				[S Christophori et com] mat
3*				S Aciscli mat
				SS general mat
	BM51 175 B		*Sant* 217 A	nocturnos fer IV
			Sal 153 A	"
			168^{v} A	nocturnos Dom de med
			Calz 2 B	

	AL
RS Iherusalem felices qui hedificant te	
RS Letare Iherusalem in filiis iustorum	
Benedictio Domini super vos (Ps 128:8)	
VR Adiciet Dominus super vos (Ps 113:22-23)	274v B
Benedictus Dominus in eternum (Ps 88:53)	
VR Sit nomen Domini benedictum (Ps 112:2)	294 B
VR Benedictus Dominus qui magnus	
RS Si ambulaverimus in viis	
Benefaciat nobis Deus (?)	
VR Inluminet vultum suum (Ps 66:2)	
Benigne fac Domini (Ps 50:20)	
VR Ut edificentur muri (Ps 50:20)	
Bethlem civitas Dei summi (Mich 5:2,5)	
VR Gaudebunt campi (Ps 95:12)	58v A
Bonum est sperare in Domino (Ps 117:9)	
VR Venite fili audite me (Ps 33:12)	291 sn
VR Brebes dies hominum	
RS Quare data est misero lux	
Caligavit ab indignatione (Iob 17:7; 16:9-10,14,19-20)	
VR Ego ad Deum aspiciam (Mich 7:7)	139 A
VR Cantabo Domino	
RS Circuibo et inmolabo	
RS Oculi mei semper ad Dominum	
Christus Ihesus qui cum in forma Dei (Phi 2:6-8,10)	
VR Christus surgens a mortuis (Rom 6:9)	183 B

A30	Silos	*BN10110*	Other Sources	Liturgical Assignment
				nubentum mat
				unoq Dom mat
	BM51 170^{v} B		*Sant* 216^{v} B	nocturnos Dom
			T35.4 144^{v} L	Dom XIV quot mat
		7 J		XLma 1 III tert
	BM51 175^{v} B		*Sant* 217^{v} B	nocturnos fer V
			Sal 154^{v} B	"
			168 B	nocturnos Dom II XLmae
92^{v} A				S Mariae mat
				unoq Dom mat
				XLma 4 V tert
			T35.4 9^{v} M	Res Dni 7 mat

AL

VR Christus surgens a mortuis
RS Christus Ihesus qui cum in forma Dei
Circuibo et inmolabo (Ps 26:6)
VR Cantabo Domino (Ps 103:33) 103^{v} B
VR Circumdederunt me aque
RS Infixus sum in limo profundi
VR Circumdederunt me canes multi
RS Omnes qui videbant me
Circumdederunt me inimici (Ps 117:12-13)
VR Quasi rupto muro (Iob 30:14)
VR Circumdederunt me inimici
RS O vos omnes qui pertransitis
VR Circumdederunt me sicut apes
RS Susceperunt me sicut leo
RS Tradiderunt me in manus impiorum
Circumdederunt nos mala (Ps 39:13)
VR Pecata nostra redundaberunt (Eccli 47:29; Apoc 18:5)
Circuminspicit Deus montes (Iob 39:8,12)
VR Qui operit caelum nubibus (Ps 146:8) 291^{v} B
VR Laudate Dominum omnes gentes (Ps 116:1)

VR Clamaberunt iusti et Dominus
RS Fulgebunt iusti et tamquam
RS Iustorum anime in manu Dei
RS Propter honorem nominis
VR Clamavi ad te
RS Per diem clamavi et nocte
Clamemus ad Dominum ex toto corde (I The 5:2-3)
VR Ecce dies Domini venit crudelis (Is 13:9) 255^{v} sn
Clamo ad te Domine (Iob 30:20-21,31)
VR Domine in volumtate tua (Ps 29:8) 129^{v} B
Clamor factus est (Mt 25:6)
VR Audite me divini fructus (Eccli 39:17) 221 G

A30	Silos	*BN10110*	Other Sources	Liturgical Assignment
				Cat S Petri mat
		91 J		XLma 5 VI sext
		27 H		XLma 2 IV sext
				unoq Dom mat
			T35.4 165 L	Dom XX quot mat
				let de clade
				XLma 3 VI mat
				SS Iustae et Rufinae mat

	AL
VR Oleum recondite in vasis (Mt)	
II Gloria et honor Patri	
Clamor noster ad te (?)	
VR Inter vestibulum et altare (Ioel 2:17)	
Clamor noster ad te (?)	
VR Peccabimus cum patribus (Ps 105:6)	129 E
Clarificatum est nomen Domini (II The 1:4-5)	
VR Deduxit eos Dominus (Ps 106:7)	249v A
Cogitaverunt adversum me (Ps 139:9)	
VR Intende in adiutorium (Ps 69:2)	
Cogitaberunt iniqui dicentes (Ier 48:2)	
VR Dixerunt venite mittamus lignum (Ier 11:19)	
VR Cogitaberunt verbum in conprehensione	
RS Conclusit vias meas inimicus	
Cognosce plebs mea (Is 52:6-7)	
VR De quo loquuti sunt prophete (Eccli 36:17)	80v A
VR Cognoscimus Domine peccata nostra	
RS Ecce quomodo defecit sacrificium	
Cognovi omnia peccata vestra (Am 5:12-13,15)	
VR Odio abuistis in porta (Am 5:10)	256 B
Columba mea quam pulchra es (Cant 4:1; 7:1)	
VR Speciem et pulcritudinem tuam intende (Ps 44:5)	78 A
Concede Domine in animas nostras (?)	
VR Deus in nomine tuo salvos nos fac (Ps 53:3)	275v B
VR Conclusit inimicus viam meam	

A30	Silos	*BN10110*	Other Sources	Liturgical Assignment
193 G				SS Iustae et Rufinae mat
	BM51 166^{v} G			med noct de virginibus
			Sal 150^{v} sn	med noct
			150^{v} G	"
		14 I		XLma 1 V sext
				XLma 3 V sext
	BM45 152^{v} E			let can mat
				SS general
			SJP 4 A	S Tirsi mat
		61^{v} H		XLma 4 IV sext
		59 I		XLma 4 IV mat
153 A				Circumcis Dni mat
				let de clade
	BM45 157^{v} B			let can tert
				S Columbae mat
				infirmis mat

	AL
RS Domine qui consoletur	
Conclusit inimicus vias meas (Thr 3:9)	
VR Replevit me amaritudinibus (Thr 3:15)	138 B
Conclusit vias meas inimicus (Thr 3:9-12,15,52-53, 59)	
VR Cogitaberunt verbum in conprehensione (?)	155^{v} B
Conclusit vias meas inimicus (Thr 3:9-12,15,52-53, 59)	
VR Sessionem eorum (Thr 3:63-64)	
VR Confitebimur tibi Deus	
RS Exaltare Domine in virtute tua alleluia	
Confitebor Domino qui salvos (Ps 7:18,11)	
VR Et psallam nomini Domini altissimi (Ps 7:18)	
Confitebor tibi Domine Deus meus (Ps 85:12)	
VR Exaltabo te Domine rex meus (Ps 144:1)	48 B 245 sn
Confortare in adventum Domini Dei tui (?)	
VR Ecce Deus noster ipse veniet (Is 35:4)	43 B
II In omnibus semper gaudete (I The 5:16-18)	43 B
VR Confusio et opprobrium	
RS Miserere et parce nobis Domine	
Congrega Domine dispersionem nostram (II Mach 1:27)	
VR Qui das salutem regibus (Ps 143:10)	295 D
Congregati sunt adversus (Ier 26:8, 14-15)	
VR Omnes in sanguine (Mich 7:2; I Mach 1:31)	

A30	Silos	*BN10110*	Other Sources	Liturgical Assignment
				XLma 4 IV sext
				XLma 6 II tert
		101^{v} I		XLma 6 III tert
	BM51 174 B		*Sant* 217 C	nocturnos fer III
			Sal 152 C	"
			168^{v} C	nocturnos Dom de med
61 B				S Leocadie mat
	5 68^{v} B		*BN13060* 145 B	S Martini vigil
	6 19 B			uno confessore mat
	BM45 146 B			S Emiliani mat
49 B				post Dom II Adv mat
				"
	BM51 170 D		*Sant* 216 D	nocturnos Dom
			Sal 166 D	"
		95 H		XLma 6 II mat

	AL
Congregati sunt adversus (Ier 26:8, 14-15)	
VR Qui custodiebant animam meam (Ps 70:10)	145 A
VR Congregati sunt adversus	
RS Facta est lingua iniquorum	
Co[n]locaberunt me quasi signum (Thr 3:12,15,16,17)	
VR Venatione ceperunt (Thr 3:52-53)	
VR Conlocabit me in obscuris	
RS Ecce inimicus meus induxit me in loco	
Conlocabit Salomon altare in medio (III Reg 9:2)	
VR Factum est autem (III Reg 8:54)	261^{v} B
VR Conplevit inimicus furorem	
RS Ecce inimicus meus circumdedit	
VR Considerabam a dextris	
RS Ecce inimicus meus circumdedit me	
Consolabitur nos Dominus Deus noster (II Mach 7:6)	
VR Miserebitur nostri Dominus et absterget (Mich 7:19)	130 F
Consolare Domine contritos corde (?)	
VR Tu subveni oppressis (?)	255^{v} A
Consolare Domine omnes flentes (Is 61:3-4)	
VR Converte nos Deus ad te (Thr 5:21)	82^{v} B
VR Consummatus in brebi explevit	
RS Homo iste custodivit in omnibus	
Contumelias et proximi mei (Ier 20:10-12)	
VR Da filios eorum (Ier 18:21)	
Convertamur ad Dominum Deum (Is 55:7)	
VR Venite adoremus (Ps 94:6)	
Convertamur ad Dominum Deum (Is 55:7)	
VR Venite exultemus (Ps 94:1)	
VR Convertatur unusquisque	
RS Querite Dominum dum inveniri	
VR Convertatur vir a via sua	
RS Derelinquat impius vias suas	

A30	Silos	*BN10110*	Other Sources	Liturgical Assignment
				XLma 5 II tert
		100 H		XLma 6 III mat
				sacr bas mat
				XLma 3 VI sext
				let de clade
158^{v} B				init anni tert
		67 H		XLma 4 VI mat
		6 H		XLma 1 III mat
		3 J		XLma 1 II tert
		21^{v} sn		XLma 2 II tert

AL

Converte Domine Deus animas (Ps 114:7)
    VR Convertere Domine aliquantulum (Ps 89:13)

Converte Domine luctum nostrum (?)
    VR Memento nostri Domine in beneplacito (Ps 105:4) 131 D
Converte nos Deus ad te (Thr 5:21)
    VR Converte nos Deus salutaris noster (Ps 84:5) 204 G

Converte nos Deus ad te (Thr 5:21)
    VR Ut quid in contemtione (Thr 5:20)
VR Converte nos Deus ad te
    RS Consolare Domine omnes flentes
VR Converte nos Deus salutaris noster
    RS Converte nos Deus ad te
    RS Nunquid in eternum repellet
VR Convertere Domine aliquantulum
    RS Converte Domine Deus animas
    RS Ecce iam Domine nobissimum tempus
    RS Miserere Domine contritis corde
    RS Peccavimus iniquitates fecimus
Convertere Domine Deus animas (Ps 114:7; Io 5:24)
    VR Secundum multitudinem misericordie (Dan 3:42)
Convertimini ad me dicit Dominus (?)
    VR Convertimini ad me et salvi (?) 111v G
Convertimini ad me dicit Dominus (?)
    VR Despexistis omne consilium meum (Prov 1:25)
Convertimini ad me domus Iacob (Is 1:18)
    VR Custodite vos a murmuratione (Sap 1:11) 115v A
VR Convertimini ad me et salvi
    RS Convertimini ad me dicit Dominus
Convertimini ad me omnis congregatio (Ier 3:12)

A30	Silos	*BN10110*	Other Sources	Liturgical Assignment
	BM51 197 B			defunct sacerd mat
				XLma 3 sabb tert
				let apost sext
	4 66 G		*A56* 11^v G	conversorum
			A60 49^v G	let apost
		13 I		XLma 1 V tert
	4 342 B			?
				XLma 1 III sext
		23 I		XLma 2 III mat
				XLma 1 sabb tert

AL

VR Adtendite ad me populus (Is 51:4)
Convertimini ad me omnis congregatio (Is 1:16-18)
VR Iudicate pupillo et egeno (Ps 81:3) 114^{v} B
VR Convertimini et agite
RS Audite me rectores
VR Convertimini et recedite
RS Exclamemus omnes ad Dominum
VR Cor meum conturbatum
RS Sicut onus grave
Cor mundum crea in me Deus (Ps 50:12)
VR Spiritum rectum innoba (Ps 50:12)

Corona sanctorum timor Dei (Eccli 25:8; 26:16,24)
VR Sit nomen Domini benedictum (Ps 112:2) 211 B
Coronavit sanctos suos (Eccli 45:9; Apoc 6:11)
VR Mansueti autem (Ps 36:11)

Curbati sunt celi dum calcaret (?)
VR Quis est iste rex glorie (Ps 23:10) 199^{v} B

VR Custodi me Domine de manu peccatoris
RS Subito vulneravit me
VR Custodi me Domine ut pupillam
RS Susceperunt me sicut leo
RS Mirifica Domine misericordias tuas
RS Vigila Domine super oves
VR Custodite leges meas
RS Timete me dicit Dominus
Custodite vos a murmuratione (Sap 1:11)
VR Non mentiemini invicem (Lev 19:11)
VR Custodite vos a murmuratione

A30	Silos	*BN10110*	Other Sources	Liturgical Assignment
		16 H		XLma 1 VI mat
				XLma 1 VI tert
	BM51 175^{v} X		*Sant* 217^{v} X	nocturnos fer V
			Sal 154 X	"
			167 X	nocturnos Dom de XLme
	BM45 9^{v} B			S Adriani mat
	BM45 136^{v} sn			SS Vinc et Cris mat
			T35.4 58 L	Ascension mat
		12 J		XLma 1 V mat

AL

RS Convertimini ad me domus Iacob
RS Unusquisque se ad proximo
VR Da filios eorum
RS Contumelias et proximi mei
VR Dabit vobis Dominus signum
RS Filia Syon consecrabis Domino
Dabo duobus famulis meis (Apoc 11:3-4)
VR Et dabo opus eorum (Is 61:8) 216v B

VR Dabo legem meam
RS Oves mee et oves gregis mei
Dabo sanctis meis primam (IV Esd 2:23,35)
VR Fulgebunt iusti sicut splendor (Dan 12:3) 239 B

Dabo vobis cor nobum (Ez 36:26,28-29)
VR Et faciam ut in preceptis (Ez 36:27) 207 A

VR Dabo vobis cor nobum
RS Amen amen dico vobis quodquumque
RS Haec dicit dominus nolite timere
VR Date Domino Deo vestro
RS Haec dicit Dominus si obtuleritis
VR Date nomini eius
RS Acceperunt prudentes oleum
De die in die benedictus Dominus (Ps 67:36)
VR Deus Israhel ipse dabit virtutem (Ps 67:36)

VR De fructu oris sui replebitur
RS Frater qui adiubatur a fratre
De manu inferni Deus libera (Ps 48:16)
VR Propter nomen tuum Domine (Ps 24:11) 146 G

A30	Silos	*BN10110*	Other Sources	Liturgical Assignment
	BM45 30v B			SS Petri et Pauli mat
				SS Cosme et Damiani mat
			T35.4 69 M	let apost sabb tert
	BM51 176 E		*Sant* 217v E	nocturnos fer VI
			Sal 155v E	"
			168 E	nocturnos Dom II de XLme
				XLma 5 III mat

De ore iusti procedet (Cant 4:11)
    VR Os iusti meditabitur (Ps 36:30) 75v B

223v B

De ore iusti procedet (Cant 4:11)
    VR Os iusti meditabitur (Ps 36:30) 251 B

    VR Dulcedo mellis est (Cant 4:11 ?)

VR De ore iusti procedunt mella
    RS Alleluia in labiis iusti
RS De ore prudenti procedunt mella
    RS Alleluia in omni loco oculi Dei
VR De profundis clamavi ad te
    RS Domine Deus ad te lebavi oculos meos
VR De quo loquuti sunt prophete
    RS Cognosce plebs mea
VR De sanctuario tuo Domine
    RS Exurge Domine miserere nobis
VR Declaracio sermonum
    RS Gressus eorum dirige Deus
VR Declina a malo et fac bonum
    RS Audi populе meus vocem Dei
VR Dedi te plebi
    RS Ex quo honorabi te
VR Dedisti mici protectionem
    RS Alleluia nunc agnovi quia voluisti me
VR Dedit Dominus capitibus
    RS Principium sapientie Dei possiderunt

A30	Silos	*BN10110*	Other Sources	Liturgical Assignment
	4 93^{v} G		*A56* 30^{v} G	consecr nov sep
	3 22 G			conm corp defunct
				S Iac frat Dni mat
				S Cucufati mat
	BM51 184^{v} B			uno iusto
	3 119c B			" mat
	BM45 53^{v} B			S Cucufati mat
			T33.3 13 N	unius iusti ad III, Dominicale

AL

VR Dedit ei Dominus sapientiam
    RS Sapientia replebit os eius
VR Dedit esurienti panem
    RS Manum suam aperuit
VR Deduc eos Domine
    RS In loco viride Domine
VR Deduc quasi torrentem
    RS Quis te consolabitur virgo
VR Deducant oculi mei lacrimas
    RS Ecce ego plorans
VR Deducant oculi mei lacrimas
    RS Vide Domine quoniam tribulor
VR Deduxit eos Dominus
    RS Clarificatum est nomen Domini
VR Defecerunt oculi mei in eloquium
    RS Vox filie Syon clamantis
Defecerunt oculi nostri (Thr 2:11)
    VR Defecit gaudium cordis (Thr 5:15-16) 258 sn
VR Defecerunt pre lacrimis
    RS Nunc venit in me dolor
VR Defecimus in ira
    RS Deprecemur Dominum dicentes
VR Defecit gaudium cordis
    RS Defecerunt oculi nostri
    RS Exurge Domine et ne repellas
    RS Facti sumus Domine tamquam alienì
VR Delectatum est cor meum
    RS Quare persequimini me
Delicta iubentutis et ignorantie (Ps 24:7-8)
    VR Vide humilitatem (Ps 24:18) 294^{v} A

Deprecemur Dominum dicentes (?)

A30	Silos	*BN10110*	Other Sources	Liturgical Assignment
				let pro plubia
				nocturnos et mat ora diei Dom
			T35.4 149 L	Dom XV quot mat

AL

VR Defecimus in ira (Ps 89:7)
Deprecemur Dominum et placabilis (Iob 33:26)
VR Venite exultemus (Ps 94:1)
Derelinquat impius vias suas (Is 55:7)
VR Convertatur vir a via sua (?) 203v F

VR Descendit cum illis
RS Sancti iter fecerunt
VR Despexistis omne consilium meum
RS Convertimini ad me dicit Dominus
VR Det tibi Dominus de rore caeli
RS Deus aperiat tibi ostium
VR Deus a Libano veniet
RS Egredietur Dominus et preliabitur
Deus aperiat tibi ostium (Col 4:3,6)
VR Det tibi Dominus de rore caeli (Gen 27:28) 270v D

VR Deus autem noster
RS Exaltare Domine in virtute tua alleluia
Deus cuius ire nemo resistere (Iob 9:13,34; 10:2-3,8-9)
VR Numquid oculi carnei sunt (Iob 10:4) 121v B

VR Deus in adiutorium
RS Ad adiubandum me festina
VR Deus in gradibus eius
RS Iherusalem civitas sancta alleluia
VR Deus in nomine tuo salvos nos fac
RS Adiu_v_a Domine sperantes in te
RS Concede Domine in animas nostras
RS Domine Deus noster pacem tuam
RS Domine qui vides universa peccata nostra
RS Dona nobis Domine laetitiam cordis
RS In loco viride

A30	Silos	*BN10110*	Other Sources	Liturgical Assignment
		18 I		XLma 1 sabb mat
		17^v J		XLma 1 VI sext
			A60 29 F	let apost mat
				ordin episcopi mat
				XLma 2 VI mat
	4 75^v B		*A56* 19 B	reconcil penit

	AL
RS Libera nos Deus [I]Srahel	
RS Ne tradas in perditione	
RS Pande manum tuam super servos	
RS Placabilis esto Domine	
RS Sana nos Domine	
VR Deus in nomine tuo salvum me fac	
RS Domine qui das salutem	
RS Libera me Domine et pone me	
VR Deus Israhel ipse dabit virtutem	
RS De die in die benedictus Dominus	
Deus Israhel propter te sustinui (Ps 68:7-10)	
VR Adversum me exercebantur (Ps 68:13)	151v A
Deus Srahel propter te sustinui (Ps 68:7-10)	
VR In multitudine misericordie (Ps 68:14)	
VR Deus meus es tu	
RS Voluntarie sacrificabo tibi	
Deus meus ne elonges (Ps 21:12)	
VR Tu autem Domine ne elonge (Ps 21:20)	
Deus meus salva me de manu impii (?)	
VR Eripe me Domine ab homine (Ps 139:2)	
Deus misereatur nobis (Ps 66:2; 84:5)	
VR Inluminet Dominus vultum suum (Ps 66:2)	256 B
Deus misereatur nobis (Ps 66:2; 84:5)	
VR Inluminet vultum suum (Ps 66:2)	
Deus noster magnus est (Iob 36:26-28)	
VR Oculis nostris vidimus magnalia (?)	294 B
Deus omnipotens suscitabit nobis (Mt 1:21)	
VR Redemit enim Deus Iacob (Is 48:20)	67 B
VR Deus pacis sanctificet vos	
RS Dominus prope est nihil	
Deus pater parvulorum tuorum (Sap 9:1,4)	
VR Quoniam elevata est (Ps 8:2)	228v B

A30	Silos	*BN10110*	Other Sources	Liturgical Assignment
				XLma 5 sabb tert
		91^{v} H		XLma 5 sabb mat
		65 H		XLma 4 V sext
		72 H		XLma 4 sabb tert
				let de clade
		19^{v} J		XLma 1 sabb tert
				unoq Dom mat
				Adv ad tert
	BM45 70^{v} B			SS Iusti et Pastoris mat

	AL
Deus qui das locum penitentie (Sap 12:10-13)	
VR Tu es Deus et in te est Deus (Is 45:18)	130 D
VR Deus qui dives est	
RS Estote imitatores Dei	
VR Deus sapientia fundabit	
RS Sapientia Dei super lapides	
VR Deus virtutum converte nos	
RS Ecce Dominus egredietur	
VR Deus virtutum converte nunc	
RS Dominator Domine Deus adtende	
RS Propitiare Domine populo tuo	
Dextera tua Domine glorificata est (Ex 15:6-7)	
VR Misisti iram tuam (Ex 15:7-8)	183^{v} B
Dicite in nationibus alleluia (Ps 95:10)	
VR Etenim correxit orbem (Ps 95:10)	184 D
VR Dies ille dies ire	
RS Ve nobis qui diligimus	
Dies mei transierunt (Iob 17:11,14,3)	
VR Induta est caro mea putredini (Iob 7:5)	277^{v} B
VR Putredini dixi pater (Iob 17:14)	
VR Dies mei velocius transierunt	
RS Militia est Domine vita mea	
VR Dies quibus peregrinatus	
RS Ecce ego viam	
VR Dilexisti iustitiam et odisti	
RS Virgo Israhel speciosa facta es	
VR Dilexisti malitiam	

A30	Silos	*BN10110*	Other Sources	Liturgical Assignment
				XLma 3 VI tert
	4 68^{v} B		*A56* 13^{v} B	penitentie
			T35.4 10^{v} L	Res Dni 9 mat
			T35.4 11^{v} L	Res Dni 11 mat
			T33.3 11 sn	Res Dni ad tert
	BM51 199 B			uno defuncto mat
	3 16^{v} B			conm corp defunct
	4 87^{v} B		*A56* 26 sn	fin hominis die

AL

RS Quid gloriaris in malitia
VR Diligam te Domine virtus mea
RS Alleluia misericordia mea alleluia
Dimitte me Domine ut plangam (Iob 10:20,21)
VR Vide humilitatem meam (Ps 24:18) 127v A
Disciplina et sapientia replebit (Eccli 17:5-6)
VR Spiritus Sanctus de caelo descendit (Act 2:2) 208 B

VR Disperde inimicos meos
RS Factus sum omni populo meo
VR Dispersit dedit pauperibus
RS Felix vir qui inventus est
RS Hic vir etate gloria mirabilis
RS Iste homo in professione sua
RS Iunior fui et senui
RS Manum suam aperuit
VR Disrupisti vincula mea
RS Alleluia laudabo te Domine semper
VR Dissipaberunt itinera mea
RS Multi Domine gemitus
VR Dixerunt venite mittamus lignum
RS Cogitaberunt iniqui dicentes
VR Dixerunt venite percutiamus
RS Viri impii dixerunt opprimamus
Dixit Ihesus discipulis suis absque (Io 16:2,33)
VR Haec loquutus sum vobis (Io 16:33) 217v G

VR Dixit Ihesus discipulis suis hec sunt
RS Recordamini qualiter
VR Dixit Ihesus Marie mulier
RS Stabat Maria ad monumentum
Doctrina Domini aperuit (Is 50:5-7)
VR Multiplicati sunt super capillos (Ps 68:5) 161v B
Dominator Domine Deus adtende (Ex 34:6; Dan 9:18)

A30	Silos	*BN10110*	Other Sources	Liturgical Assignment
				XLma 3 IV mat
			T35.4 73 L	Pentecost
				SS Petri et Pauli mat
				Cena Dni mat

	AL
VR Deus virtutum converte nunc (Ps 79:15)	119^{v} B
Domine Deus ad te lebavi oculos meos (Ps 122:1)	
VR De profundis clamavi ad te (Ps 129:1-2)	
Domine Deus noster pacem tuam (?)	
VR Deus in nomine tuo salvos nos fac (Ps 53:3)	293 B
Domine Deus virtutum beatus (Ps 83:13)	
VR Quam amabilia sunt tabernacula tua (Ps 83:2)	
VR Domine Deus virtutum convertere	
RS Aperi Domine oculos tuos	
VR Domine exaudi orationem	
RS Domine miserere nobis te enim	
Domine in caelo misericordia (Ps 35:6-7)	
VR Domine nomen tuum in eternum (Ps 134:13)	201^{v} B
VR Domine in volumtate tua	
RS Clamo ad te Domine	
Domine indulge peccatis (I Reg 26:24)	
VR Patres nostri peccaberunt (Thr 5:7)	
Domine iudica nocentes (Ps 34:1-2)	
VR Exurge Domine et intende (Ps 34:23)	
Domine loquere pro me (?)	
VR Inimici mei dixerunt mala mici (Ps 40:6)	147^{v} A
Domine miserere nobis te enim (Is 33:2)	
VR Domine exaudi orationem (Ps 101:2)	
VR Domine miserere nostri te enim	

A30	Silos	*BN10110*	Other Sources	Liturgical Assignment
				XLma 2 III sext
			Sant 213 X	med noct
				unoq Dom mat
			T35.4 160 sn	Dom XVIII quot mat
	BM51 176v C		*Sant* 218 C	nocturnos sabb
			Sal 157 C	"
			167 C	nocturnos Dom de XLme
				post Ascension fer VI mat
		37v H		XLma 3 III mat
		76 H		XLma 5 II sext
				XLma 5 IV sext
			T33.3 22 M	de XL
		24 J		XLma 2 III tert

	AL
RS Parce Domine nostris peccatis	
Domine ne in ira tua (Ps 6:2)	
VR Vide humilitatem (Ps 24:18)	276^{v} A
Domine ne intendas in delicta (IV Esd 8:26)	
VR Sit auris tua intendens (IV Esd 8:24)	128 A
VR Domine nomen tuum in eternum	
RS Domine in caelo misericordia	
VR Domine non sum dignus	
RS Salvus ero Domine	
RS Si vis Domine potes me salvare	
Domine numquid sicut dies (Iob 10:5-6)	
VR Numquid oculi carnei sunt (Iob 10:4)	125^{v} A
Domine probasti cor meum (?)	
VR Nam et si ambulem (Ps 22:4)	231^{v} B
VR Quomodo dilexi legem tuam (Ps 118:97)	252 B
VR Domine probasti me	
RS Domine tu cognobisti omnia novissima	
Domine quantus ego sum (Iob 9:14-15)	
VR Loquar et non timebo (Iob 9:35)	122^{v} B
Domine qui consoletur (Thr 1:9)	
VR Audite obsecro omnes (Thr 1:18,5)	
Domine qui consoletur (Thr 1:9)	
VR Conclusit inimicus viam meam (Thr 3:9)	141 A
Domine qui das salutem (Ps 143:10-11)	
VR Deus in nomine tuo salvum me fac (Ps 53:3)	98 B
Domine qui habitas (IV Esd 8:20-22)	
VR Excelsus super omnes gentes (Ps 112:4)	237^{v} B
VR Tronus tuus (IV Esd 8:21)	
Domine qui vides universa peccata nostra (?)	

A30	Silos	*BN10110*	Other Sources	Liturgical Assignment
	BM51 191^{v} A			uno infirmo mat
				XLma 3 IV sext
				XLma 3 II mat
				sacr S Martini mat
			BN13060 197 B	?
				unius virg confess mat
				XLma 2 VI mat
		79 I		XLma 5 III tert
				XLma 4 VI sext
206^{v} B			*SJP* 2	S Vincenti laev mat
	5 84^{v} sn			S Micaheli mat
	BM45 121^{v} A			"

	AL
VR Deus in nomine tuo salvos nos fac (Ps 53:3)	122^{v} A
Domine tu cognobisti omnia novissima (Ps 138:5-6)	
VR Domine probasti me (Ps 138:2)	272^{v} B
Dominus ab utero formabit me (Is 49:5-6)	
VR Dominum creabit me in principio (Prov 8:22)	214 A
VR Dominus confregit dentes	
RS Invocabi altissimum potentem	
VR Dominus creabit me in principio	
RS Dominus ab utero formabit me	
Dominus de Syna veniet alleluia (Deut 33:2-3)	
VR Dominus sicut fortis (Is 42:13)	35 A
Dominus de Syna veniet descendet (Deut 33:2-3)	
VR Et erit iustitia cingulum (Is 11:5,4)	
VR Exultabit ut gigans (Ps 18:6-7)	44 B
VR Dominus Deus aperuit	
RS Omnes adversarii mei persecuti	
VR Dominus Ihesus Xristus loquutus est	
RS Vigilate et orate dicit Dominus	
VR Dominus Ihesus Christus qui est	
RS Ihesum nazarenum quem unxit Deus	
VR Dominus mortificat	
•RS Tuus Domine sermo qui sanat	
Dominus omnipotens audibit vocem (?)	
VR Publicanus a longe (Lc 18:13)	
Dominus prope est nihil (Phi 4:5-7)	
VR Deus pacis sanctificet vos (I Thess 5:23)	63^{v} A
VR Dominus regnabit a ligno	
RS Obserbabitis diem istum legitimum	
VR Dominus regnabit decorem	
RS Sedet rex in trono	

A30	Silos	*BN10110*	Other Sources	Liturgical Assignment
				XLma 2 VI sext
	BM45 156^{v} A			let can sext
			T33.3 21^{v} M	de XL
				ord nat regis mat
	BM45 18^{v} A			nat S Iohannis mat
28 A				Dom I Adv
51^{v} B				post Dom II Adv mat
				"
	6 106^{v} B			Dom VI quot mat
104 A				Dom V Adv mat

	AL
VR Dominus sicut fortis	
RS Dominus de Syna veniet alleluia	
Domus tua Domine in captivitate (Hab 2:3)	
VR Humiliata est in pulvere (Ps 43:25)	53 B
Dona nobis Domine laetitiam cordis (Eccli 50:25)	
VR Deus in nomine tuo salvos nos fac (Ps 53:3)	295 A
VR Dulcedo mellis est	
RS De ore iusti procedet	
VR Dum lapidaretur Stephanus	
RS Stephanus vidit celos	
VR Ecce agnus Dei	
RS Iste qui natus est	
RS Me oportet minui illum autem	
VR Ecce constituit te Dominus	
RS Gratias agimus Deo qui elegit te	
VR Ecce Deus noster ipse est	
RS Ecce natus est nobis filius	
VR Ecce Deus noster ipse veniet	
RS Confortare in adventum Domini Dei tui	
VR Ecce Deus noster ultionem adducit	
RS Alleluia egredietur dominator	
RS Apparebit claritas Domini	
Ecce dies Domini magne (?)	
VR Quiescite agere (Is 1:17)	110 B
Ecce dies Domini veniet et quiescere (Is 13:11-12, 14; 14:1)	
VR Parate viam Domino rectus (Is 40:3)	66^{v} B
Ecce dies Domini veniet et suscitabit (Ier 33:14-15)	
VR Emittit Dominus ex [S]yon (Ps 109:2)	45 B

A30	Silos	*BN10110*	Other Sources	Liturgical Assignment
78^{v} B				post Dom III Adv mat
				nocturnos et mat ora diei Dom
			T35.4 162 sn	Dom XIX quot mat
			T33.3 21^{v} sn	de Adv, Dominicale
				XLma 1 II tert
				Adv ad tert
54^{v} B				post Dom II Adv mat

	AL
VR Ecce dies Domini venit crudelis	
RS Clamemus ad Dominum ex toto corde	
Ecce dilectus meus venit dicens mihi (Cant 2:10,12,14)	
VR Egredere quasi aurora (Cant 6:9)	254 B
Ecce Domine in toto corde suo (?)	
Ecce Dominus de Syon veniet (Ioel 3:18)	
VR Et erit in nobissimus diebus (Is 2:2)	33 A
Ecce Dominus egredietur (Zach 14:3-4)	
VR Deus virtutum converte nos (Ps 79:4)	37 A
Ecce Dominus in fortitudine (Is 40:10)	
VR In omnibus semper gaudete (I Thess 5:16-17)	67 B
Ecce Dominus in fortitudine (Is 40:10; 42:11,15-16)	
VR Ponam iudicium in pondere (Is 28:17)	36 A
VR Ecce Dominus in fortitudine	
RS Ecce testis fidelis veniet et	
Ecce Dominus veniet et omnes (Is 30:18)	
VR Salbabit Dominus (Zach 12:7-8)	31v A
Ecce Dominus veniet redemptor noster (?)	
VR Ecce Syon dominator tuus (?)	66v A
VR Ecce ego adducam cicatricem	
RS Haec dicit Dominus non cessabo	
Ecce ego plorans (Thr 1:10)	
VR Deducant oculi mei lacrimas (Ier 9:18)	
Ecce ego viam (Ier 32:27)	
VR Dies quibus peregrinatus (Gen 47:9)	
Ecce factus sum omnibus inimicis (Iob 30:9-11; 16:10; 17:3)	
VR Faretram suam aperuit (Iob 30:11)	140v B

A30	Silos	*BN10110*	Other Sources	Liturgical Assignment
				una virgine mat
73^{v} A				S Eolalie mat
			MSC 1 sn	
				ante Dom I Adv mat
33^{v} A				post Dom I Adv mat
				Adv ad tert
31 A				post Dom I Adv mat
11^{v} A				S Romani mat
				Adv ad tert
	BM51 171^{v} B			nocturnos Dom de XLme
			Sant 224^{v} B	post nocturnos
	4 85 B		*A56* 24 B	fin hominis die
	3 15 B			conm corp defunct
				XLma 4 VI tert
			T33.3 9^{v} sn	Tradit Dni tert

	AL
Ecce factus sum omnibus inimicis (Iob 30:9-11; 16:10; 17:3)	
VR Subito vulneravit me (Iob 16:8)	
Ecce iam Domine nobissimum tempus (?)	
VR Convertere Domine aliquantulum (Ps 89:13)	257^{v} B
Ecce inimicus meus circumdedit me (Iob 16:14-15,17-18)	
VR Conplevit inimicus furorem (Iob 16:10)	
Ecce inimicus meus circumdedit me (Iob 16:14-15,17-18)	
VR Ecce occupaberunt animam (Ps 58:4)	170^{v} A
II Considerabam a dextris (Ps 141:5)	170^{v} A
Ecce inimicus meus induxit me in loco (Thr 3:2-4,6)	
VR Conlocabit me in obscuris (Ps 142:3-4)	157 A
VR Ecce intelleget puer meus	
RS Auxiliabo puero meo	
Ecce natus est nobis filius (Is 9:6-7)	
VR Ecce Deus noster ipse est (Is 25:9)	71 B
Ecce non est auxilium michi (Iob 6:13; 16:9-10)	
VR Facta est hereditas (Ier 12:8)	
VR Ecce nunc benedicite Dominum	
RS Quam bone domus tuae Iacob	
Ecce nunc cithara (Iob 30:9-10,12)	
VR Aperuerunt in me ora sua (Iob 16:11)	157^{v} B
Ecce nunc tempus acceptavile (II Cor 6:2-3)	
VR Sed exibete vosmedipsos (II Cor 6:4)	110 A
Ecce nunc venit in me dolor meus (Iob 16:8-9)	
VR Suscitatur falsiloquus (Iob 16:9)	157^{v} A
Ecce occupaberunt animam meam (Ps 58:4,2)	
VR Eripe me de operantibus (Ps 58:3)	149 A
VR Ecce occupaberunt animam meam	
RS Ecce inimicus meus circumdedit me	
Ecce per omnes semitas (Is 49:9-10)	
VR Vide Iherusalem (?)	
VR Ecce quam bonum	

A30	Silos	*BN10110*	Other Sources	Liturgical Assignment
		107 H		XLma 6 IV tert
				let pro plubia
		82^{v} H		XLma 5 IV tert
				XLma 6 sabb mat
				XLma 6 III mat
123 B				Nat Dni mat
		90 H		XLma 5 VI tert
				XLma 6 III tert
				XLma 1 II sext
				XLma 6 III sext
				XLma 5 V sext
		93^{v} H		XLma 5 sabb sext

AL

RS Viri sancti vobis apertum
VR Ecce quasi filius hominis
RS Aspiciebam in visu noctis
Ecce quemadmodum (Is 31:4-5)
VR Timebunt qui ab occidente (Is 59:19) 36^{v} A

Ecce quomodo defecit sacrificium (Ioel 1:9 ?)
VR Cognoscimus Domine peccata nostra (II Esd 9:2 ?) 257^{v} sn
VR Ecce sequimur
RS Miserator et misericors
VR Ecce serbus meus
RS Famulo meo ego
Ecce Syon dominator tuus
RS Ecce Dominus veniet redemptor noster
Ecce testis fidelis veniet et (?)
VR Ecce Dominus in fortitudine (Is 40:10) 66^{v} B
VR Ecce tradidit me
RS Qui edebat panes
VR Ecce ut facta est
RS Unde mici adfuit
VR Ecce veniet in nubibus
RS Egredietur Dominus de Samaria
Ecce veniet nobis salus a Domino (?)
VR Veniet Dominus cum laude (Is 61:7) 67 B
Ecce vir impius graditur (Prov 6:12-15; 10:3,30)
VR Quum ceciderit iustus (Ps 36:24) 135 B
VR Educ de carcere
RS Intende ad orationem meam
VR Effuderunt sanguinem eorum
RS Propter honorem nominis
RS Sanguis innocens et iustus
VR Effundam super vos aquam
RS Adtende Israhel et audi

A30	Silos	*BN10110*	Other Sources	Liturgical Assignment
32 A				post Dom I Adv mat
				let pro plubia
				Adv ad tert
				Adv ad tert
				XLma 4 II tert

	AL
VR Effunde Domine super inimicos	
RS Multiplicati sunt super capillos	
VR Effunde framea et conclude	
RS Ne obduraveris aurem	
VR Ego ad Deum aspiciam	
RS Caligavit ab indignatione	
VR Ego Dominus dabo impius	
RS Elegi virum de plebem meam	
VR Ego dormibi et quiebi	
RS Angelus Domini dixit mulieribus	
RS Satiabi omnem sitientem	
Ego elegi vos dicit Dominus (Io 15:16,8)	
VR Sicut dilexit me Pater (Io 15:9)	217 B
Ego in laboribus multis fui (II Cor 11:23,25,31)	
VR Infixus sum in limo profundi (Ps 68:3)	97^{v} A
VR Ego rogabo Patrem et dabit	
Alleluia spiritum meum dedi	
VR Ego sum alfa et ω	
RS Felices qui faciunt precepta mea	
Ego sum Dominus Deus vester (Os 13:4; Is 41:5,8)	
VR Audi me Iacob et Israhel (Is 48:12)	45 B
VR Ego sum pastor	
RS Oves mee et oves gregis mei	
VR Ego sum resurrectio	
RS Amen amen dico vobis quia qui verbum	
VR Ego vero deprecabor	
RS Scio Domine quia nichil in terra	
Egredere inter lilia obbaca (Cant 4:7-8)	
VR Veni de Livano sponsa (Cant 4:8)	254 A
VR Propter veritatem et mansuetudinem (Ps 44:5)	254 A

A30	Silos	*BN10110*	Other Sources	Liturgical Assignment
	BM45 32^{v} B			SS Petri et Pauli mat
			SJP 1^{v} A	S Vincenti laev mat
53^{v} B				post Dom II Adv mat
				una virgine mat
				"
217^{v} ?				S Agate mat

AL

VR Propter veritatem et mansuetudinem (Ps 44:5)

VR Surge propera amica (Cant 2:10)
VR Egredere quasi aurora
RS Ecce dilectus meus venit dicens mihi
Egredietur Dominus de Samaria (?)
VR Ecce veniet in nubibus (?) 32 B

Egredietur Dominus et preliabitur (Zach 14:3-4)
VR Deus a Libano veniet (Hab 3:3) 55 B

VR Egredietur virga de radice
RS Alleluia emittit Dominus ex Syon
Elegi et sanctificavi vos (IV Esd 2:17,19)
VR Laudate pueri Dominum (Ps 112:1) 218 B

Elegi virum de plebem meam (?)
VR Ego Dominus dabo impius (Is 53:9) 73v A
VR Elegit Dominus tribu Iuda
RS Elegit nos hereditatem
Elegit Dominus virum de tribu Iuda (?)
VR Quisquis vestrum est sapiens (?) 261 A
Elegit eos Deus ante mundi (Eph 1:4-5)
VR Secundum divitias gratie (Eph 1:7-8) 217v B

Elegit nos hereditatem (Ps 46:5)
VR Elegit Dominus tribu Iuda (Ps 77:68) 249v B
Elemosina et fides fabricatores (?)
VR Ignem ardentem extinguit aqua (Eccli 3:33) 106v A
VR Emittit Dominus ex [S]yon
RS Ecce dies Domini veniet
VR Erans bracium
RS Virtus nostra Domine
VR Eripe me de inimicis meis Deus meus et ab insurgentibus

A30	Silos	*BN10110*	Other Sources	Liturgical Assignment
			BN13060 181 A	Adsum S Mariae
			SJP 5 A	S Agate mat
			SJP 5 A	"
14 B				ante Dom I Adv mat
83^{v} B				post Dom IV Adv mat
				SS Petri et Pauli mat
				S Stephani mat
				sacr bas mat
				SS Petri et Pauli mat
				SS general mat
				Carnes Toll mat

AL

RS A laqueo lingue inique libera me
Eripe me de inimicis meis Domine quia tu es (Ps 58:2)
VR Eripe me de operantibus (Ps 58:3)
Eripe me de inimicis meis Domine quia tu es (Ps 58:2)
VR Eripe me Domine ab homine (Ps 139:2) 148^{v} D
Eripe me de inimicis meis Domine quoniam ad te (Ps 142:9,11-12)
VR Fac mecum Deus signum (Ps 85:17) 155^{v} A
VR Eripe me de operantibus
RS Ab homine iniquo et doloso
RS Ecce occupaberunt animam meam
RS Eripe me de inimicis meis Domine quia tu es
VR Eripe me Domine ab homine
RS Deus meus salva me de manu impii
RS Eripe me de inimicis meis Domine quia tu es
VR Eripe me Domine de manu peccatoris
RS Adversum me exercebantur
VR Erravi sicut ovis
RS Vivit anima mea Deus
Esto nobis Domine (Ps 70:3)
VR Qui regis Israhel (Ps 79:2)
Estote imitatores Dei (Eph 5:1-2)
VR Deus qui dives est (Eph 2:4) 182^{v} B

VR Estote invicem benigni
RS Vox quam audistis ad initio
VR Esurivi enim et dedistis
RS Venite benedicti patres mei
VR Esuribi et dedistis
RS Beati oculi qui vident
RS Sanctis ab altissimo dicebitur
VR Et alias abeo oves
Oves mee et oves gregis mei
VR Et clamaberunt ad Dominum

A30	Silos	*BN10110*	Other Sources	Liturgical Assignment
		72^{v} H		XLma 4 sabb sext
				XLma 5 V mat
				XLma 6 II mat
	BM51 189 C			infirmis mat
			T35.4 9 L	Res Dni 6 mat

RS Iusti in Syon invocaberunt
RS Salvos fecit iustos
VR Et dabo opus eorum
RS Dabo duobus famulis meis
RS Haec dicit Dominus visitabo sanctos
RS Sancti in terram suam
VR Et effundite coram illo
RS Si Deus pro nobis
VR Et erit in nobissimis diebus
RS Ecce Dominus de Syon veniet
VR Et erit iustitia cingulum
RS Dominus de Syna veniet
VR Et eritis sicut ortus
RS Orietur in tenebris
VR Et erunt super omnem montem
RS Abundantia frugum erit in omnem
VR Et faciam ut in preceptis
RS Dabo vobis cor nobum
VR Et in umbra alarum tuarum
RS In te confidet anima mea Deus
VR Et levabit signum
RS Veniet Dominus et apparebit
VR Et magnificabit eum Dominus
RS Felix vir cuius memoria
VR Et ne nocturnis
RS Gregem tuum Domine ne desertas
VR Et non egebunt lumine
RS Alleluia absterget Deus
VR Et nunc sequimur
RS Ne nos dederis in opprobrium
RS Propter peccata nostra venerunt
VR Et occupabit salus muros tuos
RS Iherusalem confortetur cor tuum

A30	Silos	*BN10110*	Other Sources	Liturgical Assignment

AL

VR Et pater diligit eum
    RS Qui diligit me diligitur
VR Et propter honorem nominis
    RS Adiuva nos Deus salutaris noster
VR Et psallam nomini Domini altissimi
    RS Confitebor Domino qui salvos
VR Et quicumque vicerit
    RS Iustus iustificetur et sanctus
VR Et replebit splendoribus
    RS Orietur in tenebris
VR Et sapientie eius
    RS Magnus Dominus noster alleluia
VR Et tu Bethlem domus Efrata
    RS Nos omnes ambulabimus
VR Et undecim discipuli
    RS Hoc iam tertio manifestatus
VR Et videbunt faciem eius
    RS Alleluia absterget Deus
VR Etenim correxit orbem
    RS Dicite in nationibus alleluia
VR Etenim homo pacis
    RS Posuerunt inimici mei in angustia
VR Ex ore infantium et lactantium
    RS Quam admirabile est nomen tuum
Ex quo honorabi te (Is 43:4-5)
    VR Dedi te plebi (Ier 15:20) 251 sn
VR Exaltabo te Domine rex meus
    RS Alleluia laudabo te Domine semper
    RS Confitebor tibi Domine Deus meus
Exaltare Domine in virtute tua alleluia (Ps 20:14)
    VR Confitebimur tibi Deus (Ps 74:2) 202^{v} B

    VR Deus autem noster (Ps 113B:3)

A30	Silos	*BN10110*	Other Sources	Liturgical Assignment
				uno iusto mat
				Dom post Ascension mat
			T35.4 66v L	"

	AL
Exaltatus est et fulget (Eccli 50:6,8,11)	
VR Extendit super libatorium (Eccli 50:16-17)	241^{v} B
Exarcebavimus nomen tuum Domine (Ez 20:21 ?)	
VR Fac nobiscum Domine (Dan 3:42)	
VR Exaruit cor meum	
RS Sicut onus grave	
Exaudi me Domine quoniam benigna est (Ps 68:17)	
VR Secundum multitudinem miserationum tuarum (Ps 68:17)	
VR Exaudi orationem meam	
RS Adiutor et liberator meus es tu	
Excelsus super omnes gentes (Ps 112:4)	
VR Magnus Dominus noster (Ps 146:5-6)	202 B
VR Excelsus super omnes gentes	
RS Domine qui habitas	
Exclamemus omnes ad Dominum (Deut 13:17)	
VR Convertimini et recedite (Ez 14:6)	
VR Excutere de pulvere	
RS Lava a malitia cor tuum	
VR Extendit super libatorium	
RS Exaltatus est et fulget	
Exulta satis filia Syon (Zach 9:9-10,17; 10:1)	
VR Visitabit Dominus gregem suum (Zach 10:4)	47^{v} B
Exultabunt qui habitant in petrosa (Is 42:11-12)	
VR In tempore adventus Domini (Is 35:5)	62^{v} A
Exultabunt sancti cum fiducia (?)	
VR Exultabunt sancti in gloria (Ps 149:5)	93^{v} B

A30	Silos	*BN10110*	Other Sources	Liturgical Assignment
	BM45 150 B			trans corp S Satornini Aep mat
		38^v H		XLma 3 III tert
	BM51 176 B		*Sant* 217^v B	nocturnos fer VI
			Sal 155^v B	"
			169 B	nocturnos Dom de med
				post Ascension sabb mat
		28^v I		XLma 2 V tert
60 B				S Leocadie mat
100^v A				post Dom IV Adv mat
				S Sebastiani mat

AL

VR Exultabunt sancti in gloria
    RS Exultabunt sancti cum fiducia
VR Exultavit ut gigans
    RS Dominus de Synaa veniet descendet
VR Exurge Domine et intende
    RS Domine iudica nocentes
Exurge Domine et ne repellas (Ps 43:23-26)
    VR Defecit gaudium cordis (Thr 5:15) 124 A

Exurge Domine miserere nobis (Ps 101:14)
    VR Ad te lebamus oculos (Ps 122:1)
Exurge Domine miserere nobis (Ps 101:14,18)
    VR De sanctuario tuo Domine (Deut 26:15) 116^{v} B
VR Exurgentes testes
    RS [H] Eu me quod peregrinatio mea
VR Fac mecum Deus signum
    RS Eripe me de inimicis meis Domine quoniam ad te
VR Fac nobiscum Domine
    RS Exarcebavimus nomen tuum Domine
VR Facta est hereditas
    RS Ecce non est auxiliam michi
Facta est lingua iniquorum (Mich 6:12)
    VR Congregati sunt adversus (Ier 26:8-9)
Facta est Sion sicut avis volans (Is 16:2-3)
    VR Spiritus oris nostri (Thr 4:20)

Facta est Syon sicut avis volans (Is 16:2-3)
    VR Tu filia Syon summe (Ier 9:18 ?) 159 B
Facti sumus Domine tamquam alieni (Thr 5:16; Is 64:1-2)
    VR Defecit gaudium cordis (Thr 5:15-16) 122^{v} A
Facti sumus Domine tanquam alieni (Thr 5:16; Is 64:1-2)

A30	Silos	*BN10110*	Other Sources	Liturgical Assignment
	BM51 183 B			sanctis mat
				Dom II XLmae mat
			T33.3 7 M	XLma ad tert Dominicale
		11 H		XLma 1 IV sext
				Dom I XLmae mat
		88^{v} J		XLma 5 VI mat
			T35.5 62^{v} I	Dom IV XLmae mat
				XLma 6 IV tert
				XLma 2 VI tert

	AL
VR Facti sumus quasi in principio (Is 63:9)	
VR Facti sumus quasi in principio	
RS Facti sumus Domine tamquam alieni	
RS Nunquid in eternum continebis	
VR Factum est autem	
RS Conlocabit Salomon altare in medio	
Factus sum omni populo meo (Thr 3:14-15,58)	
VR Disperde inimicos meos (Ps 142:12)	
Famulo meo ego (?)	
VR Ecce serbus meus (Is 42:1)	
VR In eternum servabo illi (Ps 88:29)	246^{v} A
VR Faretram suam aperuit	
RS Ecce factus sum omnibus inimicis	
VR Favum mellis distillant	
RS Super omnia ligna campi	
Felices qui faciunt precepta mea (Apoc 22:14,16)	
VR Ego sum alfa et ω (Apoc 22:13)	87 B
Felix qui potuit transgredi (Eccli 31:10; Heb 11:25)	
VR Felix qui suscepit ludibria (Heb 11:36)	225 B
Felix qui spiritu contribulato (Ps 50:19; Prov 15:8)	
VR Os iusti meditabitur (Ps 36:30)	225^{v} B
VR Felix qui suscepit ludibria	
RS Felix qui potuit transgredi	
Felix quia deiecisti a te (Eccli 48:3-4, 11)	
VR Inpletus es quasi flumen (Eccli 24:35; 47:17)	224^{v} B
Felix vir cuius memoria (Eccli 45:1-2)	
VR Et magnificabit eum Dominus (Eccli 45:2)	225 B
Felix vir qui inventus est (Eccli 31:8-9)	
VR Dispersit dedit pauperibus (Ps 111:9)	225 A
VR Fiat auris tua	
RS Si celum et celi celorum	
Fili dilige disciplinam (Eccli 6:18-19)	

A30	Silos	*BN10110*	Other Sources	Liturgical Assignment
		25^{v} H		XLma 2 IV mat
		84^{v} H		XLma 5 V mat
	3 119c A			uno iusto mat
				S Emiliani mat
169 B			*T35.7* 121 M	Apparit Dni mat
	BM45 58^{v} B			S Felicis mat
				S Felicis mat
	BM45 56^{v} B			S Felicis mat
	BM45 57^{v} B			S Felicis mat
	BM45 57 B			S Felicis mat

	AL
VR In omni animo tuo (Eccli 6:27)	292^{V} B
Filia Syon consecrabis Domino (Mich 5:2-3)	
VR Dabit vobis Dominus signum (Is 7:13)	58^{V} B
Filia Sion facta es (Is 1:8; Lc 15:7)	
VR Gaudium erit in celo (Lc 15:10)	
Filia Syon habitabo (Zach 2:10-11)	
VR Lauda et letare filia Syon (Zach 2:10)	59 B
Filie Iherusalem audite me (Cant 3:6; 6:3,8)	
VR Quam pulcra es amica mea (Cant 6:3)	102^{V} A
Filie Iherusalem si inveneritis (Cant 5:8; 3:4)	
VR Occurrite ei virgines sapientissime (?)	220^{V} D
VR Filius quidem hominis	
RS Qui mecum ait manu	
VR Flagellabit nos ab iniquitatibus	
RS Misericordia Domini facit	
VR Florete flores quasi lilium	
RS Viri sancti germinate	
VR Foderunt manus meas	
RS Aspice Domine quia factus sum	
VR Fortissime magne	
RS Magnus es Domine et preclarus	
Frater qui adiubatur a fratre (Prov 18:19)	
VR De fructu oris sui replebitur (Prov 18:20)	228 B
Fuit homo missus a Deo (Io 1:6-7)	
VR Non erat ille lux (Io 1:8)	213^{V} D
Fulgebunt iusti et tamquam (Sap 3:7-8)	
VR Clamaberunt iusti et Dominus (Ps 33:18)	95^{V} B
VR Fulgebunt iusti sicut splendor	
RS Dabo sanctis meis primam	

A30	Silos	*BN10110*	Other Sources	Liturgical Assignment
				unoq Dom mat
			T35.4 137 L	Dom XII quot mat
91 B				S Mariae mat
		10v H		XLma 1 IV tert
93 B				S Mariae mat
72 A				S Eolalie mat
	BM45 43v B			SS Iustae et Rufinae mat
	BM45 70 B			SS Iusti et Pastoris mat
	BM45 17 B			nat S Iohannis mat
211 B				S Fructuosi Aep mat

	AL
RS In paradiso Dei requiescunt	
RS Iusti in perpetuo vivent	
Fulget celum et terra (?)	
VR Laudate Dominum omnes gentes (Ps 116:1)	85^{v} B
VR Funes extenderunt continuatis	
RS Muscipula paraberunt pedibus meis	
Funes peccatorum circumplexe (Ps 118:61,97)	
VR Quomodo dilexi legem tuam (Ps 118:97)	293^{v} A
VR Gaude filia Syon letare	
RS Audi dilecta mea propera	
Gaude filia Syon quoniam veniet (Zach 9:9)	
VR Apparebit tibi Dominus (Ier 31:3)	254 A
VR Gaudebunt campi	
RS Bethlem civitas Dei summi	
RS Montes filie Syon ramos	
Gaudete et exultate omnes populi (Lc 2:11; Is 9:7,2; 61:2)	
VR Hic est dies quem fecit (Ps 117:24)	70 B
Gaudete in Domino semper (Phi 4:4-5)	
VR Sed in omni oratione (Phi 4:6)	65 B
VR Gaudete in Domino semper	
RS Sacerdotes et levite principes	
VR Gaudium erit in celo	
RS Filia Sion facta es	
VR Germinate iusti	
RS Viri sancti germinate	
VR Gloria et honor patri	
RS Adiutorium nostrum in nomine Domini	
RS Clamor factus est	
RS Iam securus et gaudens venio	

A30	Silos	*BN10110*	Other Sources	Liturgical Assignment
			T35.7 117 X	Apparit Dni mat
				unoq Dom mat
	BM51 170^{v} A			nocturnos Dom
				una virgine mat
71 A				S Eolalie mat
121 B				Nat Dni mat
107 B				post Dom V Adv mat

	AL
Gloria magna est sequi Dominum (Eccli 23:38,37)	
VR Inquirentes autem Dominum (Ps 33:11)	290^{v} A
VR Gloriosus est aspectus eius	
RS Suscitavit Dominus regem	
Gratias agimus Deo qui elegit te (?)	
VR Ecce constituit te Dominus (Ier 1:5)	104 A
II Magna est gloria (Ps 20:6)	104 A
Gratias Domino Ihesu Christo (Apoc 1:5-6)	
VR Mortuus est Christus (Rom 4:25)	192^{v} A
Gregem tuum Domine ne deser[t]as (?)	
VR Et ne nocturnis (?)	
Gregem tuam ne desertas (?)	
VR Et ne nocturnis (?)	
Gressus eorum dirige Deus (Ps 118:133)	
VR Declaracio sermonum (Ps 118:130)	
Habeant Domine finem peccata nostra (?)	
VR Sacerdotes tui Domine (Ps 131:9)	118^{v} B
[H]Abete fidutium (Prov 3:5)	
VR Perfecti estote exortamini (II Cor 13:11)	
VR Habitabo inter vos dicit Dominus	
RS In proximo est advenire vobis	
Habitatores Iherusalem crucifigent (Zach 12:5; 13:6-7)	
VR Vivo ego dicit Dominus (Deut 32:41)	159^{v} B
VR H[a]ec cogitaberunt et erraverunt	
RS Viri impii dixerunt opprimamus	
H[a]ec dicit Dominus afflixi populum (Ier 15:7-8; Lev 25:18)	

A30	Silos	*BN10110*	Other Sources	Liturgical Assignment
				unoq Dom mat
225^{v} A				Cat S Petri mat
				"
			T35.4 33 L	Dom III post oct Pasc mat
			T33.3 11 sn	Res Dni ad tert Dominicale
	BM51 163 A			?
			T33.3 43 M	Res Dni ad non Dominicale
		108 H		XLma 6 IV sext
				XLma 2 II sext
	BM45 158 B			let can sext
		4 K		XLma 1 II sext
				XLma 6 IV sext

	AL
VR Omnes vias meas (Iob 34:27-28)	
Haec dicit Dominus civitates tuae Iudae (Ier 4:7-8)	
VR Revertere Israhel ad Dominum (Os 14:2)	255^{v} A
Haec dicit Dominus congregamini (Soph 2:1-3)	
VR Si vere utique iustitiam (Ps 57:2)	111^{v} A
Haec dicit Dominus deducam imbrem (Ez 34:26-27)	
VR Ponam sanctuarium meum (?)	290 A
Haec dicit Dominus dilectione (Ier 31:2-4)	
VR Recordatus sum tui miserans (Ier 2:2)	254^{v} A
	254^{v} A
Haec dicit Dominus domus mea (Is 56:7)	
VR Magna erit claritas domus (Agg 2:10)	262^{v} A
Haec dicit Dominus iustitia mea (Is 46:13)	
VR Veniam in Syon (Zach 8:3)	66 B
Haec dicit Dominus meus es tu (Is 43:1-2)	
VR Protector tuus ego sum (Is 43:2-3)	98 A
II Noli timere dicit Dominus (Is 43:1)	98 A
Haec dicit Dominus nolite timere (Agg 2:6,5,10; 1:14)	
VR Dabo vobis cor nobum (Ez 36:26)	209 A
Haec dicit Dominus non cessabo (Ier 31:33)	
VR Ecce ego adducam cicatricem (Ier 33:6)	289 B
H[a]ec dicit Dominus pertransibunt in mari (Zach 10:11-12,10)	
VR Volabunt in navibus (?)	195^{v} A
Haec dicit Dominus prevaricati sunt (Os 7:13-16)	
VR Quum sanare vellem Israhel (Os 7:1)	137^{v} **B**
H[a]ec dicit Dominus si custodieritis (Lev 26:3-6)	
VR Si volueritis et audieritis (Is 1:19)	289^{v} **B**

A30	Silos	*BN10110*	Other Sources	Liturgical Assignment
			T35.5 17 I	Dom II XLmae mat
				let de clade
				XLma 1 III tert
				unoq Dom mat
				una virgine mat
				"
				sacr bas mat
				Adv ad tert
207^v A			*SJP* 2^v A	S Vincenti laev mat
207^v A			*SJP* 2^v A	"
				Pentecost mat
	3 153 B			unoq Dom mat
	6 63^v B		*T35.4* 95 L	Dom II quot mat
			T35.4 43 M	S Torquati mat
				XLma 4 IV tert
				unoq Dom mat
	6 74^v B		*T35.4* 100 L	Dom III quot mat

	AL
Haec dicit Dominus si obtuleritis (Lev 2:14-15)	
VR Date Domino Deo vestro (Ier 13:16)	222^{v} B
Haec dicit Dominus visitabo sanctos (?)	
VR Et dabo opus eorum (Is 61:8)	94^{v} A
VR Haec loquutus sum vobis	
RS Dixit Ihesus discipulis suis absque	
VR H[a]ec scribo vobis ut non peccetis	
RS Si dixerimus quia peccatum	
[H]Eu me quod peregrinatio mea (Ps 119:5-7)	
VR Exurgentes testes (Ps 34:11-12)	
Heu me quod peregrinatio mea (Ps 119:5-7)	
VR Loquuti sunt adversum me (Ps 108:3)	151 B
VR Hic est dies quem fecit	
RS Gaudete et exultate omnes populi	
VR Hic est filius meus dilectus	
RS Videbitis hodie mirabilia	
Hic est vir qui servabit mandata mea (?)	
VR Homo iste in vita sua (Eccli 48:15)	231^{v} B
Hic qui advenit nemo nobit (Apoc 19:12-14)	
VR Iste formosus stola sua (Is 63:1)	80 B
Hic vir etate gloria mirabilis (II Mach 15:13-14)	
VR Dispersit dedit pauperibus (Ps 111:9)	223^{v} A
Hii ostenderunt cerimonias populo (Ex 18:20)	
VR Hii sunt qui in generationibus (Eccli 44:7)	
Hii ostenderunt cerimonias populo (Ex 18:20)	
VR Sancti in terram suam (Is 61:7)	216^{v} A

A30	Silos	*BN10110*	Other Sources	Liturgical Assignment
	BM45 49^{v} B			Primitiis mat
195^{v} A				S Fructuosi Aep mat
	BM45 129^{v} A			SS Faust, Ianuar, et Martial mat
		64 I		XLma 4 V tert
				XLma 5 sabb mat
				sacr S Martini mat
	BM45 75^{v} sn			S Mametis mat
151 B				Circumcis Dni mat
				S Cucufati mat
			MSC 18^{v} H	SS Petri et Pauli mat
	BM45 31^{v} A			SS Petri et Pauli mat

	AL
VR Hii sunt qui in generationibus	
RS Hii ostenderunt cerimonias populo	
Hoc iam tertio manifestatus (Io 21:14)	
VR Et undecim discipuli (Mt 28:16-17)	186 A
Homo iste custodivit in omnibus (Sap 4:14 ?)	
VR Consummatus in brebi explevit (Sap 4:13-14)	238^{v} G
VR Homo iste in vita sua	
RS Hic est vir qui servabit mandata mea	
RS Vir dilectus a Deo	
VR Humiliata est in pulvere	
RS Domus tua Domine in captivitate	
Humiliatus sum et curvatus (Ps 37:9,7)	
VR Quoniam anima mea (Ps 37:8)	
Iam adspirat dies (Cant 4:6-8)	
VR Speciem et pulcritudinem tuam intende (Ps 44:5)	59^{v} B
Iam securus et gaudens venio (Passio)	
VR O bona crux (Passio)	40^{v} F ?
II Salve crux que sine (Passio)	40^{v} X
II Gloria et honor Patri	
VR Ignem ardentem extinguit aqua	
RS Elemosina et fides fabricatores	
(H)ierusalem benedic Domino saeculorum (Tob 13:12)	
VR Propter fratres meos et proximos (Ps 121:8)	269 B
Iherusalem civitas sancta alleluia (Apoc 21:23)	
VR Deus in gradibus eius (Ps 47:4)	33^{v} B
Iherusalem civitas sancta exaltabitur (?)	
VR Qui descendit ipse est (Eph 4:10)	199 B

* VR incomplete.

A30	Silos	*BN10110*	Other Sources	Liturgical Assignment
			T35.4 14 L	Res Dni 15 mat
			T33.3 22^{v} sn	Res Dni
				S Hieronimi Pres mat
		57 I		XLma 4 III sext
95^{v} B				S Mariae mat
			BN13060 185 B	Adsum S Mariae mat
46^{v} F ?				S Andreae Apost mat
				"
46^{v} F ?				"
				rest bas mat
19*				S Cecilie mat
			T35.4 57 L	Ascension mat

	AL
Iherusalem civitas sancta suscipe me (Ier 18:20)	
VR Quoniam pater meus (Ps 26:10)	
Iherusalem confortetur cor tuum (IV Esd 2:17-19)	
VR Et occupabit salus muros tuos (Is 60:18)	52 A
Iherusalem ecce apparuit (Ez 26:15-16)	
VR Reges Tarsis et insule (Ps 71:10)	84v B
Iherusalem erit tibi Dominus lux (Is 60:20)	
VR Aperientur porte tue iugiter (Is 60:11)	85 G
Iherusalem felices qui hedificant te (Tob 13:16,18)	
VR Benedicti erunt qui hedificaverunt te (Tob 13:16-17)	235v B
Iherusalem letare in adventum (?)	
VR Lauda Iherusalem Dominum conlauda (Ps 147:1)	67 B
VR Letare Iherusalem quoniam (Zach 9:9)	
Ihesum Nazarenum quem unxit Deus (Act 10:38-41)	
VR Dominus Ihesus Christus qui est (Apoc 1:5)	197v A
VR In [a]eternum servabo illi	
RS Famulo meo ego	
RS Inveni unum iustum qui placuit	
In conspectu angelorum psallam (Ps 137:1)	
VR Adorabo ad templum sanctum (Ps 137:2)	295*
VR In die illa salbabo	
RS Isti sunt lapides sancti	
VR In Domino laudabitur	
RS Benedicam Domino in omni tempore	
In hoc cognobi quoniam voluisti (Ps 40:12)	
VR Propter innocentiam autem (Ps 40:13)	140v G

* VR incomplete.

A30	Silos	*BN10110*	Other Sources	Liturgical Assignment
	3 28^{v} sn			conm corp parv
				post Dom III Adv mat
				Apparit Dni mat
			T35.7 116 X	Apparit Dni mat
				S Eufimiae mat
				Adv ad tert
113 B				"
			T35.4 52 M	S Crucis mat
				nocturnos et mat ora diei Dom
				XLma 4 VI mat
	3 28 G		*A56* 36 G	conm corp parv
	4 99^{v} G			"
			LF-5 G	

AL

VR In labiis suis indulcat
    RS Unusquisque se a proximo
VR In lege Domini congregabit
    RS Adesit Domino Deo meo
In lege Domini meditemur (Ps 1:2)
    VR Venite filii audite me (Ps 33:12)

In loco viride Domine (Ps 22:1-3)
    VR Deduc eos Domine (Ps 118:35)

    VR Deus in nomine tuo salvos nos fac (Ps 53:3)
VR In multitudine misericordie
    RS Deus Srahel propter te sustinui
VR In omni animo tuo
    RS Fili dilige disciplinam
In omni loco oculi Dei (Prov 15:3)
    VR Verbum dulce (Eccli 6:5)
In omni opere suo dedit (Eccli 47:9-10)
    VR Invocabit Deum potentem (Eccli 46:6) 255 A

VR In omnibus semper gaudete
    RS Confortare in adventum Domini Dei tui
    RS Ecce Dominus in fortitudine
In paradiso Dei requiescunt (IV Esd 7:53,55)
    VR Fulgebunt iusti sicut splendor (Dan 12:3) 230v B
In principio erat verbum (Io 1:1-3)
    VR Quod factum est in ipso (Io 1:3-4) 69 D

In proximo est advenire vobis (IV Esd 2:34,14)
    VR Habitabo inter vos dicit Dominus (Ex 29:45) 64v A

A30	Silos	*BN10110*	Other Sources	Liturgical Assignment
	BM51 173^{v} A		*Sant* 216^{v} A	nocturnos fer II
			Sal 175 A	"
			166^{v} A	nocturnos Dom de XLme
	BM51 197 B			defunct sacerd mat
	3 63 B			uno defuncto mat
	BM51 170^{v} B			nocturnos Dom
				unius virg confess
			Cinc M	S Leocadiae mat
	BM45 78^{v} B			S Laurenti mat
117 B			*T35.7* 57^{v} X	Nat Dni mat
106 A				post Dom V Adv mat

	AL
In te confidet anima mea Deus (Ps 56:2)	
VR Et in umbra alarum tuarum (Ps 56:2)	
In tempore adventus Domini (Is 29:18-19)	
VR Tunc aperientur oculi (Is 35:5)	37v A
VR In tempore adventus Domini	
RS Exultabunt qui habitant in petrosa	
In tubis ductilibus (Ps 97:6-8)	
VR Psallite Deo nostro in cithara (Ps 97:5)	294v sn
In via quam ambulabam (Ps 141:4-5)	
VR Ut quid Domine repellas (Ps 87:15)	
VR Inclina Domine aurem tuam	
RS Miserere mei Domine et exaudi	
VR Incurbatus sum et humilliatus	
RS Tota die contristatus	
VR Induc super eos diem	
RS Omnes persequentes me tu	
Induta est caro mea putredine (Iob 7:5,7)	
VR Putredini dixi pater (Iob 17:14)	115v B
VR Induta est caro mea putredini	
RS Dies mei transierunt	
VR Infirmatus est in paupertate	
RS Aspice Domine quia factus sum	
VR Infirmorum adiutor	
RS Virtus nostra Domine	
Infirmus sum sana me Domine (Ps 6:3)	
VR Quoniam turbata sunt ossa mea (Ps 6:3,4)	

A30	Silos	*BN10110*	Other Sources	Liturgical Assignment
			BN10001 1^v A	
	BM51 175^v F		*Sant* 217^v F	nocturnos fer V
			Sal 154^v F	"
			169 F	nocturnos Dom de med
34^v B				post Dom I Adv mat
				nocturnos et mat ora diei Dom
		70^v J		XLma 4 sabb mat
				XLma 1 sabb mat
	BM51 174 C		*Sant* 217 C	nocturnos fer III

AL

Infixus sum in limo profundi (Ps 68:3-4,17)
    VR Circumdederunt me aque (Ion 2:6) 97^{v} B

VR Infixus sum in limo profundi
    RS Ego in laboribus multis fui
VR Ingrediar in locum
    RS Quare tristis es anima mea
Ingressus inimicus manu potenti (Iob 31:6)
    VR Tetendit arcum suum (Thr 3:12) 171 A
    II Spoliabit me gloria mea (Iob 16:15; 19:9) 171 A
VR Inimici mei dixerunt mala mici
    RS Domine loquere pro me
Iniquitates nostre et peccata (Ez 33:10-11)
    VR Peccabimus cum patribus (Ps 105:6) 119^{v} B
Iniquitates nostre et peccata (Ez 33:10-11)
    VR Peccavimus enim inique egimus (Dan 3:29-30)
VR Iniquitates nostre multiplicate sunt
    RS Habundaberunt iniquitates nostre
VR Iniquos odio abui
    RS Letor ego super eloquia
VR Inluminet Dominus vultum suum
    RS Deus misereatur nobis
    RS Misereatur nobis et benedicat nos
    RS Pacem donet Dominus
VR Inluminet vultum suum
    RS Benefaciat nobis Deus
    RS Deus misereatur nobis
VR Inpletus es quasi flumen
    RS Felix qui deiecisti a te
VR Inquirentes autem Dominum
    RS Gloria magna est sequi Dominum

A30	Silos	*BN10110*	Other Sources	Liturgical Assignment
			Sal	
			152 C	nocturnos fer III
			167v C	nocturnos Dom II XLme
205 A				S Vincenti laev mat
				XLma 6 sabb mat
				"
				XLma 2 III tert
		30 K		XLma 2 VI mat

	AL
Inquirentes Dominum non deficient (Ps 33:11-12)	
VR Magnificate Dominum mecum (Ps 33:4)	152v A
VR Instauras testes tuos	
RS Tedet anima mea vite mee	
Intellege clamorem meum (Ps 5:2)	
VR Intende voci orationis mee (Ps 5:3)	
VR Intellege clamorem meum	
RS Mane exaudies vocem meam	
Intende ad orationem meam (Ps 141:7)	
VR Educ de carcere (Ps 141:8)	
VR Intende in adiutorium	
RS Cogitaverunt adversum me	
VR Intende voci orationis mee	
RS Intellege clamorem meum	
Inter ramos arborum avium (Sap 17:17-18)	
VR Vox Domini in virtute (Ps 28:4)	293 A
Inter vestibolum et altare (Ioel 2:17)	
VR Peccabimus cum patribus (Ps 105:6)	242 B
VR Inter vestibolum et altare	
RS Amara facta est vita nostra	
RS Clamor noster ad te	
RS Isti sunt dies consolationis	
RS Vocem audivi flentis	
VR Introduxit me in cellam	
RS Invocabi proximum mici	
VR Invenerunt puerum cum Maria	
RS Stellam quam viderant	
Inveni unum iustum qui placuit (Gen 8:21; 9:15)	
VR In eternum servabo illi (Ps 88:29)	38v B

A30	Silos	*BN10110*	Other Sources	Liturgical Assignment
				Ramos mat
	BM51 174 X		*Sant* 216^{v} B	nocturnos fer III
			Sal 152 B	"
			166^{v} B	nocturnos Dom de XLme
		86^{v} H		XLma 5 V sext
				unoq Dom mat
	BM45 153^{v} B			let can tert
				S Saturnini Aep mat

	AL
Invocabi altissimum potentem (Eccli 46:6-7)	
VR Dominus confregit dentes (Ps 57:7)	251^v sn
Invocabi proximum mici (Cant 5:6-8)	
VR Introduxit me in cellam (Cant 2:4-5)	50^v E
II Per vicos et plateas (Cant 3:2-3)	50^v E
VR Invocabit Deum potentem	
RS In omni opere suo dedit	
VR Ipse super maria	
RS Omnis homo qui audit verba mea	
VR Iste formosus stola sua	
RS Hic qui advenit nemo nobit	
Iste homo in professione sua (Eccli 44:17,21)	
VR Adhesit Domino Deo suo (IV Reg 18:6-7)	244^v B
VR Dispersit dedit pauperibus (Ps 111:9)	
Iste homo supplicabat (Eccli 23:4,3)	
VR Auxiliator meus es tu (Ps 26:9)	233^v B
Iste qui natus est (Gen 5:29)	
VR Ecce agnus Dei (Io 1:29)	70^v A
Isti qui amicti sunt stolas (Apoc 7:13-14)	
VR Isti sunt qui in generationibus (Eccli 44:7)	240^v A
Isti sunt dies consolationis (?)	
VR Inter vestibolum et altare (Ioel 2:17)	204 D
Isti sunt lapides sancti (Zach 9:16; 10:7)	

A30	Silos	*BN10110*	Other Sources	Liturgical Assignment
	BM45 140^{v} B		*BN13060* 155 B	S Martini mat
	5 78^{v} B			"
				uno iusto
67^{v} E				S Eolalie mat
67^{v} E				"
				S Martini vigil
	5 61 B			"
37^{v} X				S Saturnini Aep mat
	3 131 B			confessores mat
			BN13060 191 B	?
				S Augustini Aep mat
122 A				Nat Dni mat
				SS Vinc, Sav, et Cris mat
	BM45 135 A			SS Servandi et Germani mat
			A60 48^{v} B	let apost tert

	AL
VR In die illa salbabo (Zach 8:7)	196 X
VR Isti sunt qui in generationibus	
RS Isti qui amicti sunt stolas	
Isti sunt qui non polluerunt (Apoc 3:4-5)	
VR Beati mundo corde (Mt 5:8)	92 B
Isti sunt sancti qui pro testamento (?)	
VR Sancti amabiles et decori (II Reg 1:23)	95 B
VR Iucunditatem fecisti	
RS Nunc Domine dabis populo tuo	
VR Iudicate pupillo et egeno	
RS Convertimini ad me omnis congregatio	
Iudicium rectum iudicate (Zach 7:9-10)	
VR Nolite secundum fatiem iudicare (Io 7:24)	
Iudicium rectum iudicate (Zach 7:9-10)	
VR Pauperem nolite calumniare (Zach 7:10)	113^{v} A
Iuliani dilecti mei fides hec (Passio)	
VR Propter dilectum meum Iulianum (?)	89^{v} B
Iulianus invenit gratiam coram Domino (Passio)	
VR Beati qui persequutionem (Mt 5:10)	89^{v} A
Iunior fui et senui (Ps 36:25)	
VR Dispersit dedit pauperibus (Ps 111:9)	245^{v} A
VR Os iusti meditabitur (Ps 36:30)	
Iusti in perpetuo vivent (Sap 5:16)	
VR Fulgebunt iusti sicut splendor (Dan 12:3)	249 B
Iusti in Syon invocaberunt (Eccli 48:22)	
VR Et clamaberunt ad Dominum (Ps 106:6)	230^{v} B

A30	Silos	*BN10110*	Other Sources	Liturgical Assignment
			T35.4 44^{v} L	S Torquati mat
				Allis Infant mat
	BM45 69 B			SS Iusti et Pastoris mat
198^{v} B				S Fructuosi Aep mat
		40^{v} H		XLma 3 IV mat
				XLma 1 V tert
178 sn				S Iuliani mat
				S Iuliani mat
				S Martini Aep mat
	5 77 B ?		*BN13060* 154 B	"
	BM51 185^{v} B			unius confessoris mat
				SS general
	BM45 47^{v} A			SS Sperati et Marine mat
				S Laurenti mat

	AL
Iusti omnes quasi virens (Prov 11:28; Eccli 26:2)	
VR Mulier fortis oblectat (Eccli 26:2)	211 A
Iustorum anime in manu Dei (Sap 3:1)	
VR Clamaberunt iusti et Dominus (Ps 33:18)	248 A
VR Iustus es Domine	
RS Propter peccata nostra venerunt	
Iustus iustificetur et sanctus (Apoc 22:11,14)	
VR Et quicumque vicerit (Apoc 3:5)	232v A
VR Beatus vir qui timet (Ps 11:1)	
Labia sacerdotis custodiunt (Mal 2:7,6)	
VR Sacerdos qui de ore suo (Mal 2:7)	244 B
L[a]etabitur iustus in Deo (Ps 63:11)	
VR Tota die iustus (Ps 36:26)	
L[a]etamini caeli quoniam misertus est (Ps 95:11-12)	
VR Laudem dicite Domine Deo nostro (Apoc 19:5)	193v A
L[a]etamini gentes et exultate (Ps 31:11)	
VR Nolite ante tempus (I Cor 4:5)	
L[a]etamini in Domino Deo vestro (Ps 31:11)	
VR Omnes gentes plaudete manibus (Ps 46:2)	183 B
L[a]etare deserta quem commoraris (?)	
VR Lauda Iherusalem Dominum conlauda (Ps 147:1)	66v B
L[a]etare Iherusalem in filiis iustorum (Tob 13:17-18)	
VR Benedicti erunt qui hedificaberunt te (Tob 13:16-17)	217 B
VR L[a]etare Iherusalem quoniam	

A30	Silos	*BN10110*	Other Sources	Liturgical Assignment
	BM45 10 A			S Adriani mat
				SS general mat
	BM45 99 A			S Genesi mat
	6 7v C			uno iusto mat
			T33.3 13 X	unius iusti tert
	5 42 B			S Martini vigil
	BM45 103v B			S Agustini mat
			BN13060 188 B	?
	BM45 5v F			S Hieronimi Pres mat
			T35.4 37 M	Dom IV post oct Pasc mat
			T33.3 22v sn	Res Dni Dominicale
113v A				Adv ad non
			T35.4 10 L	Res Dni 8 mat
				Adv ad tert
	BM45 33 B			SS Petri et Pauli mat

AL

RS Iherusalem letare in adventum
Laetati sunt parvuli super (Prov 3:16)
VR Lignum vite est adpropinquantibus (Prov 3:18) 227v X

L[a]etor ego super eloquia (Ps 118:162)
VR Iniquos odio abui (Ps 118:113) 295v A

VR Magnificat anima mea (Lc 1:46)
VR Lapides pretiosi omnes muri tui
RS Quam pulchri sunt muri tui
VR Laqueus contritus est
RS Adiutorium nostrum in nomine Domini
VR Lauda et letare filia Syon
RS Filia Syon habitabo
VR Lauda Iherusalem Dominum conlauda
RS Iherusalem letare in adventum
RS Letare deserta quem commoraris
RS Quam speciosa facta es Iherusalem
VR Laudabo nomen Dei mei
RS Quesibi in oratione mea
VR Laudate celi et exultate
RS Montes filie Syon ramos
VR Laudate Dominum omnes gentes
RS Circuminspicit Deus montes
RS Fulget celum et terra
RS Videte magnalia Dei
VR Laudate pueri Dominum
RS Elegi et sanctificavi vos
VR Laudem dicite Domine Deo nostro
RS Letamini caeli quoniam misertus est
Laudemus viros gloriosos (Eccli 44:1,6,5)
VR Pertransierunt quasi nabes (Iob 9:26) 195v A

Lava a malitia cor tuum (Ier 4:14)

A30	Silos	*BN10110*	Other Sources	Liturgical Assignment
				SS Iusti et Pastoris mat
			Sal 166^{v} A	nocturnos Dom
	BM51 170^{v} A			"
			T35.4 43^{v} M	S Torquati mat

AL

VR Excutere de pulvere (Is 52:2)
Lavamini mundi estote (Is 1:16-17,19)
VR Si fuerint peccata (Is 1:18)
VR Legem pone mihi Domine
RS Alleluia deduc me per semitam
VR Levabi oculos meos ad montes
RS Auxilium meum a Domino
Libera me Domine et pone me (Iob 17:3)
VR Deus in nomine tuo salvum me fac (Ps 53:3) 278 B
Libera nos Deus Srahel (Esth 15:3)
VR Deus in nomine tuo salvos nos fac (Ps 53:3)

VR Liberabo te de manu pessimorum
RS Quum essem clausus in vestibulo
VR Liberasti virgam hereditatis
RS Memento congregationis tue
VR Lignum vite est adpropinquantibus
RS Laetati sunt parvuli super
VR Loquar et non timebo
RS Domine quantus ego sum
VR Loquuti sunt adversum me
RS Heu me quod peregrinatio mea
VR Loquutus est Dominus discipulis suis dicens ascendo
RS Modicum videbitis me
VR Locutus est Dominus Ihesus Christus discipulis suis dicens surgite
RS Qui mecum ayt manum
VR Magna erit claritas domus
RS Haec dicit Dominus domus mea
VR Magna est gloria eius
RS Gratias agimus Deo qui elegit te
VR Magnificat anima mea
RS Letor ego super eloquia
VR Magnificate Dominum mecum

A30	Silos	*BN10110*	Other Sources	Liturgical Assignment
		39 H		XLma 3 III sext
		9^{v} I		XLma 1 IV mat
	BM51 199^{v} B			uno defuncto mat
	BM51 197 B			defunct sacerd mat

AL

RS Inquirentes Dominum non deficient
Magnus Dominus noster alleluia (Ps 146:5-6)
VR Et sapientie eius (Ps 146:5) 291^{v} X

VR Magnus Dominus noster
RS Excelsus super omnes gentes
Magnus es Domine et preclarus (Iudith 16:16-17)
VR Fortissime magne (Ier 32:18-19)

VR Maledicta dies in qua natus sum
RS Pereat dies in qua natus sum
Mane consurgit homicida (Iob 24:14)
VR Oculus adulteri obserbat (Iob 24:15) 161^{v} A
Mane exaudies vocem meam (Ps 5:5)
VR Intellege clamorem meum (Ps 5:2-3)

Mane nobiscum Domine (Lc 24:29 ?)
VR Sperate in eum (Ps 61:9)

VR Mansueti autem
RS Coronavit sanctos suos
Manum suam aperuit (Prov 31:20,31)
VR Dedit esurienti panem (Ez 18:7) 245 A

VR Dispersit dedit pauperibus (Ps 111:9)

Manus tue Domine plamaberunt me (Iob 10:8-9)
VR Peregrinus ego sum in terra (Ps 38:13-14) 127 B
Me oportet minui illum autem (Io 3:30; 1:27)
VR Ponam spiritum meum in eo (Is 42:1) 214 B

A30	Silos	*BN10110*	Other Sources	Liturgical Assignment
				unoq Dom mat
			Sant 216^{v} X	nocturnos Dom
			T35.4 126 X	Dom IX quot mat
			T35.5 194^{v} H	fer II de oct Pasc
				Cena Dni mat
	3 169^{v} A			fer (I)II quot mat
			T33.3 31 sn	Res Dni
				S Martini Aep mat
	BM45 140 X			"
	5 76 A			"
			BN13060 152^{v} B	"
				XLma 3 III mat
				nat S Iohannis mat

	AL
VR Ecce agnus Dei (Io 1:29)	214 B
VR Media nocte clamor factus	
RS Simile est regnum	
VR Media nocte surgebam	
RS Per diem clamavi et nocte	
Meditatus sum nocte (Ps 76:7-8)	
VR Timor et tremor (Ps 54:6)	
Memento congregationis tue (Ps 73:2)	
VR Liberasti virgam hereditatis (Ps 73:2)	280 A
VR Memento nostri Domine in beneplacito	
RS Converte Domine luctum nostrum	
RS Memento nostri Domine qualiter	
Memento nostri Domine qualiter (?)	
VR Memento nostri Domine in beneplacito (Ps 105:4)	
VR Mici absit gloriari	
RS Vir Dei sanctus dum aspiceret in celum	
Militia est Domine vita mea (Iob 7:1,3,7)	
VR Dies mei velocius transierunt (Iob 7:6)	114 A
VR Minimus erit in mille	
RS Surget dux de tribu Iuda	
Mirifica Domine misericordias tuas (Ps 16:7)	
VR Custodi nos Domine ut pupillam (Ps 16:8)	

A30	Silos	*BN10110*	Other Sources	Liturgical Assignment
	BM45 18^{v} B			nat S Iohannis mat
			Sant 213 B	med noct
			Sal 151 B	"
	BM51 166^{v} B			med noct in XLme Dominicis
	3 59 A			defunctis mat
	BM51 195 A			defunct sacerd mat
	7 17 A			defunctis mat
	BM51 194 A			defunct sacerd mat
				XLma 1 VI mat
	BM51 174^{v} F		*Sant* 217 F	nocturnos fer IV
			Sal 153 F	"
			167 F	nocturnos Dom de XLme

AL

Miserator Domine miserere (?)
    VR Ad te lebamus oculos (Ps 122:1)

Miserator et misericors (Ps 102:8)
    VR Ecce sequimur (Dan 3:41-42)
Miserator et misericors (Ps 102:8-9)
    VR Non secundum peccata nostra (Ps 102:10) 255^{v} D
Misereatur nobis et benedicat nos (Ps 66:2)
    VR Inluminet Dominus vultum suum (Ps 66:2)

VR Miserebitur nostri Dominus et absterget
    RS Consolabitur nos Dominus Deus noster
VR Miserere Deus omnium quoniam omnia
    RS Miserere et parce nobis Domine
Miserere Domine contritis corde (Is 61:1-2)
    VR Convertere Domine aliquantulum (Ps 89:13)
Miserere Domine contritos corde (Is 61:1-2)
    VR Ostende nobis Domine misericordiam (Ps 84:8) 82^{v} B
Miserere et parce nobis Domine (?)
    VR Confusio et opprobrium (Dan 3:33-35)
Miserere et parce nobis Domine (?)
    VR Miserere Deus omnium quoniam omnia (Sap 11:24) 127 A

Miserere mei Domine et exaudi (Ps 4:2)
    VR Inclina Domine aurem tuam (Ps 16:6)

Miserere quia Deus es misericors (Eccli 2:13)
    VR Ad te levamus oculos (Ps 122:1)

A30	Silos	*BN10110*	Other Sources	Liturgical Assignment
			T33.3 21^{v} N	Adv
		41^{v} H		XLma 3 IV tert
				let de clade
	BM51 176 F		*Sant* 217^{v} F	nocturnos fer VI
			Sal 155^{v} F	"
			167 F	nocturnos Dom de XLme
		27^{v} H		XLma 2 V mat
				init anni mat
		31 H		XLma 2 VI tert
				XLma 3 III tert
			T33.3 7 M	de XLma ad tert
	BM51 173^{v} B		*Sant* 216^{v} B	nocturnos fer II
			Sal 169^{v} B	"
			175^{v} B	nocturnos in Lazaro
		34 H		XLma 2 sabb sext

	AL
Miserere quia Deus es misericors (Eccli 2:13)	
VR Ad te lebamus oculos (Ps 122:1)	126 A
Misericordia Domini facit (?)	
VR Flagellabit nos ab iniquitatibus (?)	
VR Misericordia mea et refugium meum	
RS Tu Domine susceptor meus es	
Misericordiam et iudicium cantabo (Ps 100:1)	
VR Perambulabam in innocentium (Ps 100:2)	294^{v} A
Miseriis afflictus sum (Ps 37:7-8)	
VR Quoniam sagitte tue (Ps 37:3)	
VR Misisti iram tuam	
RS Dextera tua Domine glorificata est	
VR Misit Deus misericordiam	
RS Misit Dominus angelum suum	
Misit Dominus angelum suum (Dan 6:22)	
VR Misit Deus misericordiam (Ps 56:4)	145^{v} B
Misit me Dominus sanare (Is 61:1)	
VR Spiritus Domini super me (Is 61:1)	212^{v} A
VR Misit me Dominus sanare	
RS Spiritus Domini super me	
Missus est a Deo angelus Gabriel (Lc 1:26-28,35)	
VR Spiritus Sanctus superveniet (Lc 1:35)	57^{v} B
VR Mitiga Domine omnem iram	
RS Averte Domine iram tuam	
Modicum videbitis me (Io 16:16,22)	
VR Loquutus est Dominus discipulis suis dicens ascendo (Io 20:17)	198^{v} A
VR Montes exultabunt ante faciem	
RS Alienigena non transibit	
Montes filie Syon ramos (Ez 36:8)	

A30	Silos	*BN10110*	Other Sources	Liturgical Assignment
				XLma 3 II sext
		35^{v} H		XLma 3 II tert
				nocturnos et mat ora diei Dom
	BM51 170^{v} A			nocturnos Dom
		50^{v} H		XLma 4 II mat
				XLma 5 II sext
	BM45 15 A			nat S Iohannis mat
88 B				S Mariae mat
				fer IV in vesp Ascension tert

	AL
VR Laudate celi et exultate (Is 49:13)	38 B
VR Gaudebunt campi (Ps 95:12)	38 B
VR Mortuus est Christus	
RS Gratias Domino Ihesu Christo	
VR Mulier fortis oblectat	
RS Iusti omnes quasi virens	
VR Multe tribulationes iustorum	
RS Beati qui sperant in Domino	
Multi Domine gemitus (Thr 1:22,21)	
VR Dissipaberunt itinera mea (Iob 30:13)	143 A
Multi Domine gemitus (Thr 1:22,21)	
VR Omnes qui glorificabant (Thr 1:8)	
VR Multi in nativitate eius	
RS Zaccarias sacerdos dum in ordinem	
Multiplicasti misericordiam (Ps 70:21-22)	
VR Quia hostendisti mici tribulationes (Ps 70:20)	48 B
	244^{v} sn
Multiplicati sunt super capillos (Ps 68:5-6)	
VR Amici mei adversum me (Ps 37:12)	150 A
Multiplicati sunt super capillos (Ps 68:5-6)	
VR Effunde Domine super inimicos (Ps 68:25)	
VR Multiplicati sunt super capillos	
RS Doctrina Domini aperuit	
RS Tradiderunt me in manus impiorum	
Muscipula paraberunt pedibus meis (Ps 56:7)	
VR Funes extenderunt continuatis (Ps 139:6)	148^{v} A

A30	Silos	*BN10110*	Other Sources	Liturgical Assignment
35^v *				post Dom I Adv mat
			T33.3 21^v sn	Adv
				post Dom I Adv mat
				Dom post vic mat
			T33.3 9^v sn	Tradit Dni tert Dominicale
		77^v H		XLma 5 III mat
				S Leocadie
62 B	*5* 53 B		*BN13060* 132 B	S Martini vigil
				XLma 5 VI tert
		73^v H		XLma 5 II mat
				XLma 5 V tert

* VR missing.

	AL
VR Nam et si ambulem	
RS Domine probasti cor meum	
Ne abstuleris Domine misericordiam (Dan 3:35,37)	
VR Abundaberunt iniquitates nostre (Or Man 10)	242^v B
VR Ne avertas faciem	
RS Non erubescant in me	
Ne elonges a me Domine (Ps 21:20,12)	
VR Quia tribulatio proxima est (Ps 21:12)	137^v G
VR Ne irascaris Domine	
RS Ne memor fueris Deus iniquitates	
Ne memineris Deus iniquitates (Ps 78:8)	
VR Adiuba nos Deus (Ps 78:9)	120^v B
Ne memor fueris Deus iniquitates (Ps 78:8)	
VR Ne irascaris Domine (Is 64:9)	279^v F
Ne nos dederis in opprobrium (Ier 14:21)	
VR Et nunc sequimur in toto corde (Dan 3:41)	128 B
Ne obduraveris aurem (?)	
VR Effunde framea et conclude (Ps 34:3)	
Ne tradas in perditione (Ps 73:19)	
VR Deus in nomine tuo salvos nos fac (Ps 53:3)	279^v A
VR Nec fortitudo lapidum	
RS Que est enim Domine fortitudo	
VR Noli timere dicit Dominus	
RS Haec dicit Dominus meus es tu	
VR Noli timere terra exulta	
RS Oculis nostris vidimus magnalia	
VR Nolite ante tempus	
RS Letamini gentes et exultate	

A30	Silos	*BN10110*	Other Sources	Liturgical Assignment
	BM45 156 B			let can tert
	3 15 G			XLma 4 IV mat conm corp defunct
				XLma 2 IV sext
	BM51 170 F *BM51* 196 F			defunctis mat nocturnos Dom defunct sacerd mat
				XLma 3 IV tert
		55 J		XLma 4 III mat
	BM51 194 B			defunctis mat defunct sacerd mat

AL

RS Salvator noster cito veniet
VR Nolite secundum fatiem iudicare
RS Iudicium rectum iudicate
Nolite timere vos scio quia (Mt 28:5-6)
VR Quid queritis viventem (Lc 24:5-6) 185v D
VR Angelus Domini dixit mulieribus (Mt 28:5)

VR Nomen eternum dabo
RS Sanctificabo te Iherusalem
VR Non erat ille lux
RS Fuit homo missus a Deo
Non erubescant in me (Ps 68:7-8)
VR Ne avertas faciem (Ps 68:18)
VR Non mentiemini invicem
RS Custodite vos a murmuratione
Non secundum peccata nostra (Ps 102:10,14)
VR Sicut miseretur pater (Ps 102:13-14)
VR Non secundum peccata nostra
RS Miserator et misericors
RS Peccavimus Domine et facti sumus
RS Propicius esto iniquitatibus
RS Propicius esto pecatis
VR Non sum dignus ut curi filius meus
RS Surgam et ibo ad patrem
Non timebo mala Domine (Ps 22:4)
VR Virga tua et baculus tuus (Ps 22:4)

Nos omnes ambulabimus (Mich 4:5,7-8)
VR Et tu Bethlem domus Efrata (Mich 5:2) 59v B
VR Notam fecisti
RS Tu es Deus qui facis

A30	Silos	*BN10110*	Other Sources	Liturgical Assignment
				Res Dni 14 mat
			T35.4 13 L	"
		52^{v} H		XLma 4 II tert
		44^{v} J		XLma 3 V sext
	BM51 175 C		*Sant* 217 C	nocturnos fer IV
			Sal 153 C	"
			168 C	nocturnos Dom II XLme
94 B				S Mariae mat

	AL
Notus fuisti Domine parvulis (Sap 11:10-11)	
VR Quum intenderes Domine parvulos (?)	228v A
VR Nu[m](n)quid adbrebiata es	
RS Nunquid non valet	
Nu[m](n)quid in eternum continebis (Is 64:12,1)	
VR Facti sumus quasi in principio (Is 63:19)	
Nu[m](n)quid in eternum repellet (Ps 76:8-10)	
VR Converte nos Deus salutaris noster (Ps 84:5-6)	
Nu[m](n)quid non valet (Is 59:1-2)	
VR Nunquid adbrebiata es (Is 59:1)	
VR Numquid oculi carnei sunt	
RS Deus cuius ire nemo resistere	
RS Domine numquid sicut dies	
Nunc Domine dabis populo tuo (Lc 2:29-32)	
VR Iucunditatem fecisti (Ps 118:65)	80 F
Nunc venit in me dolor (Iob 16:8-9)	
VR Defecerunt pre lacrimis (Thr 2:11)	
VR O bona crux	
RS Iam securus et gaudens venio	
O vos omnes qui pertransitis (Thr 1:12)	
VR Circumdederunt me inimici (Ps 117:12)	
Obserbabitis diem istum legitimum (Ex 12:24 ?)	
VR Dominus regnabit a ligno (Ps 95:10)	191 B
VR Occurrite ei virgines sapientissime	
RS Filie Iherusalem si inveneritis	
Oculi mei semper ad Dominum (Ps 24:15)	
VR Cantabo Domino (Ps 103:33)	294v sn
Oculis nostris vidimus magnalia (?)	

A30	Silos	*BN10110*	Other Sources	Liturgical Assignment
				SS Iusti et Pastoris mat
		47 H		XLma 3 VI tert
		44 H		XLma 3 V tert
		47v J		XLma 3 VI sext
150 F				Circumcis Dni mat
		83bis H		XLma 5 IV sext
		92v H		XLma 5 sabb tert
			T35.4 28v L	Dom II post oct Pasc mat
				nocturnos et mat ora diei Dom
			T35.4 152v M	Dom XVI quot mat

	AL
VR Noli timere terra exulta (Ioel 2:21)	292 A
VR Oculis nostris vidimus magnalia	
RS Deus noster magnus est	
VR Oculus adulteri obserbat	
RS Mane consurgit homicida	
VR Odio abuistis in porta	
RS Cognovi omnia peccata vestra	
VR Oleum recondite in vasis	
RS Acceperunt prudentes oleum	
RS Clamor factus est	
Omnes adversarii mei persecuti (Iob 19:22-26)	
VR Dominus Deus aperuit (Is 50:5)	
Omnes adversarii mei persequuti (Iob 19:22-26)	
VR Scio quod redemptor meus vivat (Iob 19:25-26)	142 D
Omnes amici mei inluserunt (Abd 7; Ps 40:10)	
VR Abominati sunt me consiliari (Iob 19:19)	146^{v} A
Omnes amici mei inluserunt (Abd 7; Ps 40:10)	
VR Verbum iniquum (Ps 40:9-10)	
Omnes amici mei obliti sunt (Ier 30:14; Iob 19:19)	
VR Qui edebat panes (Ps 40:10-11)	
VR Omnes gentes plaudete manibus	
RS Letamini in Domino Deo vestro	
RS Sanctificamini odie	
RS Splendet hodie celum	
RS Universus populus ascendite	
RS Venientes de regione	
VR Omnes in sanguine	
RS Congregati sunt adversus	
Omnes iusti regem in decore (Is 33:17; 65:14)	
VR Omnes iusti videbunt (Is 33:20)	196 A
VR Omnes iusti videbunt	
RS Omnes iusti regem in decore	
Omnes persequentes me tu (?)	

A30	Silos	*BN10110*	Other Sources	Liturgical Assignment
				unoq Dom mat
		105 H		XLma 6 IV mat
				XLma 4 sabb tert
				XLma 5 III sext
		60^{v} I		XLma 4 IV tert
		86 K		XLma 5 V tert
			T35.4 45 L	S Torquati mat

	AL
VR Induc super eos diem (Ier 17:18)	139v B
VR Omnes qui glorificabant	
RS Multi Domine gemitus	
Omnes qui lugebatis (Ioel 2:23)	
VR Precipitabit Dominus mortem (Is 25:8)	46v B
Omnes qui videbant me (Ps 21:8)	
VR Circumdederunt me canes multi (Ps 21:17)	136 B
VR Omnes qui videbant me	
RS Propter te Domine sustinui	
VR Omnes vias meas	
RS H[a]ec dicit Dominus afflixi populum	
Omnibus querentibus gratiam (?)	
VR Omnis enim qui petit (Mt 7:8)	293v D
VR Omnis enim qui petit	
RS Omnibus querentibus gratiam	
Omnis homo qui audit verba mea (Mt 7:24-25)	
VR Ipse super maria (Ps 23:2)	264 B
Omnis terra letabitur (Is 14:1 ?)	
VR Qui fecit omnia (Ier 10:16)	62v A
Ora Dominum ante lucem (?)	
VR Si simplex fueris (Iob 1:1)	
Oranti in loco isto (III Reg 8:36)	
VR Respice in servos tuos (Ps 89:16)	262v B
Orabit Salomon dicens (III Reg 8:22-23,25; II Par 6:20)	

A30	Silos	*BN10110*	Other Sources	Liturgical Assignment
				XLma 4 V sext
56 B				post Dom III Adv mat
				XLma 4 III tert
				unoq Dom mat
	BM51 170^{v} B			nocturnos Dom
	3 153^{v} B			de quot mat
			T35.4 108 L	Dom V quot mat
				sacr bas mat
102 *				post Dom IV Adv mat
			Sant 213 A	med noct
			Sal 160 A	"
				sacr bas mat

* VR missing.

	AL
VR Si celum et celi celorum (II Par 6:18-19)	262 B
Orietur in tenebris (Is 58:10)	
VR Et eritis sicut ortus (Is 58:11)	
VR Et replebit splendoribus (Is 58:11)	
VR Os iusti meditabitur	
RS De ore iusti procedet	
RS Felix qui spiritu contribulato	
RS Iunior fui et senui	
Ostende in me Domine bonitatem (?)	
VR Tu es Deus salbator meus (Ps 24:5)	
VR Ostende nobis Domine misericordiam	
RS Miserere Domine contritos corde	
Ostendit Dominus sanctis suis (?)	
VR Percussit Dominus petram (Ps 77:20)	
Oves mee et oves gregis mei (Ez 34:15)	
VR Dabo legem meam (Ier 31:33)	
Oves mee et oves gregis mei (Ez 34:15)	
VR Et alias abeo oves (Io 10:16)	152 B
II Vos estis genus (I Petr 2:9)	152 sn
III Ego sum pastor (Io 10:11)	152 sn
Pacem donet Dominus (II Mach 1:5 ?)	
VR Inluminet Dominus vultum suum (Ps 66:2)	293v A
Pande manum tuam super servos (?)	
VR Deus in nomine tuo salvos nos fac (Ps 53:3)	
VR Parate viam Domino rectus	
RS Ecce dies Domini veniet et quiescere	
Parce Domine nostris peccatis (IV Esd 8:45 ?)	

A30	Silos	*BN10110*	Other Sources	Liturgical Assignment
				sacr bas mat
	3 59 C?			defunctis mat
	7 16^{v} sn			"
	BM51 197 B			defunct sacerd mat
			T35.4 156^{v} L	Dom XVII quot mat
			T33.3 12^{v} N	sanctis tert
			T35.5 111 J	Ramos mat
				Ramos mat
				"
				"
				unoq Dom mat
			T35.4 130 L	Dom X quot mat
		29 H		XLma 2 V sext

	AL
VR Domine miserere nostri te enim (Is 33:2)	127 D
Parce Domine quia tua sunt omnia (Sap 11:27; 12:1-2)	
VR Quoniam tu flagellas et salvas (Tob 13:2)	126 A
VR Pastores erant in regione eadem	
RS Angelus Domini loquutus est	
Patientiam habe in me (Mt 18:26; Gen 3:19)	
VR Tu formasti me (Ps 138:5)	
VR Patres nostri peccaberunt	
RS Domine indulge peccatis	
VR Pauperem nolite calumniare	
RS Iudicium rectum iudicate	
Peccata nostra dominantur (II Esd 9:37)	
VR Pecavimus cum patribus (Ps 105:6)	
VR Pecata nostra redundaberunt	
RS Circumdederunt nos mala	
VR Peccavi Domine peccavi	
RS Usquequo Domine non parcis	
VR Peccavimus cum patribus	
RS Abundaberunt iniquitates nostre	
RS Clamor noster ad te	
RS Iniquitates nostre et peccata	
RS Inter vestibolum et altare	
RS Peccata nostra dominantur	
RS Peccavimus Domine miserere nobis	
RS Peccavimus tibi Domine ideo	
RS Qui respicit in terra	
Peccavimus Domine et facti sumus (Is 64:6-10)	
VR Non secundum peccata nostra (Ps 102:10)	121^{v} B
Peccavimus Domine miserere nobis (Iob 7:20,16)	
VR Peccabimus cum patribus (Ps 105:6)	242^{v} sn
VR Peccavimus enim inique egimus	
RS Iniquitates nostre et peccata	

A30	Silos	*BN10110*	Other Sources	Liturgical Assignment
				XLma 3 III sext
	BM45 154 B			let can sext
				XLma 3 II tert
	4 104^{v} B		*A56* 39^{v} B	conm pres
		31^{v} H		XLma 2 VI sext
				XLma 2 VI tert
				let can sext

AL

VR Peccavimus in conspectu
    RS Ve nobis quoniam peccabimus
Peccavimus iniquitates fecimus (Dan 9:15-17)
    VR Convertere Domine aliquantulum (Ps 89:13) 120^{v} A
Pecavimus tibi Deus fac misericordiam (?)
    VR Quare in perpetuum oblibisceris (Thr 5:20)
Peccavimus tibi Domine ideo (?)
    VR Peccabimus cum patribus (Ps 105:6) 255^{v} sn
Pepercit Dominus populo suo (Ioel 2:18,21-23)
    VR Si volueritis et audieritis (Is 1:19) 290 B

    VR Audi popule meus vocem meam (Deut 28:1,11)

Per diem clamavi et nocte (Ps 87:2-3)
    VR Media nocte surgebam (Ps 118:62)

    VR Clamavi ad te (Ps 87:10)

VR Per vicos et plateas
    RS Invocabi proximum mici
VR Perambulabam in innocentium
    RS Misericordiam et iudicium cantabo
VR Percussit Dominus petram
    RS Ostendit Dominus sanctis suis
Pereat dies in qua natus sum (Iob 3:3-4)
    VR Maledicta dies in qua natus sum (Iob 3:3) 109^{v} B
VR Peregrinus ego sum in terra
    RS Manus tue Domine plamaberunt me
VR Perfecti estote exortamini
    RS [H]Abete fidutium
Perfectum est templum (III Reg 8:4-6)
    VR Venerunt cuncti senes (III Reg 8:3) 261^{v} A

A30	Silos	*BN10110*	Other Sources	Liturgical Assignment
				XLma 2 IV tert
		33 K		XLma 2 sabb tert
				let de clade
				unoq Dom mat
	6 87 B			Dom IV quot mat
			T35.4 104 L	"
			Sant 212 A	med noct
			Sal 149^{v} A	med noct Dom
	BM51 167 A			med noct Dom XLme
			T35.4 121^{v} M	Dom VIII quot mat
				XLma 1 II mat
				sacr bas mat

AL

VR Pertransierunt quasi nabes
    RS Laudemus viros gloriosos
Placabilis esto Domine (?)
    VR Deus in nomine tuo salvos nos fac (Ps 53:3)
VR Plorans plorabit in nocte
    RS Vox in rama audita est
VR Ponam iudicium in pondere
    RS Ecce Dominus in fortitudine
VR Ponam sanctuarium meum
    RS Haec dicit Dominus deducam imbrem
VR Ponam spiritum meum in eo
    RS Me oportet minui illum autem
Ponite verba Domini in cordibus (Deut 11:18-19)
    VR Adtende popule meus (Ps 77:1) 105 B

Posuerunt inimici mei in angustia (Iob 19:19 ?)
    VR Etenim homo pacis (Ps 40:10)
VR Posuerunt me in lacu
    RS Animam meam dilectam tradidi
VR Posuerunt peccatores
    RS Quod sunt dies servi tui
VR Precipitabit Dominus mortem
    RS Omnes qui lugebatis
Principes regni gentium stabunt (Dan 10:13-14,16,19)
    VR Quum Christus apparuerit vita (Col 3:4) 44v B

Principium sapientie Dei possiderunt (Prov 4:7)
    VR Dedit Dominus capitibus (Prov 4:9) 228 A

Pro defunctis offerimus (?)
    VR Requiem eternam (IV Esd 2:34,35)
Probasti nos Deus igne (Ps 65:10-12)
    VR Salvasti nos ex affligentibus nos (Ps 43:8) 95 B

A30	Silos	*BN10110*	Other Sources	Liturgical Assignment
		21^v J		XLma 2 II sext
227^v B				Dom ante intr XLme mat
		68^v sn		XLma 4 VI tert
52^v B			*BN11556* recto B	post Dom II Adv mat
				SS Iusti et Pastoris mat
	7 18^v sn			defunctis mat
199^v B				S Fructuosi Aep mat

	AL
Propitiare Domine populo tuo (?)	
VR Deus virtutum converte nunc (Ps 79:15)	242 B
Propicius esto iniquitatibus (Ps 102:3-4)	
VR Non secundum peccata nostra (Ps 102:10)	
Propitius esto peccatis (Ps 78:9; 102:3-4)	
VR Adiuba nos Deus (Ps 78:9)	122 B
Propicius esto pecatis (Ps 78:9)	
VR Non secundum pecata nostra (Ps 102:10)	
VR Propter dilectum meum Iulianum	
RS Iuliani dilecti mei fides hec	
VR Propter fratres meos et proximos	
RS (H)ierusalem benedic Domino saeculorum	
Propter honorem nominis (?)	
VR Effuderunt sanguinem eorum (Ps 78:3)	93 B
VR Clamaverunt iusti et Dominus (Ps 33:18)	93 B
VR Steterunt contra hostes (Sap 11:3)	
VR Propter innocentiam autem	
RS In hoc cognobi quoniam voluisti	
VR Propter nomen tuum Domine	
RS De manu inferni Deus libera	
Propter peccata nostra venerunt (Dan 3:28,29,35)	
VR Et nunc sequimur (Dan 3:41)	123v B
Propter peccata nostra venerunt (Dan 3:28,29,35)	
VR Iustus es Domine (Dan 3:27,30,29)	
Propter Syon non tacebo alleluia (Is 62:1)	
VR Quis reminiscimini Dominum (Is 62:6-7)	39 A
Propter te Domine sustinui (Ps 68:8-10,15)	
VR Omnes qui videbant me (Ps 21:8)	150 A
VR Propter veritatem et mansuetudinem	

A30	Silos	*BN10110*	Other Sources	Liturgical Assignment
				let can sext
		42 H		XLma 3 IV sext
				XLma 2 VI sext
	BM51 190^{v} B			infirmis mat
	7 7 B			"
	BM45 157 B			let can mat
		20 H		XLma 1 sabb sext
				Dom post Allis Infant mat
				"
186 A				"
				XLma 2 sabb tert
		43 H		XLma 3 V mat
38^{v} B				S Saturnini Aep mat
				XLma 5 VI tert

AL

RS Egredere inter lilia obbaca
VR Protector tuus ego sum
RS Haec dicit Dominus meus es tu
VR Psallite Deo nostro in cithara
RS In tubis ductilibus
VR Publicanus a longe
RS Dominus omnipotens audibit vocem
VR Putredini dixi pater
RS Dies mei transierunt
RS Induta est caro mea putredine
Qu[a]e est enim Domine fortitudo (Iob 6:11)
VR Nec fortitudo lapidum (Iob 6:12)

Qu[a]erite Dominum dum inveniri (Is 55:6-7)
VR Convertatur unusquisque (Ion 3:8)
Qu[a]erite Dominum dum inveniri (Is 55:6-7)
VR Querite Dominum et confortamini (Ps 104:4) — 114^{v} A
VR Qu[a]erite Dominum dum inveniri
RS Querite me in angustia
VR Qu[a]erite Dominum et confortamini
RS Querite Dominum dum inveniri
Qu[a]erite me in angustia (?)
VR Querite Dominum dum inveniri (Is 55:6)
Qu[a]erite me in angustia (?)
VR Scindite corda vestra (Ioel 2:13) — 113^{v} B
Qu[a]esibi in oratione mea (Eccli 51:18-20)
VR Laudabo nomen Dei mei (Ps 68:31) — 106^{v} B
Quam admirabile est nomen tuum (Ps 8:2)
VR Ex ore infantium et lactantium (Ps 8:3)

A30	Silos	*BN10110*	Other Sources	Liturgical Assignment
			Sant 224^{v} X	post nocturnos
	BM51 171 X			nocturnos Dom de XLme
		17 I		XLma 1 VI tert
				XLma 1 VI sext
		32^{v} I		XLma 2 sabb mat
				XLma 1 V sext
				Carnes Toll mat
	BM51 174^{v} A		*Sant* 217 A	nocturnos fer III
			Sal 152^{v} A	"
			169^{v} A	nocturnos in Lazaro

	AL
VR Quam amabilia sunt tabernacula tua	
RS Domine Deus virtutum beatus	
Quam bone domus tuae Iacob (Num 24:5-6)	
VR Ecce nunc benedicite Dominum (Ps 133:1)	264v sn
VR Quam pulcra es amica mea	
RS Filie Iherusalem audite me	
Quam pulchri sunt muri tui (?)	
VR Lapides pretiosi omnes muri tui (Tob 13:21)	264v B
Quam speciosa facta es Iherusalem (?)	
VR Lauda Iherusalem Dominum (Ps 147:1)	264 sn
VR Quare adversus est populus iste	
RS Adtendi et abscultabi	
Quare data est misero lux (Iob 3:20)	
VR Brebes dies hominum (Iob 14:5)	112 A
VR Quare de vulva egressus sum	
RS Quare non in vulva mortuus sum	
VR Quare in perpetuum oblibisceris	
RS Pecavimus tibi Deus fac misericordiam	
Quare non in vulva mortuus sum (Iob 3:11,13)	
VR Quare de vulva egressus sum (Iob 10:18; Ps 9:35)	111 B
Quare non tollis peccatum meum (Iob 7:21)	
VR Vide humilitatem (Ps 24:18)	119v B
Quare persequimini me (Iob 19:22-25)	
VR Delectatum est cor meum (Ps 15:9)	147v B
Quare tristis es anima mea (Ps 41:6)	
VR A me ipso anima mea (Ps 41:7)	141v F
Quare tristis es anima mea (Ps 41:6)	
VR Ingrediar in locum (Ps 41:5)	
VR Quare tristis es anima mea	
RS Anima mea cessa iam peccare	
VR Quasi rupto muro	
RS Circumdederunt me inimici	

A30	Silos	*BN10110*	Other Sources	Liturgical Assignment
				sacr bas mat
				sacr bas mat
				sacr bas mat
20 A				S Cecilie mat
				XLma 1 IV mat
				XLma 1 III mat
				XLma 2 III mat
				XLma 5 IV tert
				XLma 4 sabb mat
		69 I		XLma 4 VI sext

AL

VR Qui custodiebant animam meam
RS Congregati sunt adversus
VR Qui das salutem regibus
RS Congrega Domine dispersionem nostram
Qui dat dolorem (?)
VR Quoniam ipse flagellat (Tob 13:2)
VR Qui descendit ipse est
RS Iherusalem civitas sancta exaltabitur
Qui diligit me diligitur (Io 14:21)
VR Et Pater diligit eum (Io 14:23) — 76v A

IT Auxiliabo puero meo (Is 42:1) — 76v sn
Qui diligunt te Domine sicut sol (Iud 5:31)
VR Beati omnes qui timent (Ps 127:1) — 249 A
Qui edebat panes (Ps 40:10-11)
VR Ecce tradidit me (Iob 19:19)
VR Qui edebat panes
RS Omnes amici mei obliti sunt
VR Qui fecit omnia
RS Omnis terra letabitur
Qui mecum ait manu (Mt 26:23-24)
VR Filius quidem hominis (Mt 26:24) — 162 F
Qui mecum ayt manum (Mt 26:23-24)
VR Locutus est Dominus Ihesus Christus discipulis suis dicens surgite (Mt 26:46)
Qui non aversi sunt a Domino (Eccli 46:13-15)
VR Sapientiam eorum enarrent (Eccli 44:15) — 279 B

VR Qui operit celum nubibus
RS [A]Edificabit Dominus in celo ascensum
RS Circuminspicit Deus montes
VR Qui regis Israhel
RS Esto nobis Domine

A30	Silos	*BN10110*	Other Sources	Liturgical Assignment
	7 8^{v} sn			infirmis mat
139 A				S Ioanni Apost mat
139 A				"
				SS general mat
		112^{v} H		XLma 6 V tert
				Cena Dni tert
		110^{v} H		XLma 6 V mat
	7 29 B			defunct aep mat
	BM51 192^{v} B			defunct sacerd mat

AL

RS Qui sedes super tronum
Qui respicis in terram (Ps 103:32)
VR Ad te levamus oculos (Ps 122:1)
VR Peccavimus cum patribus (Ps 105:6)

Qui sedes super tronum (Ps 9:5,10)
VR Qui regis Israhel (Ps 79:2)
Qui sedes super thronum (Ps 9:5,10)
VR Tibi derelictus est pauper (Ps 9:35) 203v E

VR Qui sunt isti qui ut nubes
RS Vincula sanctorum iam solute sunt
VR Quia hostendisti mici tribulationes
RS Multiplicasti misericordiam
VR Quia tribulatio proxima est
RS Ne elonges a me Domine
Quid gloriaris in malitia (Ps 51:3-5)
VR Dilexisti malitiam (Ps 51:5) 147v A
VR Quid queritis viventem
RS Nolite timere vos scio quia
VR Quid retribuam Domino
RS Aput te laus mea est alleluia
RS Super acerbum lapidum
VR Quiescite agere
RS Ecce dies Domini magne
VR Quis est iste rex glorie
RS Curbati sunt celi dum calcaret
RS Suscipiamus regnum Dei nostri
Quis michi det (Iob 6:8,6)

A30	Silos	*BN10110*	Other Sources	Liturgical Assignment
	BM51 176^{v} B			nocturnos sabb
			Sant 218 B	nocturnos sabb
			Sal 157 B	"
			168 B	nocturnos Dom II XLme
		24^{v} I		XLma 2 III sext
				post Dom post Ascension fer II mat
				XLma 5 IV mat

VR Quis michi tribuat (Iob 6:8-10)

VR Quis michi tribuat
    RS Quis michi det
VR Quis reminiscimini Dominum
    RS Propter Syon non tacebo alleluia
Quis te consolabitur virgo (Thr 2:13,19)
    VR Deduc quasi torrentem (Thr 2:18)

VR Quisquis vestrum est sapiens
    RS Elegit Dominus virum de tribu Iuda
VR Quocumque ligaberis super terram
    RS Tu es Petrus
VR Quod ad humorem
    RS Alleluia erit tamquam
VR Quod factum est in ipso
    RS In principio erat verbum
VR Quod Ihesus mortuus est
    RS Reconciliati sumus Deo per mortem
Quod sunt dies servi tui (Ps 118:84)
    VR Posuerunt peccatores (Ps 118:110)
VR Quomodo dilexi legem tuam
    RS Domine probasti cor meum
    RS Funes peccatorum circumplexe
VR Quoniam anima mea
    RS Humiliatus sum et curvatus
VR Quoniam elevata est
    RS Deus Pater parvulorum tuorum
VR Quoniam ipse flagellat
    RS Qui dat dolorem
VR Quoniam observaberunt iudicium
    RS Sapientia Domini intelexerunt

A30	Silos	*BN10110*	Other Sources	Liturgical Assignment
			Sant 224 X	post nocturnos
	BM51 171 X			nocturnos Dom de XLme
			T35.5 39 H	Dom III XLmae mat
		56 I		XLma 4 III tert

AL

VR Quoniam pater meus
    RS Iherusalem civitas sancta suscipe me
VR Quoniam prevenisti eos (Ps 20:4)
    RS . . . tui Domine qui catena
VR Quoniam sagitte Domini
    RS Si adprenderetur peccata mea
VR Quoniam sagitte tue
    RS Miseriis afflictus sum
VR Quoniam tu flagellas et salvas
    RS Parce Domine quia tua sunt omnia
VR Quoniam turbata sunt ossa mea
    RS Infirmus sum sana me Domine
VR Quum ceciderit iustus
    RS Ecce vir impius graditur
VR Quum Christus apparuerit vita
    RS Principes regni gentium stabunt
Quum essem clausus in vestibulo (Ier 39:15,17-18)
    VR Liverabo te de manu pessimorum (Ier 39:17) 236 A

VR Quum intenderes Domine parvulos
    RS Notus fuisti Domine parvulis
VR Quum mici molesti essent
    RS Animam meam dilectam tradidi
VR Quum sanare vellem Israhel
    RS Haec dicit Dominus prevaricati sunt
Quumque Iulianus letaretur (Passio)
    VR A parte regis clamabatur (Passio) 89v B
Reconciliati sumus Deo per mortem (Rom 5:10-11)
    VR Quod Ihesus mortuus est (Rom 6:10) 189v A

Recordamini qualiter (Lc 24:6-7)
    VR Dixit Ihesus discipulis suis hec sunt (Lc 24:44) 185 E

VR Recordatus sum tui miserans

A30	Silos	*BN10110*	Other Sources	Liturgical Assignment
10^v A				S Romani mat
	BM45 115^v A			decoll S Iohannis mat
178^v sn				S Iuliani mat
			T35.4 24^v L	Dom I post oct Pasc mat
			T35.4 12^v L	Res Dni 13 mat

	AL
RS Haec dicit Dominus dilectione	
VR Redemit enim Deus Iacob	
RS Deus omnipotens suscitabit nobis	
Regem Dominum exercituum (Is 6:5-7)	
VR Aspiciebam in nubibus celi (Dan 7:13)	66 B
VR Reges Tarsis et insule	
RS Iherusalem ecce apparuit	
RS Sanctificate diem festum	
Regnabit Dominus Deus noster (Apoc 19:6-7)	
VR Venite exultemus (Ps 94:1)	176 A
Repleatur os meum Deus (Ps 70:8)	
VR Vide humilitatem (Ps 24:18)	295 B
VR Replevit me amaritudinibus	
RS Conclusit inimicus vias meas	
Requiem eternam (IV Esd 2:34,35)	
VR Aperiat tibi (?)	
VR Requiem eternam	
RS Pro defunctis offerimus	
VR Respice de celo et vide	
RS Resuscita Domine plantationem	
VR Respice in servos tuos	
RS Oranti in loco isto	
RS Veni clementissime Domine succurre	
Resuscita Domine plantationem (?)	
VR Respice de celo et vide (Ps 79:15)	53v B
VR Revertere Israhel ad Dominum	
RS Haec dicit Dominus civitates tuae Iudae	
VR Saccum consui super caput	

A30	Silos	*BN10110*	Other Sources	Liturgical Assignment
				Adv ad tert
				Paschae mat
			T33.3 22 M	de Res Dni
	BM51 171 B		*Sant* 216 B	nocturnos Dom
			Sal 165^{v} B	"
	4 87^{v} A			fin hominis die
	4 106 A			super sepulcrum
79^{v} B				post Dom III Adv mat

AL

RS Si dixero consolabitur
VR Sacerdos qui de ore suo
RS Labia sacerdotis custodiunt
Sacerdotes et levite principes (II Par 30:21-27)
VR Gaudete in Domino semper (Phi 4:4) — 263v B
VR Sacerdotes tui Domine
RS Habeant Domine finem peccata nostra
Sagitta vulnerans lingua inimici (Ier 9:8)
VR Annuit oculo digito loquitur (Prov 6:13-14) — 136v D
Salus nostra in manu tua (Gen 47:25)
VR Ad te lebamus oculos (Ps 122:1) — 204v B

VR Salva plebem tuam
RS Ut quid reppulisti nos Deus
VR Salvabit Dominus
RS Ecce Dominus veniet et omnes
VR Salvasti nos ex affligentibus nos
RS Probasti nos Deus igne
Salvator noster cito veniet (?)
VR Nolite ante tempus (I Cor 4:5) — 67 sn
VR Salve crux que sine
RS Iam securus et gaudens venio
Salvos fecit iustos (?)
VR Et clamaberunt ad Dominum (Ps 106:6)
Salvus ero Domine (?)
VR Domine non sum dignus (Mt 8:8)

Salvus ero Domine (?)
VR Domine non sum dignus (Mt 8:8) — 276v C

Sana nos Domine (Ps 6:3-4)
VR Deus in nomine tuo salvos nos fac (Ps 53:3) — 275v A
VR Sancti amabiles et decori

A30	Silos	*BN10110*	Other Sources	Liturgical Assignment
				sacr bas mat
				XLma 4 III sext
				let apost fer V mat
	BM45 155^{v} E			let can mat
				Adv ad tert
	BM45 39 B			S Xristofori mat
			T33.3 30^{v} L	ordo ad non
				uno infirmo mat
	3 175^{v} C			quot fer V mat
	BM51 189 A			infirmis mat

	AL
RS Isti sunt sancti qui pro testamento	
Sancti in terram suam (Is 61:7-8)	
VR Et dabo opus eorum (Is 61:8)	75 A
VR Sancti in terram suam	
RS Hii ostenderunt cerimonias populo	
RS Sancti qui iustitias erudiunt	
Sancti iter fecerunt (Sap 11:2-4)	
VR Descendit cum illis (Sap 10:13-14)	240 A
Sancti qui certamen habuerunt (?)	
VR Vidi in celo turbam magnam (Apoc 7:9)	99^{v} B
VR Vidi in Syon turbam (Apoc 7:9-10)	
Sancti qui iustitias erudiunt (Dan 12:3)	
VR Sancti in terram suam (Is 61:7)	248^{v} B
Sancti qui per fidem vicerunt (Heb 11:33-34)	
VR Steterunt contra hostes (Sap 11:3)	94^{v} A
VR Sancti qui sperant in Domino	
RS Suscipiunt sancti securi	
Sanctificabo te Iherusalem (IV Esd 2:10,12)	
VR Nomen eternum dabo (Apoc 2:17 ?)	263^{v} sn
Sanctificamini odie (Ex 19:15)	
VR Omnes gentes plaudete manibus (Ps 46:2)	67^{v} A
Sanctificate diem festum (Ier 17:24-26)	
VR Reges Tarsis et insule (Ps 71:10)	87 B
Sanctificavit rex templum (II Par 1:6,8; 6:17, 20,26-27)	
VR Stetit rex ante altare (III Reg 8:22)	260^{v} B
VR Si quis cognoberit (III Reg 8:38)	260^{v} B
Sanctis ab altissimo conceditur (?)	
VR Adduxit eos in montem (Ps 77:54)	101^{v} B
Sanctis ab altissimo dicebitur (Mt 25:34,36)	

A30	Silos	*BN10110*	Other Sources	Liturgical Assignment
				S Eugeniae mat
				SS Servandi et Germani mat
				S Babile Aep mat
	3 109^{v} B			de sanctis mat
				SS general mat
197 A				S Fructuosi Aep mat
				sacr bas mat
113^{v} *				vesp Nat Dni tert
169^{v} *				Apparit Dni mat
				sacr bas mat
				"
219 B				S Dorote mat

* VR missing.

	AL
VR Beati qui persecutionem (Mt 5:10)	219 A
VR Esuribi et dedistis (Mt 25:35)	
Sanguis innocens et iustus (?)	
VR Effuderunt sanguinem eorum (Ps 78:3)	91v B
Sapientia Dei super lapides (?)	
VR Deus sapientia fundabit (Prov 3:19)	292v B
Sapientia Domini intelexerunt (Prov 7:4; 3:4)	
VR Quoniam observaberunt iudicium (Prov 2:9)	227 X
Sapientia replebit os eius (?)	
VR Dedit ei Dominus sapientiam (?)	245v B
VR Sapientiam eorum enarrent	
RS Qui non aversi sunt a Domino	
Sapientiam suam Deus revelabit (?)	
VR Adtendite ad me popule (Is 51:4)	55v A
Satiabi omnem sitientem (Ier 31:25-26)	
VR Ego dormibi et quiebi (Ps 3:6)	181 B
VR Scindite corda vestra	
RS Querite me in angustia	
Scio Domine quia morti (Iob 30:23-24)	
VR Si ascendero in celum (Ps 138:8)	156 D
Scio Domine quia nichil in terra (Iob 5:6-7)	
VR Ego vero deprecabor (Iob 5:8)	
VR Scio quod redemptor meus vivat	
RS Omnes adversarii mei persequuti	
VR Secundum divitias gratie	

A30	Silos	*BN10110*	Other Sources	Liturgical Assignment
				SS Simonis et Iud Apost mat
	3 109 A			de sanctis mat
				Allis Infant mat
				unoq Dom mat
	6 126 B			Dom VIII quot mat
			T35.4 133^{v} L	Dom XI quot mat
	BM45 69^{v} X			SS Iusti et Pastoris mat
	BM45 84 B			S Martini Aep mat
84^{v} A				post Dom IV Adv mat
			T35.4 7 L	Res Dni 3 mat
				XLma 6 II sext
			Sant 224 B	post nocturnos
	BM51 171 B			nocturnos Dom de XLme

AL

RS Elegit eos Deus ante mundi
VR Secundum multitudinem miserationum tuarum
RS Exaudi me Domine quoniam benigna est
VR Secundum multitudinem misericordie
RS Convertere Domine Deus animas
VR Sed exibete vosmedipsos
RS Ecce nunc tempus acceptavile
VR Sed in omni oratione
RS Gaudete in Domino semper
Sedet rex in trono (III Reg 2:12; 8:56)
VR Dominus regnabit decorem (Ps 92:1) 86 B
Servi Dei benedicite (Dan 3:85)
VR ?

VR Servite Domino in timore
RS Adprendite disciplina nequando
VR Sessionem eorum
RS Conclusit vias meas inimicus
Si adprenderentur peccata mea (Iob 6:2-3)
VR Quoniam sagitte Domini (Iob 6:4)

Si affiget homo Deum (Mal 3:8)
VR Vos maledicti estis (Mal 3:9) 159 A
Si ambulaverimus in viis (?)
VR Benedictus Dominus qui magnus (Tob 13:1-2)
VR Si ascendero in celum
RS Scio Domine quia morti
Si celum et celi celorum (II Par 6:18-19)
VR Fiat auris tua (II Esd 1:6) 262v B
VR Si celum et celi celorum
RS Oravit Salomon dicens
Si consurrexistis Christo (Rom 6:8-9)

A30	Silos	*BN10110*	Other Sources	Liturgical Assignment
166 B				Apparit Dni mat
	BM51 166v			med noct de virginibus
			Sant 224 G	post nocturnos
	BM51 171 G			nocturnos Dom de XLme
				XLma 6 IV mat
		36 K		XLma 3 II sext
				sacr bas mat

	AL
VR Accedite ad Dominum (Ps 33:6)	180^{v} A
Si Deus pro nobis (Rom 8:31)	
VR Et effundite coram illo (Ps 61:9)	239^{v} A
Si diluculo surrexeris (Iob 8:5-6)	
VR Si iniquitatem que est (Iob 11:14)	120 B
Si dixerimus quia peccatum (I Io 1:8-9)	
VR Hec scribo vobis ut non peccetis (I Io 2:1)	
Si dixero consolabitur (Iob 7:13-14,21)	
VR Saccum consui super caput (Iob 16:16)	130^{v} B
VR Si fuerint peccata	
RS Lavamini mundi estote	
VR Si iniquitatem que est	
RS Si diluculo surrexeris	
VR Si non preposuero	
RS Si oblitus fuero tui	
Si oblitus fuero tui (Ps 136:5-6)	
VR Si non preposuero (Ps 136:6)	
VR Si quis cognoberit	
RS Sanctificavit rex templum	
VR Si quis sermonem meum	
RS Amen amen dico vobis quia qui verbum	
VR Si simplex fueris	
RS Ora Dominum ante lucem	
VR Si vere utique iustitiam	
RS Haec dicit Dominus congregamini	
Si vis Domine potes me salvare (Mt 8:2)	
VR Domine non sum dignus (Mt 8:8)	

A30	Silos	*BN10110*	Other Sources	Liturgical Assignment
			T35.4 6^{v} L	Res Dni 2 mat
				SS Cosme et Damiani mat
			T33.3 12^{v} *	de sanctis tert Dominicale
				XLma 2 IV mat
		34^{v} H		XLma 3 II mat
				XLma 3 sabb mat
		49^{v} H		XLma 3 sabb sext
			T33.3 30^{v} sn	ordo ad non

* VR missing.

AL

VR Si volueritis et audieritis me
    RS Audite me rectores
    RS Hec dicit Dominus si custodieritis
    RS Pepercit Dominus populo suo
VR Sicut cerbus desiderat ad fontes
    RS Anima mea desiderat te Deus
VR Sicut dilexit me Pater
    RS Ego elegi vos dicit Dominus
VR Sicut lilia munda
    RS Speciosi facti sunt sancti
VR Sicut miseretur pater
    RS Non secundum peccata nostra
Sicut onus grave (Ps 37:5,18)
    VR Cor meum conturbatum (Ps 37:11) 138v D
Sicut onus grave (Ps 37:5,18)
    VR Exaruit cor meum (Ps 72:21-22)

Simile est regnum (Mt 25:1)
    VR Media nocte clamor factus (Mt 25:6)

VR Sine iniquitati
    RS Vindica causam meam
VR Sit auris tua intendens
    RS Domine ne intendas in delicta
VR Sit nomen Domini benedictum
    RS Benedictus Dominus in eternum
    RS Corona sanctorum timor Dei
VR Speciem et pulcritudinem tuam intende
    RS Columba mea quam pulcra es
    RS Iam adspirat dies

A30	Silos	*BN10110*	Other Sources	Liturgical Assignment
				XLma 4 V mat
			T35.5 149 H	XLma 6 VI tert
			Sal 151^{v} A *	med noct
	BM51 166^{v} A			med noct de una virgine

*VR on fol. 160.

	AL
RS Veni sponsa mea	
Speciosa et decora facta es (Cant 7:6; Eccli 24:21)	
VR Vox enim tua dulcis (Cant 2:14)	48^{v} A
Speciosi facti sunt sancti (?)	
VR Sicut lilia munda (?)	90 B
Speciosi facti sunt sancti (?)	
VR Sicut lilia munda (?)	
VR Sperate in eum	
RS Mane nobiscum Domine	
RS Spes nostra in Deo est	
Spes nostra in Deo est (Ps 61:8)	
VR Sperate in eum (Ps 61:9)	
VR Ecce Deus noster	
VR Spiritum rectum innoba	
RS Cor mundum crea in me Deus	
Spiritus Domini spiritus vite (Ez 1:20)	
VR Verbo Domini celi (Ps 32:6)	
Spiritus Domini super me (Is 61:1-3)	
VR Misit me Dominus sanare (Is 61:1)	213 A
VR Spiritus Domini super me	
RS Misit me Dominus sanare	
VR Spiritus oris nostri	
RS Facta est Sion sicut avis volans	
Spiritus Sanctus de caelo descendit (Act 2:2,4)	
VR Apparuerunt illis dispertite (Act 2:3)	209 B
VR Spiritus Sanctus de caelo descendit	

A30	Silos	*BN10110*	Other Sources	Liturgical Assignment
				S Leocadie mat
				S Iuliani mat
177 sn				"
	BM51 175^{v} F		*Sant* 217^{v} F	nocturnos fer V
			Sal 154^{v} F	"
			169^{v} F	nocturnos in Lazaro
			T33.3 31 sn	de XL [ad non ?]
			T35.4 69 M	let apost sabb mat
	BM45 16^{v} A			nat S Iohannis mat
			T35.4 74^{v} L	Pentecost mat

	AL
RS Disciplina et sapientia replebit	
VR Spiritus Sanctus superveniet	
RS Missus est a Deo angelus Gabriel	
Splendet hodie celum (?)	
VR Omnes gentes plaudete manibus (Ps 46:2)	71 B
VR Spoliabit me gloria mea	
RS Ingressus inimicus manu potenti	
Stabat Maria ad monumentum (Io 20:11-12,14,18)	
VR Dixit Ihesus Marie mulier (Io 20:15)	181^{v} A
Stabat Maria ad monumento (Io 20:11-12,14,18)	
VR Dixit Ihesus Marie mulier (Io 20:15)	
Stellam quam viderant (Mt 2:9-10)	
VR Invenerunt puerum cum Maria (Mt 2:11)	86 B
Stephanus vidit celos (Act 7:56,16; Esth 7:3)	
VR Dum lapidaretur Stephanus (Act 7:60)	74 D
VR Steterunt contra hostes	
RS Propter honorem nominis	
RS Sancti qui per fidem vicerunt	
VR Stetit rex ante altare	
RS Sanctificavit rex templum	
Subito vulneravit me (Iob 16:8-9)	
VR Custodi me Domine de manu peccatoris (Ps 139:5)	
VR Subito vulneravit me	
RS Ecce factus sum omnibus inimicis	
Subveni Domine quia conturbatur (?)	
VR Ad te lebamus oculos (Ps 122:1)	255^{v} A
Super acerbum lapidum (?)	
VR Quid retribuam Domino (Ps 115:12)	74 A
Super lapidem sepulcri (Mt 28:2)	
VR Venite et videte locum (Mt 28:6-7)	182 A
Super muros tuos Iherusalem (Is 62:6)	

A30	Silos	*BN10110*	Other Sources	Liturgical Assignment
124^{v} B				Nat Dni mat
			T35.4 7^{v} L	Res Dni 4 mat
			T35.5 184^{v} H	Paschae mat
167 B			*T35.7* 119 L ?	Apparit Dni mat
132 B				S Stephani mat
		102^{v} H		XLma 6 III sext
				let de clade
				S Stephani mat
			T35.4 8 M	Res Dni 5 mat

	AL
VR Beati qui habitant in domo (Ps 83:5)	263 A
Super omnia ligna campi (Ez 31:5-7)	
VR Favum mellis distillant (Cant 4:11; Deut 32:34)	291 A
Surgam et ibo ad patrem (Lc 15:18)	
VR Non sum dignus ut curi filius meus (Mt 8:8 ?)	
Surge inluminare Iherusalem (Is 60:1,18,21,13,19)	
VR Aperientur porte tuae iugiter (Is 60:11)	269^{v} A
VR Surge propera	
RS Egredere inter lilia obbaca	
Surget dux de tribu Iuda (I Mach 3:1-9)	
VR Minimus erit in mille (Is 60:22)	43^{v} B
Susceperunt me sicut leo (Ps 16:12-13)	
VR Circumdederunt me sicut apes (Ps 117:12)	134^{v} A
Susceperunt me sicut leo (Ps 16:12-13)	
VR Custodi me Domine ut pupillam (Ps 16:8)	
Suscipe me Domine ut quum fratribus (Passio)	
VR Tu es enim Christus (Passio)	77 A
Suscipiamus regnum Dei nostri (Dan 7:18,22,27)	
VR Quis est iste rex glorie (Ps 23:10)	65^{v} A
Suscipiunt sancti securis (?)	
VR Sancti qui sperant in Domino (Is 40:31)	
VR Suscitatur falsiloquus	
RS Ecce nunc venit in me dolor meus	
Suscitavit Dominus regem (Eccli 24:34-36)	
VR Gloriosus est aspectus eius (Is 52:14-15)	86^{v} D
Suspiro ego et gemeo (Iob 3:24-26)	
VR Ve misero michi (Ier 45:3)	

A30	Silos	*BN10110*	Other Sources	Liturgical Assignment
				sacr bas mat
				unoq Dom mat
	3 172v B			quot fer III mat
				rest bas mat
50 B				post Dom II Adv mat
				XLma 4 II mat
		75 H		XLma 5 II tert
141 *				S Ioannis Apost mat
108 A				post Dom V Adv mat
	BM45 112 C			S Eufemiae mat
168 **			*T35.7* 120 L	Apparit Dni mat
			Sant 224v A	post nocturnos

*VR missing.

**VR illegible.

	AL
VR Tacui semper silui	
RS Timor quem timebam	
Tedet anima mea vite mee (Iob 10:1,6,4)	
VR Instauras testes tuos (Iob 10:17)	123v B
VR Tetendit arcum suum	
RS Ingressus inimicus manu potenti	
VR T[h]ronus tuus	
RS Domine qui abitas	
VR Tibi derelictus est pauper	
RS Qui sedes super thronum	
VR Timebunt qui ab occidente	
RS Ecce quemadmodum	
Timete me dicit Dominus (Ier 31:34)	
VR Custodite leges meas (Lev 18:5)	112v B
VR Timor et tremor	
RS Meditatus sum nocte	
Timor quem timebam (Iob 3:25-26)	
VR Tacui semper silui (Is 42:14)	113v B
Tota die contristatus (Ps 37:7-8)	
VR Incurbatus sum et humilliatus (Ps 37:9)	
VR Tota die iustus	
RS Letabitur iustus in Deo	
Tradiderunt me in manus impiorum (Iob 16:12,15,17-18)	
VR Aperuerunt contra me inimici (Iob 16:11)	
Tradiderunt me in manus impiorum (Iob 16:12,15,17-18)	
VR Circumdederunt me sicut apes (Ps 117:12)	165v A
II Multiplicati sunt super capillos (Ps 68:5)	165v sn
VR Tu autem Domine exercituum	
RS Adtende Domine ad me	
VR Tu autem Domine ne elonge	
RS Deus meus ne elonges	
Tu Domine dinumerasti (Iob 14:16-17)	

A30	Silos	*BN10110*	Other Sources	Liturgical Assignment
	BM51 171 A			nocturnos Dom de XLme
				XLma 2 sabb mat
				XLma 1 IV sext
				XLma 1 V mat
		54 H		XLma 4 II sext
		81 H		XLma 5 IV mat
				XLma 6 VI mat "

	AL
VR Verebor omnia opera mea (Iob 9:28)	129 B
Tu Domine susceptor meus es (Ps 3:4)	
VR Misericordia mea et refugium meum (Ps 143:2)	
Tu Domine virtutum cum tranquillitate (Sap 12:18-20)	
VR Aperi manuum tuam (Ps 144:16)	129 A
VR Tu es Deus et in te est Deus	
RS Deus qui das locum penitentie	
RS Venisti Domine et affacie tua	
Tu es Deus qui facis (Ps 76:15)	
VR Notam fecisti (Ps 76:15-16)	
VR Tu es Deus salbator meus	
RS Ostende in me Domine bonitatem	
VR Tu es enim Christus	
RS Suscipe me Domine ut quum fratribus	
Tu es Petrus (Mt 16:18)	
VR Quocumque ligaberis super terram (Mt 16:19)	103^{v} B 263^{v} sn
VR Tu filia Syon summe	
RS Facta est Syon sicut avis volans	
VR Tu formasti me	
RS Patientiam habe in me	
VR Tu subveni oppressis	
RS Consolare Domine contritos corde	
VR Tunc aperientur oculi	
RS In tempore adventus Domini	
Tuus Domine sermo qui sanat (Sap 16:12-13)	
VR Dominus mortificat (I Reg 2:6)	280 A

A30	Silos	*BN10110*	Other Sources	Liturgical Assignment
				XLma 3 V mat
	BM51 173^{v} B		*Sant* 216^{v} B	nocturnos fer II
			Sal 175 B	"
			168^{v} B	nocturnos Dom de med
				XLma 3 V tert
			T35.5 200^{v} H	fer III de oct Pasc
224 B				Cat S Petri mat
				sacr bas mat
				defunctis mat
	BM51 196^{v} A			defunct sacerd mat

	AL
Una sabbatorum cum sero (Io 20:19-20; Mt 28:10)	
VR Apparuit Dominus Ihesus (Io 20:26)	187^{v} A
Unde mici adfuit (Lc 1:43-44)	
VR Ecce facta est (Lc 1:44)	213^{v} B
Universus populus ascendite (?)	
VR Omnes gentes plaudete manibus (Ps 46:2)	106 A
Unusquisque se ad proximo (Ier 9:4-5)	
VR Custodite vos a murmuratione (Sap 1:11)	132 B
Unusquisque se a proximo (Ier 9:4-5)	
VR In labiis suis indulcat (Eccli 12:15)	
Usquequo Domine non parcis (Iob 7:19)	
VR Peccavi Domine peccavi (Or Man 16)	118 B
VR Ut edificentur muri	
RS Benigne fac Domine	
VR Ut quid Domine repellas	
RS In via quam ambulabam	
VR Ut quid in contemtione	
RS Converte nos Deus ad te	
Ut quid reppulisti nos Deus (Ps 73:1-2)	
VR Salba plebem tuam (Ps 27:9)	
VR Ve misero michi	
RS Suspiro ego et gemeo	
Ve nobis qui diligimus (?)	
VR Dies ille dies ire (Soph 1:15)	
Ve nobis quoniam peccabimus (Thr 5:16-18)	
VR Peccabimus in conspectu (Esth 14:6)	
VR Venatione ceperunt	
RS Co[n]locaberunt me quasi signum	
VR Venerunt cuncti senes	
RS Perfectum est templum	

A30	Silos	*BN10110*	Other Sources	Liturgical Assignment
			T35.4 18 L	Dom de oct Pasc mat
	BM45 18 B			nat S Iohannis mat
230 A				Carnes Toll mat
				Dom de med mat
			T33.3 22 sn	[de XL] Dominicale
		97^{v} K		XLma 6 II sext
				XLma 2 II mat
		49 H		XLma 3 sabb tert
	7 29^{v} sn			defunct aep mat
		46 H		XLma 3 VI mat

	AL
Veni clementissime Domine succurre (?)	
VR Respice in servos tuos (Ps 89:16)	67 B
VR Veni de Livano sponsa	
RS Egredere inter lilia obbaca	
Veni sponsa mea (Cant ?)	
VR Speciem et pulcritudinem tuam intende (Ps 44:5)	101 B
VR Veniam in Syon	
RS Haec dicit Dominus iustitia mea	
Venientes de regione (?)	
VR Omnes gentes plaudete manibus (Ps 46:2)	30 A
VR Veniet Dominus cum laude	
RS Ecce veniet nobis salus a Domino	
Veniet Dominus et apparebit (?)	
VR Et levabit signum (Is 11:12)	32^{v} B
Venisti Domine et affacie tua (Is 64:3-4)	
VR Tu es Deus et in te est Deus (?)	69^{v} D
VR Venite adoremus	
RS Convertamur ad Dominum Deum	
Venite benedicti patres mei (Mt 25:34)	
VR Esurivi enim et dedistis (Mt 25:35)	
VR Vos qui sequuti estis (Mt 19:28)	100^{v} A
II Beati qui persequutionem (Mt 5:10)	100^{v} A
Venite et audite alleluia (Ps 65:16)	
VR Venite fili audite me (Ps 33:12)	292 B
VR Venite et videte locum	
RS Super lapidem sepulcri	
VR Venite exultemus	
RS Convertamur ad Dominum Deum	

A30	Silos	*BN10110*	Other Sources	Liturgical Assignment
				Adv ad tert
				S Agate mat
70 A				S Eolalie mat
5^v A				S Aciscli
15^v B				ante Dom I Adv mat
119^v A				Nat Dni mat
214^v A				S Tirsi mat
				"
				"
	BM51 181^v A			sanctis mat
				unoq Dom mat
	6 139^v B			Dom IX quot mat
			T35.4 113 L	Dom VI quot mat

AL

RS Deprecemur Dominum et placabilis
RS Regnabit Dominus Deus noster
VR Venite fili audite me
RS Bonum est sperare in Domino
RS In lege Domini meditemur
RS Venite et audite alleluia
VR Verbo Domini celi
RS Spiritus Domini spiritus vite
VR Verbum dulce
RS In omni loco oculi Dei
VR Verbum iniquum
RS Omnes amici mei inluserunt
VR Verebor omnia opera mea
RS Tu Domine dinumerasti
Via veritas et vita (?)
VR Beati qui persecutionem (Mt 5:10) 219 A

VR Viam iniquitatis amobe a me
RS Alleluia vide humilitatem meam
Vide Domine quoniam tribulor (Thr 1:20-21)
VR Deducant oculi mei lacrimas (Ier 9:18) 91v B
VR Vide humilitatem
RS Alleluia iudicia iudicium
RS Delicta iubentutis et ignorantie
RS Dimitte me Domine ut plangam
RS Domine ne in ira tua
RS Quare non tollis peccatum meum
RS Repleatur os meum Deus
VR Vide Iherusalem
RS Ecce per omnes semitas
Videbitis hodie mirabilia (?)
VR Hic est filius meus dilectus (Mt 3:17) 80v A
Videte magnalia Dei (Ex 14:13-14)

A30	Silos	*BN10110*	Other Sources	Liturgical Assignment
				[S Christophori et com]mat
183 B				Allis Infant mat
152 B				Circumcis Dni mat

	AL
VR Laudate Dominum omnes gentes (Ps 116:1)	184 B
VR Videte nequando adgraventur	
RS Vigilate et orate ne intretis	
VR Vidi in celo turbam magnam	
RS Sancti qui certamen habuerunt	
VR Vidi in Syon turbam	
RS Sancti qui certamen habuerunt	
Vigila Domine super oves (Io 10:10)	
VR Custodi nos Domine ut pupillam (Ps 16:8)	
Vigilate et orate dicit Dominus (Mc 13:35-36; Lc 18:1)	
VR Dominus Ihesus Xristus loquutus est (Mt 26:41)	
Vigilate et orate ne intretis (Mt 26:41)	
VR Videte nequando adgraventur (Lc 21:34)	
Vincula sanctorum iam solute sunt (?)	
VR Qui sunt isti qui ut nubes (Is 60:8)	248 sn
Vindica causam meam (Ps 42:1)	
VR Sine iniquitati (Ps 57:5-6)	
Vir Dei sanctus dum aspiceret (Passio)	
VR Mici absit gloriari (Gal 6:14)	40v B
VR Vir Dei sanctus dum aspiceret	
RS Vir iste loquutus est	
Vir dilectus a Deo (Eccli 45:1)	

A30	Silos	*BN10110*	Other Sources	Liturgical Assignment
			T35.4 11 L	Res Dni 10 mat
	BM51 166^{v} F		*Sant* 212^{v} F	med noct
			Sal 151 F	"
			Sant 212 A	med noct
			Sal 150 A	med noct de XLme
	BM51 167 A			med noct de XLme Dominicis
			Sant 212^{v} F	med noct
			Sal 151^{v} F	"
				SS general mat
	BM45 2 B			S Quirici mat
		80 H		XLma 5 III sext
				S Andreae Apost mat

	AL
VR Homo iste in vita sua (Eccli 48:15 ?)	251v B
VR Vir iste conservabit legem	
RS Vir iste in populo suo	
Vir iste in populo suo (II Mach 15:13-14)	
VR Vir iste conservabit legem (Eccli 44:20-21)	251 X
Vir iste loquutus est (Passio)	
VR Vir Dei sanctus dum aspiceret (Passio)	40 B
VR Virga tua et baculus tuus	
RS Non timebo mala Domine	
Virgo Israhel speciosa facta es (Cant 7:6)	
VR Dilexisti iustitiam et odisti (Ps 44:8)	254 B
Viri impii dixerunt opprimamus (Sap 2:1,10,12; Prov 1:12-14; Ier 11:19)	
VR Dixerunt venite percutiamus (Ier 18:18)	
Viri impii dixerunt opprimamus (Sap 2:1,10,12; Prov 1:12-14; Ier 11:19)	
VR Hec cogitaberunt et erraverunt (Sap 2:21)	136 B
Viri sancti germinate (Eccli 24:19 ?)	
VR Florete flores quasi lilium (Eccli 39:19)	241 B
VR Germinate iusti (Eccli 39:19)	
Viri sancti qui habitas (Bar 1:13 ?)	
VR Vos sancti Domini (Is 61:6)	248v A
	265 sn
Viri sancti vobis apertum (IV Esd 8:52-54)	
VR Ecce quam bonum (Ps 132:1)	239 A

A30	Silos	*BN10110*	Other Sources	Liturgical Assignment
				uno iusto
			BN13060 169 B	S Emiliani mat
				uno iusto
				S Andreae Apost mat
				una virgine
				"
			BN13060 183 B	Adsum S Mariae mat
				"
			T35.5 88v I	Dom V XLmae mat
				XLma 4 III tert
				SS Vinc, Sav, et Cris mat
			SJP 8 B	SS Emeteri et Celedoni mat
				SS general mat
				sacr bas mat
				SS Cosme et Damiani mat

AL

Virtus nostra Domine (?)
    VR Ad te lebamus oculos (Ps 122:1) 275 A
    VR Erans bracium (Is 33:2)
    VR Infirmorum adiutor (?)

VR Visitabit Dominus gregem suum
    RS Exulta satis filia Syon
Vivit anima mea Deus (Ps 118:175)
    VR Erravi sicut ovis (Ps 118:176)

VR Vivo ego dicit Dominus
    RS Habitatores Iherusalem crucifigent
Vocem audivi flentis (Apoc 18 ?)
    VR Inter vestibulum et altare (Ioel 2:17)
VR Volabunt in navibus
    RS H[a]ec dicit Dominus pertransibunt in mari
Voluntarie sacrificabo tibi (Ps 53:8-9)
    VR Deus meus es tu (Ps 117:28) 294v A

VR Vos estis genus
    RS Oves mee et oves gregis mei
VR Vos maledicti estis
    RS Si affiget homo Deum
VR Vos qui sequuti estis
    RS Venite benedicti patris mei
VR Vos sancti Domini
    RS Viri sancti qui habitatis
VR Vox Domini in virtute
    RS Inter ramos arborum avium
VR Vox enim tua dulcis
    RS Speciosa et decora facta es

A30	Silos	*BN10110*	Other Sources	Liturgical Assignment
				infirmis mat
	3 53 A			"
	BM51 189 A			"
	7 6^{v} A			"
	BM51 176^{v} C		*Sant* 218 C	nocturnos sabb
			Sal 157 C	"
			169 C	nocturnos Dom de med
		48^{v} H		XLma 3 sabb mat
				nocturnos et mat ora diei Dom

	AL
Vox filie Syon clamantis (Ier 4:31; 5:1)	
VR Defecerunt oculi mei in eloquium (Ps 118:82)	91 B
Vox in rama audita est (Ier 31:15)	
VR Plorans plorabit in nocte (Thr 1:2)	91 A
Vox quam audistis ab initio (I Io 2:24,28)	
VR Estote invicem benigni (Eph 4:32)	67v A
Zaccarias sacerdos dum in ordinem (Lc 1:8,19,13,17)	
VR Multi in nativitate eius (Lc 1:14-15)	212v B

A30	Silos	*BN10110*	Other Sources	Liturgical Assignment
182 B				Allis Infant mat
181 A				Allis Infant mat
				Adv ad tert
	BM45 16 B			nat S Iohannis mat

BIBLIOGRAPHY

For further bibliographical information, the reader is referred to the items by Millares Carlo and Mora Ontalba cited below.

Anglés, Higinio. "La música medieval en Toledo hasta el siglo XI," *Spanische Forschungen der Görresgesellschaft*, Erste Reihe, VII (1938), 1-68.

Antifonario Visigótico Mozárabe de la Catedral de León, Monumenta Hispaniae Sacra, Serie Litúrgica, Vol. V, 2, *Facsímiles Musicales,* I. Madrid-Barcelona-León, 1953.

Ayuso Marazuela, Mons. Dr. Theophilo, ed. *Psalterium Uisigothicum-Mozarabicum, Biblia Polyglotta Matritensia,* Series VII, *Uetus Latina* L. 21. Madrid, 1957.

Bishko, Charles Julian. "Gallegan Pactual Monasticism in the Repopulation of Castile," *Estudios Dedicados a Menéndez Pidal*, II (Madrid, 1951), 513-553.

_______. "Salvus of Albelda and Frontier Monasticism in Tenth-Century Navarre," *Speculum,* XIII, No. 4 (1948), 559-590.

Bishop, W. C. *The Mozarabic and Ambrosian Rites: Four Essays in Comparative Liturgiology,* edited from his papers by C. L. Feltoe. London, 1924.

Brockett, Clyde Waring, Jr. "Antiphons, Responsories, and Other Chants of the Mozarabic Rite." Unpubl. diss. Columbia, 1965.

Brou, Louis, O. S. B. "L'Alleluia dans la liturgie mozarabe," *Anuario Musical,* VI (1951), 3-90.

_______, and José Vives, eds. *Antifonario Visigótico Mozárabe de la Catedral de León, Monumenta Hispaniae Sacra, Serie Litúrgica,* Vol. V, 1. Barcelona-Madrid, 1959.

_______. "Un antiphonaire mozarabe de Silos d'après les fragments du British Museum," *Hispania Sacra*, V (1952), 341-366.

_______. "L'Antiphonaire wisigothique et l'antiphonaire grégorien du VIIIe siècle," *Anuario Musical,* V (1950), 3-10.

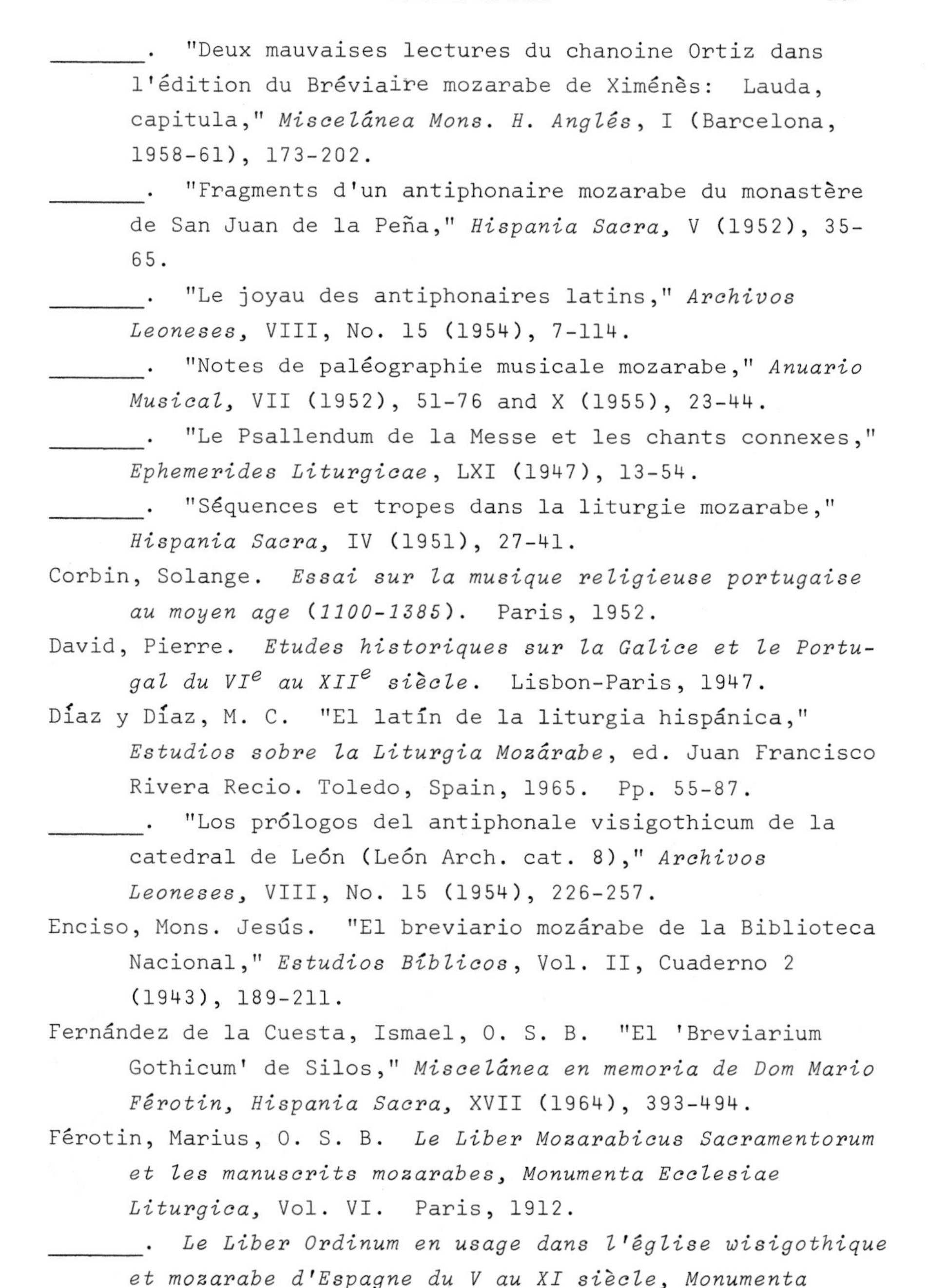

_______. "Deux mauvaises lectures du chanoine Ortiz dans l'édition du Bréviaire mozarabe de Ximénès: Lauda, capitula," *Miscelánea Mons. H. Anglés*, I (Barcelona, 1958-61), 173-202.

_______. "Fragments d'un antiphonaire mozarabe du monastère de San Juan de la Peña," *Hispania Sacra,* V (1952), 35-65.

_______. "Le joyau des antiphonaires latins," *Archivos Leoneses,* VIII, No. 15 (1954), 7-114.

_______. "Notes de paléographie musicale mozarabe," *Anuario Musical,* VII (1952), 51-76 and X (1955), 23-44.

_______. "Le Psallendum de la Messe et les chants connexes," *Ephemerides Liturgicae*, LXI (1947), 13-54.

_______. "Séquences et tropes dans la liturgie mozarabe," *Hispania Sacra,* IV (1951), 27-41.

Corbin, Solange. *Essai sur la musique religieuse portugaise au moyen age (1100-1385)*. Paris, 1952.

David, Pierre. *Etudes historiques sur la Galice et le Portugal du VIe au XIIe siècle*. Lisbon-Paris, 1947.

Díaz y Díaz, M. C. "El latín de la liturgia hispánica," *Estudios sobre la Liturgia Mozárabe*, ed. Juan Francisco Rivera Recio. Toledo, Spain, 1965. Pp. 55-87.

_______. "Los prólogos del antiphonale visigothicum de la catedral de León (León Arch. cat. 8)," *Archivos Leoneses,* VIII, No. 15 (1954), 226-257.

Enciso, Mons. Jesús. "El breviario mozárabe de la Biblioteca Nacional," *Estudios Bíblicos*, Vol. II, Cuaderno 2 (1943), 189-211.

Fernández de la Cuesta, Ismael, O. S. B. "El 'Breviarium Gothicum' de Silos," *Miscelánea en memoria de Dom Mario Férotin, Hispania Sacra,* XVII (1964), 393-494.

Férotin, Marius, O. S. B. *Le Liber Mozarabicus Sacramentorum et les manuscrits mozarabes, Monumenta Ecclesiae Liturgica,* Vol. VI. Paris, 1912.

_______. *Le Liber Ordinum en usage dans l'église wisigothique et mozarabe d'Espagne du V au XI siècle, Monumenta*

Ecclesiae Liturgica, Vol. V. Paris, 1904.

Ferretti, Paolo, O. S. B. *Esthêtique Grêgorienne.* Paris, 1938.

Franquesa, Adalberto, O. S. B. "El códice emilianense 60 y sus piezas litúrgicas," *Hispania Sacra,* XII (1959), 423-444.

García Villada, Zacarías, S. J. *Paleografía Española.* Madrid, 1923.

Gilson, J. P., ed. *The Mozarabic Psalter* (British Museum Add. 30851), The Henry Bradshaw Society, XXX. London, 1905.

Gros, M. S. "Les fragments parisiens de l'antiphonaire de Silos," *Revue Bênêdictine,* LXXIV, Nos. 3-4 (1964), 324-333.

Huglo, Michel. "Mélodie hispanique pour une ancienne hymne à la croix," *Revue Grêgorienne,* XXVIII, No. 5 (1949), 191-196.

Husmann, Heinrich. "Alleluia, Sequenz und Prosa im altspanischen Choral," *Miscelânea Mons. H. Anglés*, I (Barcelona, 1958-61), 407-415.

Jammers, Ewald. *Tafeln zur Neumenschrift.* Tutzing, 1965.

López Calo, José. "Das Responsorium in Spanien," *Die Musik in Geschichte und Gegenwart,* Vol. XI, art. "Responsorium." Kassel, 1963.

Martín Patino, José M.[a], S. J. "El breviarium mozárabe de Ortiz: Su valor documental para la historia del oficio catedralicio hispánico," *Miscelânea Comillas,* XL (1963), 205-297.

Millares Carlo, Agustín. *Los códices visigóticos de la catedral toledana: Cuestiones cronológicas y de procedencia.* Madrid, 1935.

_______. *Manuscritos visigóticos: Notas bibliográficas, Monumenta Hispaniae Sacra,* Subsidia: Vol. I. Barcelona-Madrid, 1963.

Moll Roqueta, Jaime. "Nuevos hallazgos de manuscritos mozárabes con neumas musicales," *Anuario Musical,* V (1950), 11-14.

Mora Ontalba, José María. "Bibliografía general, ediciones de textos, trabajos y repertorios," *Estudios sobre la Liturgia Mozárabe*, ed. Juan Francisco Rivera Recio. Toledo, Spain, 1965. Pp. 165-187.

Mundó, Anscari M., O. S. B. "La datación de los códices litúrgicos visigóticos toledanos," *Hispania Sacra*, XVIII (1965), 1-25.

Pérez de Urbel, Justo, O. S. B. "Antifonario de León: El escritor y la época," *Archivos Leoneses*, VIII, No. 15 (1954), 115-144.

_______. *Historia del condado de Castilla*. Madrid, 1944.

_______. "La reconquista de la Rioja y su colonización espiritual en el siglo X," *Estudios dedicados a Menéndez Pidal*, I (Madrid, 1950), 495-534.

Pinell, Jorge M., O. S. B. "Las *Missae*, grupos de cantos y oraciones en el oficio de la antigua liturgia hispana," *Archivos Leoneses*, VIII, No. 15 (1954), 145-185.

_______. "El oficio hispano-visigótico," *Hispania Sacra*, X (1957), 385-427.

_______. "Los textos de la antigua liturgia hispánica," *Estudios sobre la Liturgia Mozárabe*, ed. Juan Francisco Rivera Recio. Toledo, Spain, 1965. Pp. 109-164.

Porter, W. S. "Monasticismo español primitivo," *Hispania Sacra*, VI (1953), 3-36. Excerpted and translated from the articles by the same author entitled "Early Spanish Monasticism," *Laudate*, Vols. X-XII (1932-34).

_______. "Studies in the Mozarabic Office I: The Verona Orationale and the Leon Antiphoner," *Journal of Theological Studies*, XXXV (1934), 266-286.

Povés, María Luisa. "Los fragmentos de códices visigóticos de la catedral de Santo Domingo de la Calzada," *Revista de Archivos Bibliotecas y Museos*, LVIII (1952), 517-520.

Prado, Germán, O. S. B. "Estado actual de los estudios sobre la música mozárabe," *Estudios sobre la Liturgia Mozárabe*, ed. Juan Francisco Rivera Recio. Toledo, Spain, 1965. Pp. 89-106.

Rojo, Casiano, O. S. B. and Germán Prado, O. S. B. *El Canto Mozárabe*. Barcelona, 1929.

Suñol, Grégoire M., O. S. B. *Introduction à la paléographie musicale grégorienne*. Paris-Tournai-Rome, 1935.

Vives, José. "En torno a la datación del antifonario legionense," *Hispania Sacra,* VIII (1955), 117-124.

_______. "Fuentes hagiográficas del antifonario de León," *Archivos Leoneses,* VIII, No. 15 (1954), 288-299.

_______, ed. *Oracional Visigótico, Monumenta Hispaniae Sacra, Serie Litúrgica,* Vol. I. Barcelona, 1946.

Wagner, Peter. *Einführung in die Gregorianischen Melodien.* Hildesheim, 1962. First edn., 3 vols., Leipzig, 1911-1921.

_______. "Der mozarabische Kirchengesang und seine Ueberlieferung," *Spanische Forschungen der Görresgesellschaft,* Erste Reihe, I (1928), 102-141.

_______. "Untersuchungen zu den Gesangstexten und zur responsorialen Psalmodie der altspanischen Liturgie," *Spanische Forschungen der Görresgesellschaft,* Erste Reihe, II (1930), 67-113.

Werner, E. "Eine neuentdeckte mozarabische Handschrift mit Neumen," *Miscelánea Mons. H. Anglés*, II (Barcelona, 1958-1961), 977-991.

Whitehill, Walter M. and Justo Pérez de Urbel, O. S. B. "Los manuscritos de Santo Domingo de Silos," *Boletín de la Real Academia de la Historia*, XCV (1929), 521-601.